The Dō of Cooking

The Dō of

introduction by
Herman Aihara

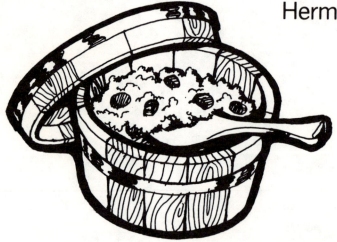

Complete Macrobiotic Cooking for the Seasons

Cooking
Cornellia Aihara

GOMF Press

First published in 1971 as four volumes.

© Copyright 1982
  George Ohsawa Macrobiotic Foundation
  902 14th Street, Oroville, California 95965.

ISBN 0-918860-39-3

Cornellia Aihara was born in Fukushima, northern Japan, in 1926. When she was twelve years old, her mother gave birth to a baby boy. Since her mother did not have enough milk to nurse, her mother was kept very busy with his care and it became Cornellia's responsibility to cook for the family. She also learned Chinese-style cooking around 1946 after many Japanese exiles returned home from Manchuria after World War II ended.

She learned macrobiotics from George Ohsawa when he came to her town (Aizuwakamatsu) for lectures. This incident changed her life. Soon after this, she left home and went to Ohsawa's school. In this school she didn't learn cooking, but she learned that if someone dislikes you, then that is a mirror reflection of your arrogance or exclusivity. This learning helped her to be a macrobiotic teacher later.

At that time she also began corresponding with Mr. Aihara, who was living in New York. He invited her to New York in 1955. Trusting Herman Aihara only through exchanged letters, she came to America with only ten dollars in her pocket. Soon after her arrival in New York they were married. There they engaged in retail businesses until Mr. and Mrs. Ohsawa came to the United States from Europe. Then she studied macrobiotic cooking by helping Mrs. Lima Ohsawa at the first macrobiotic summer camps at Long Island in 1960; at the Catskill Mountains in 1961; at the University of California at Chico in 1963; at the Big Sur camp in 1964; and at many other of Mrs. Ohsawa's cooking classes.

Since 1961 Cornellia has devoted her life to the teaching of macrobiotic cooking, childcare and home remedies, and philosophy. She has travelled extensively with her husband since 1970, giving cooking classes and lectures throughout the United States and Europe. Together they have organized fourteen macrobiotic summer camps in California since 1965. In these camps, Cornellia's cooking has been the biggest attraction. She has become a foremost teacher of macrobiotic natural foods cooking.

Besides *The Do of Cooking,* her other cookbooks are *Macrobiotic Kitchen* (Japan Publications, formerly published as *The Chico-San Cookbook* by GOMF Press), and *The Calendar Cookbook* (GOMF Press).

This book is dedicated to my teachers George and Lima Ohsawa, to my mother and father, and to all my friends.

The following friends have sent their original recipes to us, and many of them are included in this book along with my own. I deeply appreciate their help.

Claude Abehsera	Marilyn Fryer	Charlotte Palumbo
Amy Alexandre	Lorraine Harr	Susan Richards
Minnie Brady	Ann Harris	Lillian Russell
Ann Burns	Nan Jones	Gilbert Savaria
Ann Canty	Mary Jo Kline	Grace Walcott
Marilyn Cristifori	Joanne Kowalenok	Donna West
Dorothy Duncan	Margie Lehman	Sheryl White
Yvette de Langre	Hilda Lewis	Durbin Yamaguchi
Alice Feinberg	Cheryl Loskutoff	Kazuko Yamazaki
	Claire Okada	

Many people have helped to realize this publication, and I am especially thankful to them. In the original editions, Norman Katz, Eunice Katz, Fred Pulver, Alice Feinberg, Mary Kyger, and Agnes Dolence worked tirelessly to transform my 'Japanese English' to better English; Susan Jacobowitz, Linda Baker, Betty Patterson, and Maya Edwards typed the manuscripts; Carl Campbell did the interior drawings; and Hiro Fukuda photographed the New Year's dinner. For this new edition, I am most thankful to Carl Campbell who did the wonderful cover design as a donation; to Paul Orbuch who took the professional color photographs (backdrop courtesy of Roger Barber); to Carl Ferre, who designed the format and typeset the copy again and again each time I made changes in the recipes; to Sandy Rothman for editing and proofreading the final manuscript; to Julia Karlen, who added suggestions to help American readers understand unfamiliar recipes; and to Annette Hafer for her accurate typing and work on the index which helped complete the book.

Cornellia Aihara

Contents

Spring

Summer

Autumn

Winter

Preface

When the George Ohsawa Macrobiotic Foundation was started in San Francisco in January 1971, we planned to publish our own version of a macrobiotic cookbook. Cornellia Aihara wrote a complete book after intensive work and concentration of thought. However, she gave the manuscript to Chico-San, Inc., when Bob Kennedy, president of the company and a long-time friend of hers, expressed his wish to publish a company cookbook.

Therefore, in order to publish our own book we began in June of 1971 to gather macrobiotic recipes from our members to compile a cookbook to be published by GOMF. Although most of the recipes in this book were written by Cornellia, many have been contributed by other members of the Foundation (as seen in her acknowledgments). All contributors studied macrobiotic cooking with Cornellia and have followed the macrobiotic diet for several years. They are also experienced in giving cooking classes and cooking for large groups, at the GOMF summer camps and other occasions. Since many of these recipes were given by American macrobiotic cooks, they are more acceptable to many Americans than just her own recipes.

Then, Cornellia divided these recipes into four seasons and actually cooked them by herself. After many hours of work and thought, she made the final recipes and wrote how to cook them. Her work was not finished here. After writing the recipes and way of cooking, she added the seasonal cooking hints which make this the most complete macrobiotic cookbook available today. At this time we received a book in Japanese, *The Secret of Zen Cooking* (I. Kajiura, Korinkaku Publishers), from Mrs. Lima Ohsawa, and she suggested I translate it to English. After reading it I found it a very interesting book but I didn't translate it. Many materials used in this book were not available in most of the United States, and most of the cooking is Zen cookery using tofu, natto, various rice misos, etc.; I thought it would be best for more advanced macrobiotic students or for occasional cooking. However, the general advice for the Zen style of cooking in this book was very macrobiotic. Therefore, it was the inspiration for a chapter in our book.

When the book was done, we printed it by the season in four small volumes. Our press was small and our printing technique was poor. Ten years later, however, in order to compete with other macrobiotic cookbooks available on the market and to encourage the general public to accept macrobiotic cooking, we decided to combine the four volumes to one. This meant better quality and a very complete macrobiotic cookbook.

While Cornellia was in Japan, I took over her cooking classes and used this cookbook at our Vega Study House. I found that the recipes were easy to follow and the meals were delicious and health-giving. Many of my students enjoyed them too. Therefore, I am sure you will find that this cookbook will be one of the most useful kitchen tools in your life for many years to come.

Herman Aihara
June 1982

Introduction

by Herman Aihara

Do ("dough"), or tao, is the essential concept not only of the *Tao Te Ching,* written by Lao Tsu, but also of the Chinese mentality. According to R. B. Blakney it means, "A road, a path, the way by which people travel, the way of Nature and finally the way of ultimate reality." (*The Way of Life: Tao Te Ching,* 1955 Mentor N.A.L.) The Chinese character for tao is composed of a head, symbolic representation of a thinking man or ideal order, and another part that primitively depicted the process of walking. Therefore, tao can be said to be the way of nature manifested, or the way man should follow.

George Ohsawa explains do or tao in the *Book of Judo* as follows:

"War cannot be prevented by force. One has only to use the antipode of force; that is, supreme judgment. This is the principle of judo which is a unifying concept of the world or rather a concept of the universe. Such judgment is called do. Judo, sado (tea), kendo (fencing), kado (flower arrangement), ido (medicine), and all the traditional schools indicate that they are based on the do. They are nothing other than different paths toward the same end – namely, an understanding of the order of the universe, the key to the kingdom of heaven." Then what is the order of the universe? He explains in the same book, "In the universe there is an order. This order was named 'tao' by the great Chinese thinkers some thousands of years ago. I have translated it to 'the order of the universe' for a new edition in the 20th century."

According to Ohsawa, the order of the universe has seven theorems, as follows:

1. What has a beginning has an end.
2. There is always a front to a back.
3. The greater the front the greater the back.
4. Nothing is identical in this world.
5. Change is produced by the two antagonistic forces yin and yang, centrifugal and centripetal force.
6. The antagonistic yin and yang can be nothing else than the right and left of oneness, which is infinite, absolute, eternal, dialectical, and is polarized in yin and yang forces.
7. The universe, reality, or oneness is unchangeable, unchanging, constant, boundless, and omnipotent. It is eternity itself, which produces, increases, destroys and produces anew all that is found within.

Therefore, all traditional schools are dojo (jo is a place or building) where students study, comprehend, and acquire the principles of the order of the universe, applying them to the deeds of daily life, as well as trying to achieve an aesthetic sense of shibui (elegance) and the ethical values of modesty and humility.

Since do is an education aiming at Ohsawa's supreme judgment, supreme beauty, shibui, modesty and the humility of human virtue, it does not impart knowledge. Usually the students have no books to read. They must practice and find or acquire the ultimate goal by themselves. This is also true in cooking. There have been no cookbooks in Japan. Teachers rarely teach the quantities of the ingredients and seasonings. Therefore, the students must discover these by themselves. This is the best way of education because students learn the principles as well as the techniques, and as a result they improve their creativity. If only knowledge is given, students learn techniques but not principles. This will cause danger sometimes, as Ohsawa said.

A macrobiotic student left my house to live by himself after having lived with us for about six months. When he visited a few months later he said our food had been a little too salty and too yang for him and that this had caused him to go out and eat ice cream often. Many Americans are like him, especially those who have eaten much animal food before starting the macrobiotic diet. They cannot eat salty foods or yang vegetables even though these foods may not taste overly salty to other people. For example, if I eat at an American macrobiotic home the cooking is often dull due to their use of less salt than is used in my home.

There are three reasons, in my opinion, why some people cannot eat salty foods or why foods may be too salty for one person and not another. The first reason is that some people have a high content of salt in their body cells due to a previous large consumption of animal food. Because of this, the recent Japanese macrobiotic recommendation has been to take shiitake mushrooms (black Japanese mushrooms) or konnyaku (a gelatin-like cake made from yams) cooked with a little salt or no salt. We should have given our friend shiitake or konnyaku without soy sauce when he was staying in our home. However, he didn't tell us about this craving for ice cream until after he left.

A second reason may be weak kidneys. The kidney controls the amount of minerals in the body, especially sodium. If the kidneys are weak, excess sodium circulates in the blood and will cause much stimulation to the parasympathetic nerves; this causes thirst, and inhibition of the heart, kidney, liver, spleen, and pancreas functions which in turn can result in depression, 'hang-ups,' and dragging behavior.

The third reason one cannot take salty foods, or may think foods are salty even though they are not too salty for others, is a psychological one – that of judgment. When depression, hang-ups, cravings, dragginess, or other physical symptoms appear, a macrobiotic student usually thinks he is eating too yang or too salty. However, this is not always true. In most cases the kidneys may be too weak to discharge the toxins and/or excess sodium. While the kidneys are failing to discharge the toxins and salts, these remain in the bloodstream and body cells and cause reactions or psychological effects. Then a person thinks he is eating too salty or yang and may crave some yin foods. He tends to blame the foods but not his condition. He may not be aware of the need to repair his kidneys, and he may stop the symp-

toms of the kidney disease by taking yin food or drink. Therefore, the kidney condition does not improve but stays the same, even if he has been on the diet for many years. The solution for such a case is very difficult. The person may blame and resent the diet or may give up the diet, thinking it is not right for him.

In order to avoid such trouble and to prevent such unhappiness from happening, we should teach the macrobiotic diet carefully. One solution for this is not to give any quantities of ingredients in cookbooks so that everyone cooks by his/her own taste or need. Then when mistakes are made, we will have no one to blame but ourselves. This way of education is do. It is one of the quickest ways to improve judgment.

Since most Americans are not trained in this way, we give quantities for each ingredient mentioned in the recipes. However, you should disregard the quantities after you have tried a recipe once or twice so that you will find the quantity best suited for you or your family.

In short, however skillfully or well you prepare your food, some people may not like your cooking. You must learn that what is good for one is not good for another. What tastes delicious to someone may not be delicious for someone else. This is frustrating at times. Can we learn a technique which will satisfy everyone? Is there any cuisine which is delicious or nutritious to everyone? The answer, unfortunately, is no – because everything is different in this relative world. Then what is the highest cooking? Knowing that everyone and everything is different, to cook and to serve with the best materials available within the limits of space and time, and to prepare with modesty and humility is the supreme cooking – shibui. Learning such an art is do. One who has reached such a state of cooking will be able to overcome any difficulties in life and create a happy and free life. This is the tao of cooking, or ryori-do.

The Macrobiotic Diet

Many people give up the macrobiotic diet after following it for awhile. Some may stay on it only for a month. Some may give it up after several years. There are many reasons for giving it up, and for each individual the reason may be different. One of the most common reasons is that changes resulting from the diet may be too confusing and too surprising. As one observes the diet, he starts to change his constitution, character, likings and desires – in short, his ego or self. Such changes cause uncomfortable or annoying feelings. One faces the dualistic confusion of two egos. One is the conservative self and the other is the radical, idealistic self. One is the sentimental ego, which has been molded by school or family education. This ego is very much concerned about status, income, living conditions, comforts, etc. He feels uncomfortable and unhappy giving these up. The other ego is the aspiration or the striving of his higher judgment by which he reveals his real self. If his understanding of the real self, or the desire to reveal his real self, is not profound, one does not want to change himself. This is one reason why he may give up the diet. Therefore, in order to continue the macrobiotic diet, one must have a motive which drives him to his higher self.

In Japan, many people – including students, businessmen, politicians, scientists, and many other kinds of people – go to Zen monasteries to practice zazen (Zen meditation). Why? What will they learn from zazen?

They learn how to change themselves in a most simple way. Many of these people have mental or psychological problems stemming from disharmony in family life, sexual or financial troubles, etc. They go to Zen temples after trying without success to solve those problems through modern conventional methods. Their minds are always occupied. Therefore, there is no room for inspiration, a new idea, or imagination to enter. They are 'hung-up,' trapped and rigid.

In the Zen temple, one sits and breathes deeply from the abdomen which settles the blood down. As a result, the overabundant blood in the brain is distributed to the lower parts of the body. One begins to feel less nervous, and as the brain starts to function better one can think more clearly. Then the body relaxes and fresh ideas can flow. Zen is an Eastern style of psychiatry. Zen masters do nothing to the student. The student changes himself. He finds the solution by himself.

Simple meals were traditionally eaten in the Zen temples. The meals consisted of macrobiotic foods such as whole grains, miso soup, seaweeds, pickles, and vegetables. Preparation of simple meals has been practiced in Zen temples for hundreds of years. This is called 'shojin ryori,' which means 'judgment-improving-cooking.' The most sophisticated cuisine in Japan today is called shojin ryori. You have to pay extremely high prices to eat this cuisine if you dine in one of the best shojin ryori restaurants.

This shojin ryori is not only delicious but also nutritious and spirit-developing. One who stays in Zen temples will benefit not only from zazen but also from the spiritual foods they serve. However, students do not rely on the diet or even on the masters. They solve all problems by themselves. They do not depend on anything except themselves. They really know that no one can help them to be a happy man – a real self – except themselves; that sitting zazen does not give them the solution but is only a help.

This is true in the case of the macrobiotic diet. One should not depend on anything, not even his mastery of the macrobiotic diet itself. Neither master nor diet can change him into the real self, a happy man. They are only aids. However, the diet is really a great help, for without it the task can be almost impossible.

Many macrobiotic followers make a mistake and think that on the macrobiotic diet one automatically realizes his real self, the happy man, and as a result they depend on the macrobiotic diet but not on themselves. Depending on something outside of oneself is a great mistake which is often followed by disappointment or resentment. I say this especially because there are often misunderstandings in this respect. Don't rely upon the diet to solve your problems, to make you happy, or to help you to realize your true self. However, for one who struggles to be happy for himself and by himself, the macrobiotic diet can be a great help if not the greatest.

There are two types of people who quit the macrobiotic diet. One type is afraid of the changes the diet will bring, and the other is ungrateful for the changes the diet has brought. I have already written about the first type of person earlier in this introduction. We cannot do anything about this type of person because he doesn't want to change himself.

The other type of person is very important to us because as long as there is such a person, our teaching is neither perfect nor correct. I have met many people who cured their sickness or solved their problems or changed to happier lives, yet quit the diet. Most people start the macrobiotic diet because of their suffering or unhappiness. However, they often forget their suffering and unhappiness when they feel better. When they feel normal, they easily forget the benefit they received. They have not suffered enough to acquire an appreciation big enough so that the importance of the diet becomes unforgettable. One who has gratitude and humility is happy. Therefore, he is happy to continue the diet. One who has no gratitude is unhappy, even though he is not sick anymore. Therefore, he does not continue the diet. This is the right thing. This happens because our ultimate goal is happiness which is manifested by appreciation. If there is no appreciation, there is no happiness. If you don't gain any appreciation, there is no happiness. If you don't gain any appreciation for anything, something must be wrong – including the diet.

To be happy, grateful, and humble you must not be tired, you must sleep well, have a good appetite, no constipation, no allergies. However, fulfilling these conditions does not necessarily always bring gratefulness or humility. In other words, some key point exists in our life which causes the switch-over from unhappy feelings (lack of gratitude and humility) to happy feelings (gratitude and humility). How, when, and where this key point is found is an individual matter. This exists beyond description, beyond foods, and beyond cooking techniques. However, the individual key for you to use must be modified to fit your lock. Discovering and modifying this key is left up to each person.

. . . .

The entire issue of *House Beautiful* magazine, August 1960, was devoted to Japan. Writing about Japanese cuisine, the editors said they found it to be the best of the twenty-nine countries they had visited. Macrobiotic cuisine should be even better than those dishes the editors tasted in Japanese restaurants because macrobiotic cuisine uses no chemicals, no chemically produced condiments, no artificial flavoring agents, no preservatives, no other artificial agents – while most Japanese restaurants use chemically grown white rice, sugar, monosodium glutamate, dyed tea, and miso and soy sauce that have been produced by processed methods. Macrobiotic cooking requires much skill. However, once you learn it, the macrobiotic cooking method will be far superior to restaurant cuisine in taste and nutrition.

The editors of *House Beautiful* went on to say:

We discovered some basic truths which are above and beyond cost. Such a one is the new world of soup stocks and cooking stocks made of dried kelp and dried bonita and loaded with trace elements;

dipping sauces and marinades that give new zest to familiar foods; preserved chestnuts that are better than candy. There was a whole world of tender sprouts and leaf tips: fern fronds, ginger sprouts, lotus roots, lily bulbs, trefoil (a long-stemmed three-leaf clover), pepper tree buds, horseradish sprouts, soybean sprouts, young chrysanthemum leaves.

Some ingredients basic to their cuisine we literally have no counterpart for. Such a one is miso, a paste made from soybeans that may be sweet or salty or red or white, and can make a dressing for green vegetables, a marinade for meats, or the filling body of a soup. All delicious!

But there was an over-riding element, more important than these details. The total syndrome of Japanese ingredients and methods – the way all the parts fitted lyrically with all the other parts – towered like the Himalayas in the world's gastronomy. I had previously felt that the classic French cuisine, which you meet in the finest French homes (rather than in the famous restaurants that put a strain on your liver) was the purest, most elevated, and sensitive form of cooking extant. But my 149 meals in Japan made me shift gears very decidedly.

The editors ate in many Japanese restaurants while in Japan. The foods they ate were not whole grains or authentically produced foods. The macrobiotic diet contains a much higher nutritional value than what they ate in Japan. Even so, they said:

For not only is the Japanese cuisine worthy of the attention of the most serious gourmet, but it is nutritionally big news at this time in science's unfolding of our nutritional needs. For it is low in calories, low in animal fats, high in calcium, phosphorous, loaded with vitamin A, and loaded with trace elements, thanks to their heavy use of the products of the sea – dried seaweeds and dried shrimp, fishes – and to the prevalent use of nut and vegetable oils. . . .

Assuming you would blend Japanese foods with our American diet . . . you would have an ideal way to lower your total intake of calories and fats while raising the intake of the wanted nutrients. If we are all at least 20 pounds overweight, as the new figures from the actuaries say we are, here is the answer to how to eat agreeably and heartily while getting our weight down to where it ought to be.

This cookbook is designed and written to teach you such cuisine and such methods of cooking.

. . . .

Since ancient times, wise men knew of the relationship between food and health, happiness, and freedom in men. They advised a diet which creates a healthy body and a happy life. Such a diet developed later as medicine. Foods were medicine for the ancient Greeks, Hindus, Chinese, and Japanese. In the Japanese tea ceremony, a dinner is called 'yaku seki' which means 'medicinal drug.' The 'gokanmon,' Zen chant given before meals, says 'to eat food is to keep the body healthy.' According to *The Secret of Zen Cooking,* many Zen temples in Japan kept memoranda of cooking for the sick. Miss T. Nagasaki, a modern Japanese nutritionist, recommends Zen cookery, saying that fucha-ryori, a type of Rinzai Zen cooking, has high nutritional value. Her report was published at Wohbaku Temple, Uji, Kyoto, Japan, 1967 entitled: *Fucha-ryori and its Nutritional Value.*

Although delicious taste is important in daily meals, if such meals deteriorate health, such cooking is not right for us. Therefore, the purpose of cooking is the development of tasty meals, health, and higher judgment for mankind.

The macrobiotic diet and way of cooking strengthens the life force because of the purity and naturalness of the foods and seasonings used. They calm the mind, protect us from sickness, raise our judgment – provided we study the principles of life and contemplate humility. Therefore, mastering macrobiotic cooking is very important in life for both men and women. We do not say that the macrobiotic diet and cooking are the solution to every problem, but they certainly may serve as two of the most important factors for creating and maintaining a healthy body and a happy life.

The Dō of Cooking

Selecting Good Foods

First of all, freshness is a primary factor in the selection of vegetables. Vegetables just brought from the market are still wet. Open the bundles of fresh vegetables and dry in a dark place for about three to four hours. Then, put in plastic bags so that the vegetables will retain their freshness and not dry out. If wet vegetables are kept in a refrigerator they will quickly spoil.

The taste of vegetables is always better when they are in season. They are also much cheaper then. Get into the habit of using vegetables when they are in season. Most vegetables are sold in markets all year round. This indicates that most of them are produced in faraway places or grown in hothouses. It is therefore important to learn which vegetables are produced in each season. If you use seasonal foods, they will be grown in nearby places. This allows your body to adapt to your environment.

Spring to Summer Vegetables——————

Cauliflower (Oct.–June): Choose a head with a green outside and closed flower buds. When the buds are open, the taste is not so good. A reddish color indicates age. Yellow color means the vegetable is overripe. Cook in wheat flour water as for asparagus. Good in salads, sauteed, or with wheat sauce and vinegar.

Broccoli (Oct.–June): If the flower is opened too much, it is too mature and the taste is not good.

Mustard greens (Feb.–April): The distinguished bitter taste of mustard greens neutralizes excess yang accumulated during the cold winter season. The best time to eat them is in the beginning of spring. Good boiled, with sesame seeds, pickled, and in miso soup.

Dandelion (Feb.–April): Wild vegetables should not exceed more than ½ the weight of other vegetables when prepared (they should always be eaten along with garden vegetables because of the high potassium content). Dandelion is good sauteed with cabbage. If you find a large root, wash it thoroughly and slice very thin. Saute it with sesame oil (use slightly more oil than for garden vegetables) for a long time over a low flame. The root can be eaten year round. Good for yin and anemic persons.

Asparagus (May–July): Varieties that grow in cooler climates are softer, rounder, and have better taste. Vertical fibers indicate a harder, less tasty variety. Prepare asparagus by boiling in 5 cups of water with 1 Tbsp. whole wheat flour and 1 tsp. salt. Cook until tender and rinse. Drain and serve with French dressing or mayonnaise. Very good as tempura or prepared with sesame seeds.

Red Cabbage (May–June) or (Oct.–Dec.): Brush with salt, then wash. (This makes a nice color.) Good for salads, or serve with French dressing.

Bell pepper (May–Sept.): The short, round varieties have more seeds and are harder. The triangular variety is longer and has fewer seeds; select the latter. They are delicious when stuffed and baked in the oven, boiled, deep-fried with batter, or used raw in salads. Discard the seeds after cutting. Rich in vitamins A and C.

Cucumber (May–Sept.): Those with a smooth shape have a better taste; a bent top indicates that the cucumber dried on the stalk in the field. Also, avoid those with a yellow color, because this indicates a hard skin. Cucumbers that still have a flower are fresh and taste good.

Eggplant (May–Sept.): Large eggplants are good for boiling, baking, and sauteing. Smaller eggplants are good for pickles. Autumn eggplant is good for mustard pickles and miso pickles because it contains less water.

Peas and string beans (May–Nov.): If the size is very small, the taste is not so good. Just before maturity is when the beans taste best. Suitable for boiling, steaming, tempura, and miso soup.

Summer squash (June–Sept.): Zucchini, yellow crookneck, patti-pan should be young and tender.

Tomato (June–Sept.): Well-ripened tomatoes are strongly acidic. Therefore, they are best for cooking purposes rather than raw. Greenish tomatoes are good for salad, or they may be pickled. To remove skin, drop vegetable in hot water, then peel off skin with your fingers. For salad, use a knife to remove the skin.

Potato (June–Aug.): Those varieties with a rough skin are produced in a warmer climate. Small and hard varieties taste better.

Cabbage (June–Aug.): This is one vegetable that is easily available all year round. However, the best season to eat cabbage is between June and August. A tightly rolled hard head is good for cooking. Soft, loosely rolled heads are best for making pickles, soup, stuffed cabbage rolls, and salad.

Corn (Aug.): Those with yellowish, well-ripened kernels fresh from the field taste best. Those with a wrinkled skin and cornsilk should be avoided. Good for soup, tempura, or corn on the cob.

Autumn to Winter Vegetables

Satoimo (albi or taro)-(Aug.–Nov.): Wash it with a tawashi (vegetable brush) to remove the loose feathery skin. If the potato shows white underneath, it is good. If the color is green and the shape is more elongated, the potato was grown too near the surface. These do not taste as good. Around November, many stores have big albi. These are the original parent plants (oyaimo or kashiraimo). They are harder, so they are better for stews. Small albi are better for miso soup and nitsuke.

Winter squash (Sept.–Nov.): Squash tastes best when picked exactly at its time of maturity. Unripe squash is not very sweet, but over-matured squash is very porous. Usually, those grown in a large flower bed around a raised center taste good. Squash should be hard and heavy and have a nice color. Good for soup, sauce, and tempura.

Yams (Sept.–Nov.): The best are usually harvested at this time, but they are available all year. These are good for kanten (desserts), nitsuke, tempura, and miso soup.

Daikon radish (Sept.–Nov.): The less watery, hard, straight ones with smooth skins are best. Big daikon should be heavy. If they are not, then something is wrong. The inside may be empty or dried out. This vegetable has innumerable uses, all delicious. They are good for nitsuke, pickles, stew, miso soup, or salad.

Turnips and Rutabagas (Sept.–Feb.): Turnips can grow all year in lower California, but the best-tasting ones mature from autumn to early winter. Small ones are good for pickles, salads, and miso soup. Big turnips are good for nitsuke, stews, and mushi mono (a steaming process). They have the best sweet turnip taste if you cook them for a long time until they fall apart easily. After April-May, the small turnip variety gets big and tough. The cellulose gets hard and the taste is less flavorful.

Chinese cabbage (Sept.–March): Those with the best taste appear around November after the frost. The frost makes the cabbage tender and sweet. They are good for pickles, sauteing, nitsuke, stew, and miso soup. Heavy heads are best. They are more yang and compact.

Burdock (Oct.–Dec.): If possible you should use it as soon as you take it from your garden. When you choose it from the market, select ones as thick as your thumb, straight and long. Don't choose fat ones because many times the center can be hard and woody. Some stores have fresh burdock during the summer (July–Aug.). This is younger and sweet, still all right.

Leeks (Nov.–April): This vegetable is similar to scallions. Those harvested from November to April have the best taste. Good for miso soup, clear soup, cooked with celery, or in vegetable stews.

All Year Vegetables

Carrots: If carrots planted in June, July, or August are allowed to pass through the winter they will blossom in early May. At this stage, however, they are too woody and tough to use as food. Otherwise they are good all year round, though the best season is autumn. Carrots are good in nitsuke, stew, salads, miso soup, and clear soup.

Jinenjo: This amazing vegetable grows wild in the mountains of Japan. It has such a strong life force that it will pass through cracks in rocks, splitting them apart as it grows. It grows very slowly, in a zig-zag pattern. After planting, it takes a few years to grow to usable size (about 1½ feet). The pulp is very sticky. It is used in tororo soup (jinenjo ground in a suribachi and served raw), and also good for making jinenjo kinpira or tekka miso, a condiment good for heart disease and rheumatism or any disease caused by an excess of yin. Jinenjo gives much strength and energy, and helps people with weak sexual appetite. It may be found in America growing wild in the mountains – perhaps you can discover it. It is included here for the adventurers who want to search for this extremely strengthening food.

Nagaimo: This is available all year round in Japanese markets, though autumn is the best season for it. Nagaimo is cultivated jinenjo. It is hairy, light tan, and firm with a sticky white center. It is around two feet long. It has less flavor and taste than jinenjo and is not as yang, but it is still very yang. It is good in stew, soup, nitsuke, fried, or steamed.

Bean sprouts (moyashi): There are two kinds of sprouts: mung bean and soybean. If these have grown into leaves in the store, or have turned reddish-brown, don't buy them; they are too old. Bean sprouts spoil very quickly, so don't get too large a quantity at one time (just enough for three or four days use). Keep them in the refrigerator in a plastic bag. They are good for salads and sauteing, but don't overcook; if you do, they will shrink. Keep them crispy for the best taste.

Ginger: Ginger helps neutralize animal food poisons. It helps digest oily foods and generally stimulates digestion. It makes the fishy taste disappear from your seafood dishes, and gives a good flavor to all meat, poultry, or fish dishes. In the summertime from July to September, fresh ginger arrives in the Oriental markets. The skin is softer and lighter and does not have to be removed for cooking. It is good for making salted plum juice pickles. These are pink and look especially nice in chirashi-sushi (see *Calendar Cookbook,* GOMF, #196). Ginger pickles (similar to #82) are good condiments for baked fish and egg omelettes.

To keep ginger fresh: Fill a small box with sand, moisten it, and keep the ginger covered with sand. In this way the ginger will keep fresh for a year.

Scallions: Scallions are most delicious from autumn to winter. Scallions pulled after frost are best; these are the most tender and sweet, and are good for nabemono and other stews. Summer scallions are quite hard, not so good for cooking, but they make a good condiment for noodles. Scallions with a dark green color are best. Those that are yellow or white are not so good. Scallions are good through the winter if stored properly. To do this, dig a hole five inches shorter than the scallions, stand them up in the hole and fill with earth. The earth will slowly turn the scallions white due to the absence of light, and will keep them crisp. This makes them taste better. You can keep them all winter in the warmer states by doing this.

You can keep burdock the same way as scallions. Cover the burdock with sand about one inch above the tops. Later the burdock leaves will push through and grow.

You can do the same with daikon, but don't cover the greens. Leave them and one inch of the top of the daikon exposed. They will keep all winter like this where there is no snow. Carrots can be preserved in the same way with the greens exposed outside the earth.

Onions: Onions are a very good vegetable for all sorts of dishes, because the taste and flavor lends itself well to so many different foods. Small onions are good for stews (used whole) and salads (sliced). Large onions are watery and do not taste so good – avoid them. Buy the small ones; they are more nutritious and have a sweeter, more delicious taste. Onions kept in storage during the spring sprout very quickly, so don't store too many at this time or you may find your supply has become an onion patch.

Small red radish: Clear bright red ones with smooth skin and no black or white spots are best. Black spots indicate old radishes. Good for salad and fried food decorations, nitsuke, and miso soup.

Spinach: The best-tasting spinach ripens from autumn to the end of April. After that it goes to flower. Rich soil makes it grow darker. A yellowish-green color means the soil was not so good. Good for ohitashi, aemono, boiled salads, and clear soup or miso soup.

Lotus root: Lotus root is available all year round, but fresh lotus arrives in the Oriental markets around July. Lotus should have a uniform brownish-tan color and smooth skin. If it has dark areas it is not so good. Try to get those with the most yang shape.

Dried Foods

Bonita (katsuobushi): Good bonita is completely dry. It looks like a piece of dry wood, about 8″ long and 2″ wide at the center. If there is a little bit of green mold on the bonita, this is good; it helps keep the bonita fresh. When you buy unshaved dried bonita, don't wash it in water. Use a dry tawashi or dry towel to rub off the green mold. You should shave bonita just before using with a bonita shaver, which is a wooden box with a blade. If you cannot get one, you can use a fish knife. Shave it in the same way you sharpen a pencil. Shavings do not keep long – even one hour later they lose flavor if not used. Use immediately to get the best fresh taste.

Bonita flakes (kezu ri bushi): These are made from broken pieces of bonita or mackerel or bass, made into flakes by a machine which shaves them very thin. The taste is sometimes heavy and somewhat acid, and has a strong fish smell, so packaged bonita flakes are not used in good cooking. They are easy to use because they are already shaved, so use them when you are in a hurry, but only when it is not possible to shave the katsuobushi yourself.

Chuba iriko (niboshi): This is a baby sardine, which has been boiled and then dried. Since they have already been cooked, you can eat them without further cooking. When you are shopping for chuba iriko, choose the fish that are 1½″ long with a silver color. The bigger chuba (2″-3″ long) have a very fishy taste, so they are not good for soup stock. If they are reddish or brown and oil comes out of the body, you should not buy them. This means they are old. If you want to keep the chuba for a long time, dry them completely in the sun, and store in a can with a tight cover.

Dried tofu (koya tofu): This is made during the cold season by first freezing fresh tofu in natural cold weather and then drying it. Fresh koya tofu has an ivory color. As the color gets darker it loses its taste, so keep it in a dry place.

Kampyo (gourd strips): Kampyo is made into strips in the summer. When fresh, it is pure white, but turns yellowish after awhile. Keep it fresh by hanging it in an airy place.

Kanten (agar-agar, or jelly seaweed): Kanten is made from a variety of seaweed called 'ten gusa.' After cooking ten gusa it is frozen during the cold season and then dried. This forms the kanten. If you wrap it in paper, tie it, and hang it in a dry airy place, you can store it for 10 years.

Kombu: If it has a deep dark color, is covered with a white powder, and is thick, then it is really good kombu. The surface of kombu has the best taste. If you wash the surface with water you remove this good taste, so to clean kombu just open the folded pieces and brush off the sand and dust with your fingers by slapping each piece with your hands. Then pour water down both sides, catching it in a pan. Save this water to use in cooking. If you soak kombu in water, all the kombu taste will dissolve in the water.

To keep kombu fresh, tie a bunch in the center and hang it from the rafters or in an airy place. If mold grows on the kombu, don't throw it away. Remove the mold by washing it with your finger under running water. The mold makes the kombu soft and gives it a good taste. You don't need to throw the molded kombu away. To cook it, cut it in 1″ square pieces and cook it in water seasoned with soy sauce to your taste. Cook it a long time until the kombu becomes soft and the soy sauce and salt flavor saturate each piece. This is called 'shio kombu' in Japanese. It makes a good condiment for rice or is used in the center of rice balls instead of a piece of salted plum.

Sesame seeds (goma): There are three kinds of goma: black (kuro goma), brown (cha goma), and white (shiro goma). (In Japan, there are whole – unhulled – sesame seeds that are white, but in America the white ones are usually hulled.) The black are the most yang, the white the most yin. Black goma are grown in a colder climate. White seeds are used more in salads. Black sesame seeds are usually used in gomashio (sesame salt) in Japan, on steamed sweet brown rice and azuki beans (seki han), and on azuki rice (azuki gohan). Black sesame seeds are usually used on these foods because they give more flavor, and the contrast of red and black looks very nice.

Sesame seeds should have a round shape and all be the same size. If they are different colors and flat instead of round, then the taste is not very good. When washing sesame seeds, some seeds stay on the surface of the water. These are not completely ripe. Since we are concerned with economy we use them too. They don't have as much oil, protein, or minerals, but there is no reason not to use them.

Shiitake (Japanese dried mushroom): Mushrooms with short or medium-sized stalks are best because the button is more meaty. If it has a long stalk, there is usually little meat in the button part, which is the most delicious part. Shiitake doesn't like sun, so it is best to dry it in a shady place. After it is completely dry, keep it in a plastic bag or covered can.

Wakame: Wakame grown in the cold season has the best taste. The best wakame comes from turbulent waters where the ocean churns and waves swirl. Fresh wakame is dark blackish green; if it is completely black, then it is old. Nowadays some companies dye the wakame with artificial color. Test for dye by soaking it in water. If the water changes to a green color suddenly, this is dyed – don't use it. Natural wakame does not color the soaking water.

Choosing Fish and Fowl────────────

Choose fish according to the season when they are most plentiful and delicious. Most fish tastes best during the spawning season because there is fat meat on the back and stomach at this time. During this time, the fish have more energy. So fish at this time taste good prepared in any way – raw, baked, fried, etc. Also, since they are plentiful, they are cheaper to buy.

When you buy fish it is important to get fresh fish; cooking methods are of secondary importance. So please train your eye to recognize and choose well. Try to shop at a busy store to insure getting fresh fish.

Fresh fish has a good firm shape, natural color, moistness, shininess, clear eyes, and no missing scales. Mackerel and bass will have a clear blue color. The stomach of a fresh fish should be firm to the touch – springy, bouncing back when pressed with the finger. Hold the fish in the middle to test for freshness; it should remain flat on the hand. If the head and the tail bend downward, it is old. The fins on the back and the chest of fresh fish are firm and stand up. A small amount of laying-down is all right. Fresh fish from the ocean have a good clean ocean smell. Freshwater fish have little or no odor, just a good clean smell. Sliced fish you buy in the stores should also have a good smell, color, natural shine, firmness and be fairly moist – should not be soft or in broken pieces.

If you see a mackerel or bass that is not a clear green color but looks whitish, then it is getting old. If the fins are soft and weak and the eyes are red or white, it is old. If you press the stomach and fluid comes out of the anal pore or organs are coming out of the stomach, then the fish is too old. Old fish have a strong offensive fishy smell. If the fish scales are changing to a whitish color or are falling out, do not buy it – it is old.

Ocean fish are usually quite oily, so serve them raw or cook them simply. Try to bring out the natural fish taste. Freshwater fish are not oily, so cook them with oil to improve the taste.

If you have caught or bought a lot of fish, pickle them in salt. Then, before serving, roast them over a gas flame on a metal toaster or frying pan. This gives them a very good taste. When you have whole fish, be sure to wash thoroughly, remove the scales and internal organs; then keep cool or in a refrigerator until ready for use. If you keep whole fish in the refrigerator that have not been cleaned, they will spoil quickly. So clean them first before putting in the refrigerator.

Before cooking fish with green skins, wash them first with salt water. This also improves the taste. This method is for fresh fish.

Different seasons are better for different fish. In spring, the best are red snapper, sardine, herring, bass, and most shellfish with two shells. In the summer, look for flounder, salmon, trout, abalone, and eel. In autumn, there are bass, red snapper, sardines, steelhead, mackerel, shrimp, and oysters; oysters are best September to March. Scallops are good in spring. In winter, you find tuna, flounder, cod, carp, and mackerel, as well as oysters and scallops. Sole, perch, whitefish, smelt, halibut, catfish, and mullet are plentiful in fish stores when in season.

Stale fish giving off a strong fishy smell will taste all right if cooked, so it is best to broil it in the oven, then cook it in soy sauce-water or saute it with oil in a fry pan. You can use a sweet-sour kuzu sauce to cover the fish or use a bit of spice to make the fish more delicious. If you have a fish that is not so fresh and you want to fry it, another method is to sprinkle it all over with rice vinegar and let sit for 5 minutes before frying. This will remove any fishy smell. Another method is to sprinkle fresh ginger juice and salt over the fish and set aside for 1 hour. Then wash it under running water, cleaning off any blood. Dry with a paper towel before frying.

To tell fresh shellfish: If the shells are wide open, the shellfish is dead. If partly open, then they are not so fresh. Sometimes, they have half-opened mouths. If they close when you beat on the shell, they are living and okay. Sometimes the shellfish body is out of the shell. If you touch your finger to the body and it goes back suddenly into its shell, then it is living and is all right to eat. Sometimes the shell is closed but the shellfish is dead inside. To tell if the shellfish is living inside, take one shellfish in each hand and knock them together. If the sound is "katchi-katchi" then this sound tells you they are living. If the sound is "boke-boke" this means the shellfish is dead. So be careful when you choose and cook shellfish; one dead one will make the whole batch taste bad.

If you want to keep living shellfish fresh in the cold season, it is possible to do so for about a week only. Do not use water. Set them in a wooden or porcelain container and cover with a small wooden dish with a small stone on top for light pressure. The cover should be a little smaller than the container so that it can go down with the pressure.

When buying oysters, be sure the oyster body edges are a clear black, not greyish or white. The meat should be ivory or greenish white. Only like this are oysters fresh.

Fresh abalone can be recognized when the meat sits inside the shell firmly. When you press it with your finger it springs back to its original shape. If the meat comes out of the shell easily and is soft, it is dead and not good to eat.

When buying fresh shellfish without the shells, check for natural shine and firmness.

Chicken: Whole young chickens should be fat on the hips and back and have a smooth cream-colored skin. If the breastbone is soft, this means the chicken is young and the meat is tender. The meat in fresh chicken has a clear color in both the white and the red areas. If the gallbladder breaks, it will color the flesh purple or green. Remove meat parts that have this color.

Eggs: Fresh eggs have an evenly rough shell. Old egg shells get smooth from handling. If the egg appears dark when held up to the light, it is old. Examine the egg when you break it; if the yolk is higher than the white and the white part is jelly-like, this is fresh. Old eggs have a watery white part. A small red spot near the yolk means the egg is fertile.

Techniques for Cooking Fish

Before boiling fish, take 1 cup of water and mix it with 2 Tbsp. of salt. Marinate fish in this mixture for 30 minutes. This will make the fish contract and become firmer, so that it won't break easily on cooking. Prepare the fish sauce (see recipe below) and bring to a boil. Add the fish and bring to a boil again, then cook over a medium flame uncovered for 20 minutes. Turn fish on the other side and cook for 10 minutes longer. The fish sauce should just cover the fish. If you cook old fish, add mirin (sweet Japanese sake) or yinnie syrup. This makes it taste sweet. Season fresh fish with soy sauce and a little bit of ginger juice to bring out the fresh flavor.

Flounder is a very soft fish. To cook it, first prepare fish sauce and bring to a boil. Add the fish, then turn the flame to medium and cook for 30-40 minutes. Then let the fish sit in the cooking pan until cold. Remove to serving plate.

If you boil cod in this way, it breaks up easily. So for cod, add 1 tsp. of arrowroot or kuzu in preparing the fish sauce. Cooked in this manner, the cod will not fall apart.

Fish sauce:
    1 cup water or soup stock
    2 Tbsp. natural soy sauce
    1 Tbsp. sake
    1 Tbsp. mirin or yinnie syrup (if you like it sweet)

When using kombu stock, make it the following way: To 10 cups of cold water add 1 piece of 4″ × 12″ kombu and boil for 30 minutes. Remove the kombu and reserve the stock. Don't use bonita or chuba iriko soup stock. The taste is too heavy to combine with cooked fish. It is best to use kombu stock or plain water. Natural macrobiotic soy sauce adds a nice flavor.

Fish can be seasoned with miso. When boiling or broiling fish, before you add the miso, bring 1 cup of soup stock to a boil. Add the cooked fish and bring it to a boil again, then cook over a low flame for 10 minutes. Add 3 Tbsp. of barley miso (or 1½ Tbsp. of rice miso and 1½ Tbsp. of barley miso). Before adding it to the stock or water and fish, make a paste of the miso and some of the stock or water. Miso fish stew is prepared the same way. The fish is cooked first.

When you use kuzu or arrowroot for a thick sauce, first transfer the cooked fish from the cooking pan to a serving dish. Then dilute the kuzu or arrowroot by adding 2 times as much water. Bring it to a boil, pour sauce over fish, and serve sprinkled with scallion or parsley.

If your fish has a really strong fish smell after cooking it, add ginger juice or lemon peel and mix it with the cooked fish. Then shut off the flame. This helps to give it a good flavor. You can also use lemon, orange, or tangerine juice. When using citrus juice, remove the cooked fish from the heat before adding the juice. Do not cook it.

To soften the bones of freshwater fish, broil or bake it first, then dry in the sun. Cover fish with plain water and cook for about 1 hour. Add soy sauce for seasoning. This method makes all the bones soft, including the head.

When you bake fish in the oven, it must be broiling hot – 450°. First heat up a cookie sheet, oil lightly, then set the fish on the sheet. Put it in the oven and bake for 20 minutes. Then carefully turn the fish over and bake on the other side for 30 minutes more until both sides are slightly browned. If you are cooking sliced fish, bake the meat side first, then turn over and bake the skin side. When you are cooking oily fish (sardines or mackerel) in season (at which time they are the oiliest), sometimes the oil burns and makes black smoke. This black smoke makes the fish dirty. So, take out the cookie sheet several times, air out the oven and bake some more. This gives the fish a good naturally brown color, instead of smoky and black.

If you bake in a fireplace, barbecue style, when camping or picnicking, heat up the metal grate first, then coat it with vegetable oil. Soak up the excess water from the fish with a paper towel, then bake. This method makes a beautiful baked fish. If you use a metal skewer with the fish, take it out carefully right after baking, when the fish is still hot. Hold the fish with one hand and remove the skewer by turning it. When you are finished cooking, wash the skewer and put on a little oil before storing it away.

Traditionally, when serving whole fish it is customary to place the head of the fish to the left on the serving plate, with the stomach facing you.

When frying fish, it is best to use a heavy frying pan. First heat the pan hot, add oil, then fish, and cook covered over medium flame. Cook for about 15 minutes, then turn over once and cook for another 15 minutes uncovered. If you wish to steam-cook, after adding the fish add ½ cup boiling water, pouring it around the edge of the pan. Then cover. The lid must fit tightly, otherwise steam escapes. Fry over medium heat until tender.

Shellfish already contain much water which tends to dilute the taste of the sauce in which they are cooked. If you cook shellfish for a long time, they become hard. This is not good. To keep them soft and make them taste good at the same time, cook the following way:

Prepare the fish sauce first (see page 22). Divide the fish sauce into 3 portions. Place one portion in a saucepan, bring to a boil, add the husked shellfish, bring to boil again and strain shellfish from sauce. Add another portion of fish sauce to the pan. Bring the sauce to a boil, add shellfish and once more strain out the shellfish. Add the remaining portion of fish sauce to the pan and cook uncovered on a high flame until ½ evaporates. Then add the fish again, cook over a high flame for 5 minutes, and remove from heat. Then set shellfish in a pan for about 1 hour. It is now ready to serve and will be very tender, tasty shellfish.

To cook squid, rub the whole body of the squid with salt. This helps to remove the skin. After removing the skin, wash off the salt. Cut the squid tentacles in 1″ strips. Bring salted water to a gentle boil (2 cups water to 1 tsp. salt). Add the squid and bring to a boil once more. Remove the pan from the heat. Leave the squid in the pan until the water cools. Strain and save the cooking water. Bring the cooking water to a boil, add 2 Tbsp. soy sauce, 1 Tbsp. mirin or yinnie syrup and bring to a boil again. Remove from the heat, add the cooked squid and soak in this hot sauce for 2 hours. Turn squid over every 30 minutes. It is then ready to serve. This method makes it very tender. Use the leftover squid sauce in cooking vegetables.

The Secret of Cooking

Seasons and Locality of Foods

An important principle of the macrobiotic diet is to eat locally-grown foods in season (see *Macrobiotics: An Invitation to Health and Happiness,* GOMF). Therefore the best cook always uses vegetables which grow nearby (backyard products are best), and those in season. One who serves such foods to family and guests will be the best cook. A Japanese word for feast is 'gochiso,' meaning 'running back and forth.' In other words, a feast is a service, part of which consists of going back and forth to the garden to pick vegetables and wild grasses which are often cooked immediately before serving.

At a feast you give the best of what you have, which are natural products – the healthiest foods. Cooking requires thought and care. If you cook only for sensory pleasure and use condiments and spices a lot, you will not develop into a good cook. In our modern convenience-oriented society, traditional cooking seems outdated. However, this way of cooking may be the answer to our present alienation from nature. Real ecology should start in the kitchen.

Grains and vegetables can be eaten during all four seasons in most areas. Winter-grown vegetables should be eaten in winter, summer-grown vegetables in summer, etc. Fruits also should be eaten during the season in which they grow.

In most cases vegetables should be eaten in season. However, one who has no nearby source of seasonal vegetables may eat out-of-season vegetables. Your cooking technique will help balance the nutrients of the vegetables used. Natural grains and seaweeds can be eaten even if they come from foreign countries; the reason is that grain and seaweed can be grown in most of the temperate zones. In time, condiments such as miso and soy sauce will be more and more domestically produced.

The Principle of No Waste

Another macrobiotic principle of cooking is no waste. Cook with whole grains, whole grain flours, whole vegetables, and whole fish. However, in some cooking techniques you may need to separate parts, such as leaves and roots of a vegetable, and cook the roots separately because they take a longer time to cook than the leaves.

Another exception to this principle is not to use fish liver because toxins from polluted waters accumulate in the liver of the fish.

An example of how to use the whole is the use of daikon radish. The best (middle) part of the daikon is used for nitsuke vegetable, and both end parts of the daikon are either grated or used in miso soup. Radish leaves are good for pickles. In short, macrobiotic cooking adapts the way of cooking to the part of the vegetable that is being cooked.

When cooking fish, use the whole fish; the bones and head can be used for making soup stock. Hard fish bones can be barbecued on the stove until they become brown and crispy. If you waste a lot of food, your cooking is not good. In daily cooking, it is not always necessary to prepare gourmet food; this kind of food is more suited to special occasions.

The Yin Yang Game (Selection of Foods)

Another principle of macrobiotic cooking is the

yin yang principle. In order to master macrobiotic cooking you have to master this. However, don't be too nervous about it. Enjoy the game! To begin, carefully observe the length of cooking time, the amount of salt to be added, how much miso or soy sauce to be used, how the dish should taste – delicious, sweet, salty, hot, sour, etc.

What combination of foods will bring the best results? Such a study is the same as a chemist's experimentation in his laboratory. Most chemists learn by trial and error. Most recipes are created in a similar way. However, if you know the yin yang principles, these things become interesting and easy. You become a scientist of life, using the kitchen as a laboratory.

Then what is yin and what is yang? Lao Tsu says in the *Tao Te Ching:* "Tao produces one. The one produces two. The two produces three, and from three all things are produced. All things carry the yin outside and hold the yang inside, and through blending (complementing their antagonistic forces) yin and yang achieve harmony." (Chapter 42.)

Cooking is a way to achieve this harmonious blending of yin and yang, which is manifested everywhere. For more detailed information, please read the various publications on macrobiotics. A thorough understanding involves much study, but it deepens your life without a doubt.

For cooking, it is necessary to understand yin yang differentiation. First of all, we divide foods into two categories: vegetable foods and animal foods. Vegetable foods are yin and animal foods are yang. (Here the yin represents: expansive, quiet, cold, green, blue, etc., and the yang represents: contractive, active, hot, red, yellow, etc.) Alcohol, vinegar, and most drugs are yin. All animals are dependent upon vegetables for their survival, including carnivorous animals, because their prey eat vegetables. In the vegetable kingdom, grain is the most abundant and popular food.

The following chart is a guide for classifying foods according to yin and yang.

Yin and yang are not absolute. They change in degrees according to origin of the food, the manner of growth or production, season, and even which part of the animal or vegetable is used in cooking. Therefore, it is necessary to look at the chart as a guide, rather than an exact breakdown. Heat, time, pressure, and amount of salt used in preparing foods also affect their yin yang qualities.

very yin	drugs
	vinegar (commercial)
	sugar
	alcoholic drinks
yin	fruits
	nuts
	vegetables (and seaweed)
	seeds
balanced	grain (cereals)
	buckwheat and jinenjo
yang	shellfish
	white meat fish
	red meat fish
	fowl
	egg
	meat
very yang	salt

The Three Stages of Cooking

There are three stages of cooking – beginner, skillful, and master cook. Although beginners make many mistakes due to their lack of experience, they do not make big mistakes because they follow the directions carefully and faithfully.

As they improve their skill and experience in cooking and receive more praise for their cooking, they start to consider themselves masters of cooking. Such pride tends to make them overconfident and arrogant. Then, although they are skillful, they may make serious mistakes. This is the second stage in the art of cooking. Their mistakes come from their overconfidence and neglecting to follow the advice of others. In this stage, their cooking is neither attractive nor all-embracing, even though it is advanced in technique. Their arrogant attitude may be destructive to family or friendship in spite of their good cooking. In fact, their skill or knowledge in cooking may bring them misery and unhappiness. This is the most crucial time in the mastering of cooking. The way to overcome this stage and to become a master is through humility. Humility accepts all complaints even when they are very sentimental and emotional. It embraces unwelcome friends along with other friends and changes disagreeable foods into delicious cuisine. After one thousand and one humiliations they become masters of cooking, and at the same time become masters of their home – on which our happiness and health depend.

Don't Hurry

Don't cook in a hurry. Cooking and eating are the sacred act and art which create life. We should neither cook nor eat in a hurry. In modern society, we tend to live with a hurried mentality which produces faster mass production, faster communication, faster travel, faster education, faster cooking, and faster eating.

When modern people go picnicking or camping they eat canned or frozen foods. They never enjoy making a fire, cooking with wood, or eating under a blue sky. Speed and convenience are the symbols of modern society. Therefore, people marry in a hurry and separate in a hurry. They are like jet plane travelers who see the whole world, but do not enjoy life as much as their ancestors who did not leave their home towns.

Today, some miso and soy sauce sold on the market are the product of only a few months aging. We recommend using only those which are produced by at least eighteen months of aging and authentic fermentation. This advice does not apply to cooking. If you cook miso soup too long the taste will spoil. Miso should be added only after all the vegetables are cooked. The same is true in making tea. The tea leaves should be added last, and just simmered.

If you are in a hurry, don't cook. Eat warmed-up leftovers instead. Also, don't throw away vegetable or seaweed juices from cooking or soaking. They contain valuable minerals and can be used later in cooking.

Make your kitchen orderly. If your kitchen is messy, this creates chaos in your cooking and subsequently in your family. You need to have an orderly kitchen, otherwise your family receives the disorder of the kitchen in the food.

Basic Suggestions

Main foods should be whole grains such as rice, barley, wheat, millet, buckwheat, whole oats, corn, and rye with seasonal and climatic vegetables, beans, and fruit. For seasonings use traditional, naturally fermented miso and soy sauce, sea salt, and high quality vegetable and seed oils. Tekka, gomashio, shiso, kinpira, hiziki, and shio kombu can all be used as table condiments. Use kinpira, hiziki, and shio kombu to balance a yin meal.

Daikon pickles, miso pickles, or some pickled vegetables should be eaten with each meal. Use a piece of pickle to clean your plate and bowl, then pour in some tea and drink everything. Don't waste anything. It is better to make takuan (rice bran pickles) and miso pickles yourself. Takuan contain lots of vitamin B and help produce bacteria in the intestines that promote better digestion.

Older people and children should eat less salt and a smaller quantity of food. If you are cooking for older people and children at the same time, cook with less salt and use gomashio made with less salt for children. Older people and children should have one-half the adult quantity of food. Use less miso for older people and children. The menus in this book include party food, so I have included fish recipes. Usually we are vegetarian, but for special occasions we serve fish or fowl. You can omit fish and fowl from these recipes; instead, use dashi kombu on the bottom of the pan and later add soy sauce. This makes a delicious taste. This is just an example. Experiment with different vegetables. Study yin and yang balance and create new dishes.

To eat in the macrobiotic way, drink one mouthful of miso soup first, then eat a mouthful of rice, and then vegetables. Then rice, soup, vegetables and so on in that order. Or else, you can eat all of your miso soup first and then the rest of your meal. After you have a mouthful of rice, put down your chopsticks and chew well. Everyone should chew fifty to one hundred times per mouthful. Chew quickly, not slowly; this is more yang. For a yin person or a person with a yin sickness, chew three mouthfuls of rice to one mouthful of side dish.

Don't use salt at the table – use gomashio instead. Don't add soy sauce to rice.

Condiments and Spices

In macrobiotic cooking we use condiments such as soy sauce, miso, sesame oil, corn oil, olive oil, and salt; avoid strong spices which may better be used in tropical countries.

There are three kinds of salt: unrefined salt, salt without magnesium, and table salt which has calcium bicarbonate added to keep it dry. Commercial salt also contains dextrose. Table salt is hard to dissolve in water and is not good for either cooking or table use. During ancient times people kept crude salt in a vase for a year. The magnesium absorbed water from the air and went down. The remaining top salt became less salty and was then used for cooking. This salt is roasted in a frying pan and ground in a suribachi before being used. It can be used in cooking or to make gomashio.

Salt tastes better as it cooks more. Therefore, add salt early in cooking. Pickles also develop a better taste with aging because salt loses its saltiness with time.

Soy sauce is made of soybeans, wheat, and salt. Avoid chemically produced soy sauce. To examine the nature of a soy sauce, add hot bancha tea to 1 tsp. of soy sauce. If the result is clear, it is good natural soy sauce. If the result is dark, it is chemically produced. Another method for examining soy sauce is to drop it in cold water. If the soy sauce sinks gradually, it is good. If it expands immediately, it is chemically produced.

Soy sauce is usually added at the end of cooking (except in tsuku dani dishes which use soy sauce in cooking such as shio kombu – kombu cooked throughout with soy sauce), because otherwise the soy sauce loses its flavor.

There are three kinds of miso: Hacho (soybean) miso, mugi (barley) miso, and kome (rice, white or brown) miso. Hacho miso is the most yang. Barley miso is the most delicious and is used all year round. The miso sold in Japanese stores is white rice miso (white or red in color), which is aged about two months or less. Less salt is used in this miso and therefore may be used for those who have eaten much meat. However, much rice miso is made from beans which have had the oil extracted from them, and from potatoes. For these reasons, rice miso can be served with fish on occasion, but frequent use is not recommended. It can also be used mixed with barley miso in salads or to make a fish-miso dish. In summer it is to be kept in a cool spot.

Rice vinegar is made from the residue of rice wine (sake) or rice. It is a weak acid. Chemically produced vinegar is too yin and not tasty. To make orange vinegar, cut a green (unripened) orange or lemon in half and squeeze out the juice immediately – all of it at once. Squeezing out all the juice in one stroke is the secret of making good vinegar. Otherwise, the vinegar will be bitter. Keep this vinegar in a bottle with a little salt and then bury it in clay. This way it can keep for a year. It is very good for cooking fish.

Sake is used in cooking to increase the flavor of dishes and to aid self-reflection. A proper use of sake elaborately increases the taste of cooking. Add sake in the beginning so that the smell of alcohol dis-

appears completely.

Mirin is a rice wine made of sweet rice and has a sweet taste. It will tighten the foods cooked with it and therefore should not be used when it is desired to have soft foods. Use only good quality mirin.

In macrobiotic cooking, we only use vegetable oils. There are many kinds of oil on the market today. Therefore, you should choose oils according to their use such as frying, sauteing, or in salads. Oils distinguish themselves also according to taste and ease of digestion. You should select the proper oil for the proper purpose. Light sesame oil is the best from the standpoint of fragrance and taste. However, since it is expensive, it is best to use it with thirty percent other oils for daily use. It is very good for sauteing vegetables. Corn oil is a universal oil used in frying, sauteing, and as a salad dressing oil. Olive oil is good in salad dressings because of its taste, easy digestion, and density. It is also good in mayonnaise. Safflower oil is very light. It is not good to use for deep frying because it requires a longer cooking time. Therefore, it is best to mix it half and half with corn oil for deep frying. Salad oils commercially available are usually made with chemicals and are not recommended for use.

Here is some useful information on spices. Karashi is a powdered mustard made from the mustard seed. It can be used in making eggplant pickles. Peppers: the small red pepper is the hottest one. Use the red-skinned peppers only. The inside seeds cause a bad taste and have a bad effect on the body, so they should not be eaten. Adding five or six red peppers, either whole or chopped, to your nuka pickles in summer will prevent the growth of undesirable bacteria in the crock. Ginger is useful in removing the fish and oil smell from foods. In summer, grated ginger with miso or soy sauce makes a good appetizer. Roasted poppy seeds are used in baked or boiled foods to add fragrance. They are good on top of bread. White and black sesame seeds have hundreds of different uses in cooking. They can be added to soups, boiled foods, vegetables, baked goods, etc.

Fragrant foods have many uses also. Yuzu (citron), before they become ripe, can be used for fragrance in cooking. The juice is used the same way as lemon or orange juice. The rind of the citron makes an attractive serving shell for salads. Cut off the top, scoop out the flesh and stuff with your favorite salad.

Shiso leaves come in two varieties – purple and green. Green leaves have a better fragrance than the purple, but the purple leaves contain more minerals.

The white part of big scallions is used for sashimi or clear soup. Soba (buckwheat noodles) or udon (wheat noodles) are good with small scallions; chop the white and green sections into small pieces. This is also used in soup, or foods prepared with vinegar.

Roasted sheets of nori cut into thin strips with a kitchen scissors can be used with vinegared food, clear soup, or as garnish. Powdered nori seaweed is used in jinenjo (mountain potato) sauces.

Food Combination

When selecting foods, you must understand the importance of making combinations. Every food has its own characteristics. Good combinations will enhance the taste, but a bad choice of just one food will destroy even the good ones. Using such a guide for combining, the Chinese add up hundreds of combinations for herbal teas. Their effectiveness is dependent upon exact combination of certain herbs.

Food combination is not as critical as preparing herb tea. However, it is very important from the standpoint of nutrition and taste. Yin and yang classification of food will be a great help for this.

In combining foods we consider shape, color, and taste. Contrasting foods – salty food with non-salty food, animal food with fruit, mochi or tempura with grated daikon – makes food more appealing. The white meat of fish such as flounder and herring can be cooked with vegetables.

A poor combination may be fresh fish cooked with chuba and bonita, which taste bad cooked together. The cook uses only fish or fish products and does not create balance. Even beans cooked with just water and salt need a sensitive touch, or they will taste bad. Never use sugar or MSG. Bring out the natural taste of whatever you cook. In combining foods, we balance and create harmony in our meals. It is said that macrobiotic cooking uses seven leaves and seven roots to make peace and great art in our lives.

Lunch Box and Other Tips

A mother or wife must be very attentive in preparing a lunch box. If she mixes hot and cold food, the food will become sour by the time it is opened. Use hot food only or cold food only. Keep different foods separate. When the lunch box is opened, everything should not be mixed up; keep things separated

with tinfoil or pieces of wood. Try to have a different menu every day so it appeals to your husband or children. Otherwise they will be attracted to restaurant food and their health will diminish. To create a happy home, use your imagination with food every day. Occasionally, have a picnic outdoors. An attractive special dinner makes everyone happy. Most important, the wife or mother should be cheerful, and she will impart her happiness to her family. If your husband is violent, he is too yang. Feed him shiitake mushroom, kampyo, konnyaku, water chestnuts, and green vegetable ohitashi (cooked in salt water only). These foods are good for an angry woman too.

Kitchen Hints

If your kanten is yellow and old, add 1 tablespoon of salt to 3 cups of warm water and wash the kanten in this. The yellow color will disappear. Squeeze the kanten and soak in plain water. Then you can use it in your recipes.

Cook fresh green asparagus in a tall coffee pot. Then you can stand the asparagus up in it, and the tops will steam gently.

When you are about to remove the cover after steaming food, first take the steamer to the table. Then take off the cover. If you take the cover off when the steam is still coming out you can burn yourself. When you take off the cover hold it like a shield so that no remaining steam burns you or others at the table.

When you are reheating leftovers, it is best to steam-heat them. Then they have the same taste and saltiness. If you heat them up in a pan they get a more salty taste because the juices escape and the salt becomes more concentrated. Stale bread tastes very good when steamed, and the flavor is quite different from that of fresh bread. You can even steam an entire, uncut loaf of stale bread and everyone will enjoy the new taste and different texture from the steaming. Steamed bread is better for babies and small infants and children than regular bread as it is easier to digest, and it is even more satisfying to them. The infant's bread should be prechewed, as with their rice, grains, cereals, and vegetables.

If someone is coming in late for dinner, prepare a dinner plate for him, then cover it with a pie pan and keep it in the oven. You can keep food warm for 2 or 3 hours and serve it whenever they arrive. This works best in a gas oven because the pilot keeps the oven the ideal warmth. An electric oven would need to be kept on at the lowest temperature possible.

You can keep gas burners clean by putting silver foil around the burner plate. Then when you have to clean them, just remove the silver foil.

Sometimes when you deep-fry foods, the oil may catch fire. Don't lose your head. Take any kind of green vegetable leaf, salt, or flour, and quickly put it in the burning oil. This will put out the flame. Don't use water, because it will spatter the oil.

Sometimes you may have an empty jar with a tight-fitting cover which is perfect for gomashio, umeboshi, shio kombu, or other condiments. But it may have a strong lingering smell that cannot be washed out. If so, add mustard powder and boiling water and set it aside uncovered for a few hours. Then all the smell will go away and it will keep condiments very fresh.

If your vegetable oil has a strong smell or flavor, then bring 5 cups of oil to a boil, add one 5″ scallion cut into 1″ pieces, and add 3 or 4 pieces of fresh sliced ginger. Before the scallion burns, shut off the heat and remove the scallions and ginger with a strainer. Then this oil no longer has a strong flavor.

After deep frying, use a strainer covered with thin absorbent cotton and strain the hot oil through it. This removes all fine crumbs and cleans it completely. Be sure to strain it when it is hot. Cold oil gets thick and doesn't strain easily. Store it in a bottle or can. You can use this oil many more times. If you don't remove the oil from the pan after cooking the oil it is exposed to air and becomes acid. So store it in a can or bottle, it will stay fresher longer.

Kitchen Utensils

Good cooks need good utensils. This section lists and explains the necessary ones.

Cutting boards – at least 12″ wide. If possible have 2 boards, one for vegetables and one for fish and fowl. If not possible, use one side for vegetables and the other for fish and fowl.

Knives – see Cutting, (pg. 32). For vegetables – rectangular and thin. For fish – thick and pointed.

Kitchen towels – at least five. Keep those for food preparation separate from those used for dishes. Towels are used for making sarashinegi (washed scallions), for filtering kombu water, for squeezing water out of tofu, and for covering bread dough.

Clean ones are better and so they should be kept separate.

Bonita shaver – available in Japanese or other Oriental markets.

Salad bowls – may be wood, stainless steel, porcelain, enamel-covered iron, or glass: 10″, 9″, 8″, 7″, 5″, 4″ diameters.

Enamel-covered metal plates – 8″, 7″, 6″ diameters – round or square.

Rice paddles – always keep dry, otherwise they may begin to smell.

Oil skimmer – small, used for cleaning (filtering) tempura oil

Bamboo mats – several sizes, used for sushi and ohitashi.

Japanese metal toaster – use this over the burner or on an asbestos pad over the flame for cooking fish, toasting bread, or heating rice balls or mochi. Useful on camping trips also.

Bamboo skewers – 1 package of 5″ size is most useful.

Suribachi and suricogi – for grinding and mashing foods; especially for making gomashio.

Graters – several kinds and sizes; porcelain is best, can be found in Japanese stores.

Wire wisk – for mixing lumpy batter or sauces.

Kitchen brush – small, for oiling foods and containers or to brush egg on breads.

Vegetable brush – for cleaning vegetables; available in Japanese stores.

Cooking chopsticks – longer and thicker than usual, for fried foods or nitsuke.

Measuring spoons and cups – one set of each.

Ladles – for soup.

Flour sifter.

Spongecake pan.

Bread pans – 2 to 4 as needed.

Pudding mold – for special occasions.

Jelly molds – one large and several small ones.

Tart pans – as needed.

Cookie sheets and pie pans – as needed.

Rubber spatulas – different sizes and shapes as needed.

Cookie cutters – as needed.

Apple corer.

Nutcracker.

Metal spatula – for turning pancakes.

Rolling pin.

Foley food mill.

Rice-cooking pot – stainless steel pressure cookers

are best. Use 4- or 6-quart size depending on how many people you are cooking for.

Boiling pot – a big, deep pot is best. Thick sides are not needed. Enameled iron or stainless steel are best, but aluminum is all right.

Nishime pot – iron is best. If possible the sides should be curved, the bottom should be small and the top larger. You will need less salt, soy sauce, or other seasoning with this type of pot, since the seasoning collects in the bottom of the pot and steams through all the food more thoroughly.

Rice steamer – the Japanese type of Oriental steamer is very good. The best, however, is a Chinese steamer which uses a wok on the bottom and a bamboo top. The Chinese steamer does require more gas heat and so is not as economical. The choice is yours. Choose a large steamer because it holds more water. A 4-quart size is enough for five servings but the 5-quart size will hold much more. If you choose a Chinese wok with a bamboo steamer, the latter should be 1½″ smaller than the wok. If the steaming tray is the same size, most of the steam will escape. If it is smaller, the pan will not hold enough water. Since the Chinese steamer is made of bamboo and wood, it should be washed and dried immediately after use. Keep thoroughly dry when not in use.

Frying pans – one small and one large. A thick heavy pan is best, either iron or stainless steel. The 10″ size is the most convenient. It is used mostly for sauteing foods and roasting grains or seeds.

Deep-frying pot – heavy iron is best because the heat is evenly distributed and also because the oil evaporates more slowly in this type of pot.

Pyrex dishes – with covers, size and number as desired.

Casseroles – with covers, size and number as desired.

Asbestos pad – as needed, to use over flame burners to prevent burning foods.

Dinner set.

Cookware care

The best cooking pans and pots are thick-bottomed because these distribute the heat evenly and prevent burning over high heat. Enamel-covered iron or aluminum pans heat quickly and so are good for boiling water or making ohitashi (boiled vegetables).

After using, wash them in hot water and then dry completely with a dish towel. If there is an oily residue, add some washing soda to the boiling water, cool slightly and dip a cloth in this to use to clean off the oil.

If food burns on the bottom of a pan, add water and bring to a boil. This will usually take off the burned areas; if not, try a scraper or a scouring brush.

After cooking with your frying pan, clean off the excess oil while the pan is still hot. If you wait until the pan is cool, it may become sticky. After cleaning with a paper towel, put a little fresh oil on a towel and coat the pan. Then go over it once more with a dry towel. This oil protects your pan and helps season it. Keep the cover on the pan or turn it upside down to protect against dust when not in use.

Porcelain – mix wood ashes with cold water and bring to a boil, then put in the plates. It will make them really clean. It is a good idea to boil the dinnerware in this solution when first bought, before use. It makes them stronger and cleans them thoroughly. After 6 months or so of use, boil in the same type of solution to restore their whiteness. After daily use, the dinnerware can be washed in soapy water, rinsed well, and dried thoroughly with a clean cotton towel.

Japanese lacquerware – to keep beautiful forever, do not leave in the sun or near heat like the stove or fireplace. Also, do not keep in the refrigerator. Either extreme will make it crack.

To clean new lacquerware, make a mixture of 10 cups water and 2 cups rice bran (nuka). Bring to a boil for 20 minutes. Set aside to cool to body temperature. Wet the lacquerware in cold water. Then put it into the rice-bran water and wash with a cotton cloth. This removes the odor. Rinse twice in warm water and let dry on a cotton cloth until shiny. To store, cover with Japanese rice paper or a cotton cloth bag to keep it dry.

To clean lacquerware after using, bring a mixture of 10 cups water and 3 cups nuka to a boil. After 20 minutes of boiling, set aside and cool to body temperature. Wash the used lacquerware in this, rinse in warm water, and drip-dry on a cotton cloth as above. With a dry cotton cloth, buff until shiny. Cover, as above, to store.

If your lacquerware is square and you find it difficult to clean the corners, use a bamboo chopstick with the end wrapped in a piece of cotton cloth. When washing lacquerware, place one hand against the bottom as you wash the other side to prevent breaking through the fragile pieces.

Cleaning glass dishware – add soap to warm water and wash with a cotton cloth. Then rinse in cold water, warm water, and finally in hot water. Hot water does not remove soap as well as cold water does, so it is best to follow the above steps for your better glassware. This method prevents breakage and the glassware dries more quickly. (Do not use hot and cold water at the same time as this will cause breakage.) Dry with a cotton cloth until shiny and no finger marks remain. Do not stack wet glassware as it sticks together and is hard to separate.

Cleaning plastic dishes – boiling water will sanitize new plastic dishes but may melt them in the process, so hot soapy water is best. New plastic ware usually has a chemical smell; if yours does, wash it well and let it air for a few days. This will usually make the smell go away.

After using plastic dishes, clean immediately with soapy water as they accumulate dirt easily. Do not use dirty water as it will make the plastic dirty. Use clean soapy water. Do not scrub with a brush since plastic scratches easily.

Silverware – add baking soda (sodium bicarbonate) to soapy water and wash with a clean cloth. Rinse in hot water and dry with a cotton cloth. Avoid leaving fingerprints. Silverware tends to become tarnished after prolonged contact with air, so keep it covered with rice paper or some other soft paper. If your silverware gets tarnished, use commercial tooth powder or silver polish.

Kitchen cabinets, walls, and other areas get greasy and smoky from cooking. To clean them, take 7 cups of boiling water and 1 tablespoon of ammonia. Use rubber gloves on both hands. Dip an old cotton towel or cotton rag in the ammonia water, squeeze it, and clean the whole kitchen – shelves, everywhere. Ammonia removes dirty oil and the smoky color, so your kitchen becomes bright.

Cutting

Cutting has three purposes: The first is to make cooking easier. The second is to make better taste. The third is for decoration.

Shape is important in cooking. There are many shapes to choose from: quarter moon, chrysanthemum, matchstick, flat rectangles, diced, half moon, shaved, etc. If you always cut vegetables the same way,

you don't develop art in your cooking. Your cooking loses taste and life force.

Before cutting, have a clean board and knife; with each different vegetable you cut, wash your knife and board. Never cut two or three vegetables at a time without washing the knife and board. Each vegetable has a different balance of yin and yang, so if you don't clean the board and knife, this gets all mixed up. As you cut the vegetables, use them. Don't leave them on the board, because it will soak up some of the vegetable juices; thus they lose their taste. If you cut all your vegetables alike but plan to cook them differently, using some for sauteing and some for deep frying, this is not a good practice. In making stew, all vegetables are cut larger. If you don't have enough time, cut them thinner or smaller. For a vegetable soup, whether miso or clear, the thinner and smaller you cut the vegetables the better. For a vegetable stew, a medium-sized cut is best; for long cooking, such as oden, or Russian soup, large chunks are good. Think how to cut vegetables according to yin and yang. Use everything, don't throw anything away. Vegetables are whole foods, they receive minerals from the soil. We show our thanks to nature by using the whole vegetable. Macrobiotic cooking is different from other cooking in this respect also: we use the tops and roots of vegetables – for example when using scallions, everything is used.

Never peel vegetables; these peelings make our own skin stronger. Don't soak vegetables in water – they lose their minerals that way. Try to cut them uniformly for each dish – that is, not some thick and some thin.

Sometimes we cut incorrectly, not according to yin and yang. In cutting an onion, the top part is yin and the root is yang. If cut horizontally, some people receive only the yin part, some only the yang part of the vegetable. Therefore, the pieces must be cut from the top to the bottom in the shape of a half moon. Then everyone receives both the yin and yang parts of the vegetables. Vegetables which have long roots, such as daikon and burdock, are difficult to cut so that each piece is balanced. The point is more yang, so give this to the more yin members of the family. The top is more yin, so give this to the more yang members of the family. At first this is confusing, but as you study and cook, you learn to make a good balance.

Spring

#243 – Rice Balls (Azuki Rice, #100). #57 – Fried Tofu with Buckwheat. #124 – Vegetable Kabobs with mayonnaise dressing.

Grains

1. Pressure Cooked Brown Rice
2. Boiled Brown Rice
3. Baked Rice
4. Green Pea Baked Rice
5. Rice Cream Cereal
6. Thick Rice Cream
7. Sweet Rice Cream
8. Rolled Oats

Noodles

9. Soba Roll
10. Custard Noodles
11. Casserole Noodle Soup
12. Macaroni Gratin
13. Fried Whole Wheat Spaghetti
14. Homemade Noodles with Miso Soup

Vegetables

15. Mustard Green and Onion Nitsuke
16. Onion Miso
17. Rolled Cabbage
18. Rolled Cabbage with Age
19. Vegetable Fritters
20. Green Pea and Shrimp Nitsuke

Wild Vegetables

21. Mugwort
22. Horsetail Nitsuke
23. Horsetail Balls
24. Horsetail Rolls
25. Aster Nitsuke
26. Onion Aster Boats
27. Dandelion Nitsuke
28. Dandelion Roots
29. Bracken Nitsuke
30. Chickweed
31. Wild Scallion Nitsuke
32. Wild Scallion in Soup
33. Thistle Nitsuke
34. Thistle Root Condiment
35. Boiled Licorice
36. New Zealand Spinach
37. Plantain
38. Pigweed

Soups

39. Kombu Stock
40. Kombu Stock with Fish
41. Bonita Stock
42. Fish Stock
43. Chicken Bouillon
44. Oyster Chowder

Wheat Gluten

45. Wheat Gluten
46. Seitan
47. Fresh Wheat Fu
48. Boiled Fu
49. Fried Fu (Gluten Cutlet)
50. Shish Kebab

Tofu

51. Tofu Making
52. Quantity Tofu Preparation
53. Nigari Making
54. Okara Vegetables
55. Tofu with Kuzu Sauce
56. Fried Tofu
57. Fried Tofu with Buckwheat
58. Scrambled Tofu
59. Tofu Rolled with Nori
60. Stuffed Age

Special Dishes

61. Barbecued Chicken and Vegetables
62. All-Purpose Barbecue Sauce
63. Barbecued Fish
64. Sukiyaki
65. Thick Omelette

Deep-Fried Foods

66. Tempura
67. Mock Goose *(Ganmodoki)*
68. Mock Chicken with Cream Sauce *(Kashiwamodoki)*

Salads

69. Bean Sprout Salad
70. Cole Slaw with Bean Sprouts
71. Cucumber Carrot Salad
72. Asparagus Sesame Salad
73. Sour Cabbage
74. Mustard Green Ohitashi

Sauces and Dressings

75. Mayonnaise
76. Tartar Sauce
77. French Dressing
78. Other Dressings

Pickles

79. Rice Bran Pickles
80. Chinese Cabbage Rice Bran Pickles
81. Onion Pickles
82. Onion Vinegar Pickles
83. Mustard Powder Pickles

Breads and Snacks

84. Rice Bread
85. Ohsawa Bread
86. French Bread
87. Special French Bread
88. Gyoza
89. Vegetable Pancakes

Desserts

90. Kanten Jello
91. Whole Wheat Pudding
92. Raisin Pie
93. Apple Chestnut Twist

Beverages

94. Bancha (Twig) Tea
95. Mu Tea
96. Ohsawa Coffee *(Yannoh)*
97. Pearled Barley Tea *(Hatocha)*
98. Dandelion Coffee *(Tan Po Po)*

Spring Cooking

In 1961 thirteen macrobiotic families, about 36 people, moved from New York to Chico, California. Each family drove in a car and the trip took around two weeks. We passed many states and towns. I was surprised; in each town we saw the same foods – nothing special in different places. Hamburgers, hot dogs, pizza – all the same. I realized how the old Japanese history and the young American history are so different. Even travelling by train, in Japan, at each big station different kinds of foods are served. Japan is about the same size as California, but the north and south have much different foods. Also in Japan the four seasons are very clearly separate, and vegetable produce is different in each season.

I grew up in northern Japan, at Aizuwakamatsu, with long winters – about five months under big snows. Before the snow, each family stores fresh vegetables for winter underground in the backyard. They make a large hole, line the inside with rice straw, then place daikon, Chinese cabbage, burdock, and carrots inside. This is covered with rice straw and then one foot of soil. The vegetables do not freeze; they are always fresh, even when snow covers everything, so fresh vegetables can be eaten anytime all winter. Otherwise, if daikon stays in the kitchen it soon freezes because the kitchen is so cold. When I was growing up there were no heating systems in Japan.

At the end of March the snow melts and the new soil is very black and fresh. The black soil seems like nice energy to us after the long white winter. The first vegetables are tender mustard greens with stems the diameter of large asparagus. The stems are repeatedly cut and harvested all spring, and we eat mustard stems and leaves until the flowers blossom. Tired of daikon, cabbage, and the winter vegetables, we eat mustard greens sauteed, steamed, ohitashi, nitsuke, and in miso soup every day.

In Japan we say in spring it is good to enjoy the bitter taste. Summer is the sour taste, autumn hot, winter salty. In spring try to use more leafy green vegetables, some having a slightly bitter taste: dandelion, watercress, mustard greens, turnip greens, collards, and kale. Wild vegetables such as dandelion, mustard, aster, chickweed, and mugwort grow in springtime. George Ohsawa said, "In springtime you must eat the bitter taste, because during the cold wintertime we have eaten more animal foods, salt, and oil. The bitter vegetables 'melt' or decrease this overstock. Then the body can prepare for the coming hot summer when we take in less fat, salt, and oil." In summer, wild vegetables have a slightly sour taste, so sour foods in summer naturally make it more comfortable to pass the hot season – lots of tossed salad, vinegar salads (sunomono), etc. In autumn it becomes cold, so we take the hot taste: mustard, hot pepper, green pepper. These help to open the blood vessels and the body becomes warm by increased circulation. In winter we naturally take more animal food, salt, and oil such as during holiday meals or parties.

Here in the United States markets have the same vegetables all year round, but in springtime you should eat more wild vegetables (dandelion, chickweed), the leafy greens mentioned above, and other special macrobiotic foods. If you don't like the bitter taste, try making tempura with these vegetables.

Mugwort is a very helpful wild plant – it has lots of iron, good for anemia and also for cleansing intestinal parasites. In early spring, pick mugwort when it is about 3″ to 4″ tall; dip in boiling salted water, squeeze out, and form into small balls. Dry these in the shade and they can be stored for a long time in a glass jar. Seasonal wild vegetables, including ceremonial foods, all help remove heavy proteins, salt, and oil stored over the winter. Mugwort also contains fiber, good after winter eating as an intestinal cleanser.

I am surprised our ancestors were so clever. They knew we would never eat mugwort, so special days were created to remind us. Mugwort mochi is traditionally served in Japan on Girls Day, March 3; mugwort dango is served on Boys Day, May 5. I still serve these foods on these days and I pray that everyone has one year of peace and happiness with no problems. Knowing mugwort is so useful, perhaps you can make mugwort mochi on ceremonial spring days. If mochi is difficult for you, you can make a mugwort bread with a beautiful green color.

A friend visited us in San Francisco with her whole family and I served mugwort mochi to her children. The next day she called me to say that her three-year-old boy, to whom she had often given cow's milk, had had three eliminations that night and that his face was very clear. Another time, in Chico, I served mugwort mochi to many friends at a Boys Day ceremony; a friend's daughter eliminated many parasites. I think all macrobiotic kids eat a lot of fruit, which removes the body's salts, and also do not get enough salt in cooked foods. Therefore, they all have parasites. I suggest mugwort bread for children.

Bracken is another good wild mountain spring vegetable, strong in potassium. In Japan, wood ash is used to remove the excess potassium. Wild vegetables have such a strong life power – people walk over them and they grow again. Please serve some wild greens at your table in springtime.

During springtime sometimes a hot day comes, like summer. Your body feels tired and fatigued. This means you are still carrying the winter storage of salt and fats. Try eating cold kanten jello with vinegar or lemon soy sauce. In my country at the spring equinox around March 20, even though it is still cold, tokoroten is served. This is kanten cut like noodles, served with lemon or vinegar soy sauce. This food is very refreshing. If you have no kanten, you can serve green salad with lemon dressing, or sauerkraut.

If you have picnics in spring, hunt wild vegetables. If possible, cook and serve them at that time. Wild vegetables are very good for the study of yin and yang.

So please enjoy spring wild vegetables and individual cooking at your table.

Grains

1. Pressure Cooked Brown Rice

3 cups brown rice
4-4½ cups water
½ tsp. salt

Rinse the rice gently in a pan of cold water; keep changing the water and rinsing until the water is clear. If your pressure cooker does not have much pressure, it is best to soak the rice overnight. Add the salt just before cooking. Cook on a low heat for 20 minutes. Then turn to high until pressure comes up to full. Lower heat and cook 45-60 minutes. Then turn off heat and allow pressure to return to normal, 20-30 minutes. Remove cover and mix rice thoroughly before serving. (When cooking over 10 cups of rice, decrease amount of water.)

2. Boiled Brown Rice

4 cups brown rice
6-8 cups water
1 tsp. salt

Ideally, a porcelain-coated cast iron or heavy cast iron pot is best, although a stainless steel pan can also be used.

Rinse the rice as in #1 and soak overnight in 6-8 cups water. Add salt just before cooking. Cook on low heat for 30 minutes, then turn heat to high until boiling point is reached. Now cook for 20 minutes on a medium high heat and 40 minutes on low heat. Turn off heat again and let sit for 20 minutes. Remove cover and mix rice thoroughly before serving.

3. Baked Rice

2 cups brown rice
4 cups boiling water
½ tsp. salt

Preheat oven to 350°. Wash the rice, then dry roast in a heavy skillet over a medium flame until golden colored. Place the rice in a casserole and add salt and cover with boiling water. Cover pan and set in oven. Bake for one hour. This preparation is very soft and light and a pleasant change from pressure-cooked rice. Because the rice comes out so light and fluffy it prevents overeating.

4. Green Pea Baked Rice

2 cups brown rice
¼ cup dried green peas
5 cups water
1 tsp. salt

Wash peas and soak overnight, or for about 5-6 hours in one cup of water. Wash and dry roast the rice and place in a casserole with peas and soaking water. Boil the remaining water with the salt and pour over rice. Cover casserole and place in a preheated 350° oven and bake for one hour.

If using fresh green peas, cook rice as in regular baked rice recipe (#3) and add 1 cup fresh green peas, 2 Tbsp. soy sauce and ¼ tsp. extra salt during the last 10 minutes of cooking.

Rice Cream – Prepared rice cream powder can be purchased in natural food stores and at macrobiotic outlets, but it is very easy to prepare at home and tastes much fresher. To make the powder, wash the rice and dry roast in a heavy skillet (without oil) until it is a golden color and begins to pop. Either grind in an electric blender set on high speed, or grind by hand in a grain mill.

5. Rice Cream Cereal

1 cup rice cream powder
3½-4 cups boiling water
¼ tsp. salt

Dry roast the powder in a heavy skillet over a medium flame until it gives off a nut-like fragrance. Bring the pan to the sink, cool and add boiling water and salt. Mix thoroughly to remove lumps, and return pan to heat. Cook over a low heat with a cover for 40-50 minutes, stirring occasionally to prevent burning. Mix thoroughly before serving.

6. Thick Rice Cream

1 cup rice cream powder
2 cups boiling water
¼ tsp. salt

Roast the powder as in #5. Bring pan to sink to cool, then add salt and one cup boiling water. Mix quickly to prevent lumping. Return pan to heat and push aside the dough mixture with a rice paddle and add second cup of boiling water so that the dough floats above the water and avoids contact with the bottom of the pan. Cover with a close-fitting lid and let rice steam over a low heat for 30-45 minutes. Mix thoroughly before serving.

7. Sweet Rice Cream

1 cup rice cream powder
½ cup sweet brown rice
    cream powder
4-4½ cups boiling water
⅓ to ½ tsp. salt

This rice cream powder is not available to be purchased. I created this recipe and served it at a breakfast at GOMF. Prepare the brown rice per instructions in the introductory paragraph to Rice Cream recipes. Wash and roast the sweet brown rice separately, as it requires less roasting time. Combine with the roasted brown rice in proportions of two parts brown rice to one part sweet brown rice. Cook as in #5, after grinding into rice cream powder.

8. Rolled Oats

2 cups rolled oats
5 cups water
1 tsp. salt

Roast oat flakes in a dry skillet over a medium flame until golden in color. Cool, and add 4 cups of water, and salt. Return to stove. Bring to a boil, then add remaining cup of water and bring to boil again. Lower flame, cover, and cook until desired consistency is reached. (Adding cold water after the first boil makes a smoother cereal.) Stir occasionally during cooking. Serve with sesame salt. This cereal can be cooked the night before, or slowly simmered overnight. To cool quickly, fill sink with about 2″ cold water and place pan in this.

Noodles

9. Soba Roll

2 8oz. pkgs. soba noodles
5 sheets of nori
Bamboo mat

A soba roll is made by rolling soba in nori (seaweed). Sometimes we enjoy noodles with soup, but this recipe gives a new taste served with sauce. This dish is enjoyed served at room temperature all seasons of the year and is especially good for parties as it can be prepared in advance.

Bring 8 cups of water to a boil and add the soba noodles. Bring to a boil again. Add 1 cup of cold water and bring to a boil again. Shut off heat and let sit for one minute. Then strain the buckwheat noodles and rinse quickly with cold water until noodles are completely cold. After about two minutes when noodles are thoroughly drained, place them on a clean cotton towel in strips about 1½″ wide and ½″ thick to drain more.

Cut sheets of nori in half, crosswise. Holding both halves of nori together roast very lightly on the outsides only. Place one piece of nori on the bamboo mat, close to the bottom of the mat, unroasted side down. Place strips of noodles on nori leaving a ¾″ margin at top and bottom. Using the mat to manipulate the nori and, pressing down firmly, roll the nori like a jelly roll, pressing as you roll to get the proper shape. While rolling, the mat never comes in contact with the noodles. Remove the mat and slice roll into pieces 1¼″ wide using a wet knife – about 6 pieces per roll. Serve these slices laid flat on a plate.

Soba Sauce

3 Tbsp. soy sauce
3 Tbsp. bonita flakes
2 Tbsp. soup stock (see #39)
Served with chopped scallions

Combine soy sauce, bonita flakes, and broth in a saucepan. Bring to a boil on a low flame. Remove from heat and let cool. Mince scallions. Serve sauce in individual small dishes for dipping and serve scallions in a small bowl.

10. Custard Noodles

2 8oz. pkgs. whole wheat noodles
⅓ cup thinly sliced raw chicken
   or seitan
1 tsp. soy sauce over the chicken
3 scallions sliced thin, diagonally
5 med. dried mushrooms or
   10 small fresh mushrooms
4 cups soup stock (see #39)
1 Tbsp. soy sauce
1 tsp. salt
2 eggs

Soak dried mushrooms 10 minutes. Remove hard parts of stem to be used later in soup or vegetable dish, and cut mushrooms in half.

Put noodles in 8 cups of boiling salted water, bring to a boil again, add 1 cup of cold water and bring to a boil again. Remove from heat and drain immediately. Place hot noodles into large porcelain bowl with cover.

Bring soup stock to a boil in a covered pan. Add salt and cook 10 minutes. Add soy sauce, bring to a boil, and remove from heat to cool. Mix well-beaten eggs into lukewarm soup stock.

Add one or two pieces of sliced chicken, a few pieces of mushroom, and the scallions to the noodles. Pour the egg mixture over the noodles until the bowl is ¾ full.

Place the covered bowl in a heated steamer and steam for about 10 minutes or until the custard is firm. Test in center with a chopstick. Remove contents of bowl to individual plates and serve.

11. Casserole Noodle Soup

2 8oz. pkgs. whole wheat noodles
2 pieces fried wheat gluten (½″
   thick – see #45) or tofu
   if you have no gluten
5 med. dried mushrooms or
   10 small fresh mushrooms
1 bunch watercress (or scallions),
   ½″ diagonals
5 cups soup stock (see #39)
3 Tbsp. soy sauce
½ tsp. salt
2 eggs (optional)

Prepare the whole wheat noodles and mushrooms as in #10.

Place hot noodles in a casserole, top with fried gluten (or tofu), mushrooms, and watercress (or scallions). Add soy sauce and turn off flame.

Bring soup stock to a boil, add salt and simmer 10 minutes. Add boiling soup stock to noodles. Cover and bring to a boil again for 5 minutes.

Beat eggs and pour over the top of the noodles. Cover and continue to cook until eggs are half cooked.

Serve immediately.

12. Macaroni Gratin

½ lb. whole wheat macaroni
½ cup cooked crab
10 small white mushrooms
1 tsp. lemon juice
1 Tbsp. oil
1 heaping Tbsp. pastry flour
⅔ cup milk or water
1 Tbsp. white wine
⅓ cup grated natural cheese or
   1 Tbsp. tahini or
   ⅓ cup seitan
1 Tbsp. bread crumbs

Wash mushrooms. Cook them in 2 cups boiling water to which lemon juice has been added, until tender or about 15 minutes. Reserve liquid and chop each mushroom into about five pieces.

Bring about 6 cups of salted water to a boil and cook macaroni about 15 minutes. Drain thoroughly.

To make a sauce, heat oil, add flour and roast until fragrant (medium light color). Cool. Add mushroom water or milk and stir until smooth and thickened. Bring to a boil and add salt to taste. Add wine. Thin the sauce if necessary.

Mix two thirds of sauce with macaroni and put into casserole. Mix remaining sauce thoroughly with crab and mushrooms and pour over the top of the macaroni. Sprinkle grated cheese or seitan (see #46) over macaroni and top with bread crumbs.

Bake in 450° oven without cover until crumbs are lightly browned.

Note: If you do not wish to use cheese or seitan, mix 1 Tbsp. sesame butter with macaroni.

13. Fried Whole Wheat Spaghetti

2 8oz. pkgs. whole wheat spaghetti
1½ cups onion, thin crescents
4 cups cabbage, thin matchsticks
1 cup celery, thin diagonals
4 cups bean sprouts
⅓ cup chopped seitan
1½ tsp. salt
3 Tbsp. oil
2 Tbsp. soy sauce

Prepare the noodles as in #10. Rinse once quickly in cold water. Shake strainer to dry completely.

Heat 2 Tbsp. oil in cast iron skillet. Put noodles in skillet and cover. Cook over medium heat about five minutes. Remove cover and turn noodles over. They should be light brown. Replace cover and cook another five minutes. Repeat this once more, cooking twice on one side until thoroughly hot. Sprinkle soy sauce, cover, and shut off heat.

Heat 1 Tbsp. oil. Saute onion. When half transparent, add cabbage and celery. When celery is bright green, add sprouts and seitan. Cook a few more minutes on high flame without cover to keep a crispy crunchy texture. Remove from fire. Mix vegetables with noodles and serve.

Variation: Prepare vegetables as above. Add to cooked noodles (not fried) and heat until noodles are hot.

14. Homemade Noodles with Miso Soup

3 cups whole wheat flour
1½ tsp. salt
⅔ cups cold water

Soup
1 med. burdock, shaved
2 med. onions, crescents
1 med. carrot, shaved
2 age, sliced ¼"
1½ tsp. sesame oil
½ tsp. salt
½ cup barley miso

1 bunch scallions, thin diagonals
2 sheets nori, roasted and crushed

Mix flour, salt, and water. Knead well and make into a ball. Place in plastic bag, then into a paper bag or in folds of newspaper and knead dough barefoot for 20 minutes. Roll dough out on floured board very thin.

Fold dough in half, sprinkle lightly with flour. Continue to fold dough in half, sprinkling with flour, until dough is 3" wide. Slice very thin. Separate strands.

Bring 8 cups of unsalted water to a boil, add noodles and bring to a boil again. Shut off heat and let sit one minute. Drain and rinse with cold water and allow to get completely cold.

Heat oil, saute burdock over medium flame until some of the smell is gone, add onion, and carrot. Add ½ tsp. salt. Cover vegetables with hot water and bring to a boil. Remove cover, add age and cook two to three minutes.

Add 4 additional cups of hot water and cook with a cover until the vegetables are tender. Then drop in the noodles and bring to boil. Cream miso with a little stock from the soup and stir into rest of soup. Bring soup to a boil, then immediately remove from heat.

Serve noodle soup hot with a sprinkling of chopped scallions and roasted crushed nori.

Note: If soy sauce is preferred for seasoning, omit miso.

Vegetables

15. Mustard Green and Onion Nitsuke

1 bunch mustard greens, stems
   1″ pieces, leaves 1½″, and
   then cut across
3 med. onions, ¼″ crescents
1 Tbsp. sesame oil
¼ tsp. salt
1 Tbsp. soy sauce

Remove the spoiling leaves from the mustard before washing it. Fill a large container with cold water and wash the mustard greens, especially the inside of the stems. Wash them quickly and let them drain.

Heat the oil and saute the onions until they are transparent. Add the stems and cook them uncovered until they turn bright green. Add the leaves, then add the salt and the soy sauce. Stir and continue to cook the vegetables until they are tender.

16. Onion Miso

10 small whole onions
3 Tbsp. miso
1 Tbsp. oil
1-2 cups cold water

Saute the onions in oil for at least five minutes. Cover with water, bring to a boil, and cook over a low flame for one hour. After the onions have cooled, quarter them about two thirds of the way down towards the root, so that the onion opens like a flower. Dissolve the miso in a little of the onion juice left over from cooking, and add to remaining juice. Cook until it is thick and creamy and serve it as a sauce over the onions. Allow two onions per serving.

17. Rolled Cabbage

10 cabbage leaves
2 pieces French bread (see #87)
1 cup onions, crescents
⅓ cup carrots, matchsticks
5 strands of kampyo (gourd strips)
1 6″ piece of kombu
1 tsp. oil
1 tsp. salt
Parsley for garnish

Place the cabbage leaves in boiling water until their color changes. Take out and let cool, reserving water. Remove hard section from core.

Oil a pan and fry the bread on both sides until browned. Cut into ⅓″ squares. Saute the onions and carrots in the same pan for a few minutes. Add salt to taste, turn off flame, add bread cubes.

Place a spoonful or two of this mixture in each cabbage leaf and fold the leaf into a package. Tie it with kampyo that has been softened with warm water.

Place the kombu on the bottom of a pan, lay cabbage rolls on top; cover with water, bring to a boil, and season with salt. Cook until tender, remove and cover with bechamel sauce and parsley. Cabbage rolls may also be used in oden, stews, and nabemono in place of fish.

Bechamel sauce

2 heaping Tbsp. whole wheat
   pastry flour
1 Tbsp. oil
½ cup water
¼ tsp. salt

Heat oil in a saucepan and toast flour until it has a nut-like fragrance, stirring constantly to prevent burning. Cool the flour, add water and return to flame. Bring to a boil, add salt and cook five more minutes. Pour over cabbage rolls.

18. Rolled Cabbage with Age

1 head cabbage, cored
1 handful string beans
4 med. onions, crescents
2 age, matchsticks
4" piece of carrot, matchsticks
2oz. bean threads
1 Tbsp. oil
2 tsp. salt
Soup stock (see #39 or #40) or water

Place the whole cabbage in boiling water until it becomes soft. Separate leaves and set aside to cool. Boil string beans in boiling salted water for about four minutes, then slice on the diagonal. Soak bean threads in boiling water 5-6 minutes.

In a skillet heat 1 Tbsp. oil and saute the onions until they are transparent. Add age, carrot, bean threads, and 1 tsp. salt, and cook until half done. Add string beans.

Place a small amount of mixture in each cabbage leaf and roll into a package, securing with a toothpick. Return rolls to pan, cover with a little soup stock or water and season with remaining salt. Bring to a boil. Cover with bechamel sauce and serve.

Bechamel sauce

2 cups whole wheat pastry flour
2 Tbsp. oil
7 cups water
1 tsp. salt

Heat oil in a small saucepan, and toast the flour until it has a nut-like fragrance. Cool the flour, add liquid left from boiling cabbage leaves, bring to a boil, and add salt. Cover cabbage rolls with sauce and garnish with parsley.

19. Vegetable Fritters

1 cup burdock, thinly cut
    on the diagonal
1 cup carrot, thinly cut
    on the diagonal
⅓ cup whole wheat flour
2 Tbsp. oil
1 tsp. salt
1½ tsp. soy sauce

Place flour in a plastic bag. Add burdock and shake vigorously. Remove burdock from bag. Heat oil in a skillet, place floured burdock in pan and cover. Cook over medium heat for five minutes. Turn over and cook another five minutes with a lid.

Place carrots in flour mixture and shake as above. Add to burdock when it has become soft and cook until the carrots are soft. Add salt, soy sauce. Sprinkle water in a spiral beginning from the outer edge of the skillet. Add ¼ cup more water if necessary. Cook until tender.

Adjust seasoning. Remove from flame. This method of cooking is similar to French fritter cooking and it is very delicious.

20. Green Pea and Shrimp Nitsuke

1 lb. fresh green peas
1 lb. shrimp
3½ cups soup stock (#39)
1½ Tbsp. soy sauce
1½ tsp. salt
1 Tbsp. arrowroot

Bring the soup stock to a boil, add salt and peas and cook uncovered until half done. Add soy sauce. Clean and de-vein shrimp and add when the peas are almost done. Do not cook too long. Bring to a boil and add starch that has been dissolved in a little cold water. Bring to a boil again and cook until thickened and transparent. Serve in deep bowls.

Wild Vegetables

During the spring and summer it is very easy to pick out wild vegetables when we go to the country for a picnic or a hike. These vegetables are very rich in minerals and help to strengthen the body. Wild vegetables have a slightly bitter taste and are most helpful in removing excess salts, oil, and protein from the body. Eat wild vegetables during the spring and summer for more energy and vitality.

When serving wild vegetables, always use one part wild vegetables to three parts domestic garden vege-tables, so their strong flavor will not overpower a meal.

Many wild vegetables grow in abundance in fields and meadows all over America. With a little experimenting you can soon learn to pick out the edible varieties. This section deals with their various beneficial qualities and preparations.

Jinenjo, taro, and burdock are discussed on page 18.

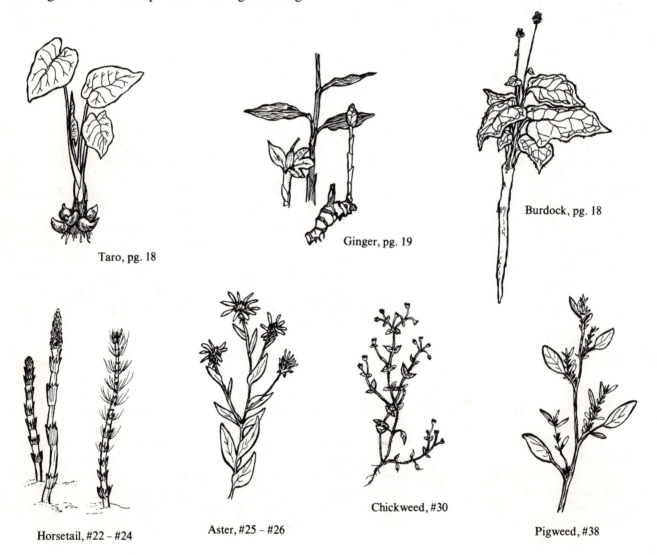

Taro, pg. 18

Ginger, pg. 19

Burdock, pg. 18

Horsetail, #22 – #24

Aster, #25 – #26

Chickweed, #30

Pigweed, #38

Dandelion, #27 – #28

Bracken, #29

Thistle, #33 – #34

Beefsteak, #138

New Zealand Spinach, #36

Goosefoot, #136

Wood Sorrel, #137

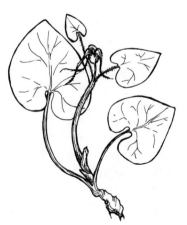

Wild Ginger, #139

Jerusalem Artichoke, #277

Purslane, #135

> **Mugwort** – Mugwort grows in early spring and can be eaten until the beginning of June. In early spring, harvest about 3″ to 5″ from the top of the plant, but later when it's tall, eat only the soft top part. Mugwort contains a lot of iron. It is good for cleaning parasites and treating anemia. Even though mugwort is a spring vegetable, George Ohsawa said it is a very yang grass that can be eaten all year round. I remember keeping some for 3 years that I found in New York.

21. Mugwort

Mugwort
Water
Salt

Dip mugwort in boiling salted water, then squeeze with each hand into small balls. Store these in a clean, dry place. In 2-3 weeks they will be dry. These dried mugwort balls can be stored a long time in a glass jar.

Mugwort is good for tempura, for use in mochi, noodles, or baking bread. For mugwort bread, use one handful mugwort to 14 cups flour. Boil the mugwort uncovered in salted water, squeeze out the liquid, and cut into small pieces. Add to the dough before the last kneading. Knead, let rise for the last time, and bake.

> **Horsetail** – Horsetail contains more available calcium than any other vegetable. It is especially good for people who are suffering from lung problems, or have weak bones resulting from calcium deficiences. The edible part of the horsetail grows only for about one month in early spring. Only the tender stems are used; the head and the hard brownish sections are removed before cooking. After the brief growing season in early spring, the leaves begin to form and the plant should not be eaten. Horsetail can be prepared in a variety of ways: tempura, nitsuke, with age (fried tofu), nori, and fried in dough.

22. Horsetail Nitsuke

Horsetail stems, cut ¼″
Oil
Soy sauce

Wash carefully and remove the brownish section from stem. Cut the stems and saute in a little sesame oil. Add a small amount of water, season with soy sauce, cover pan and cook about 20 minutes. Remove cover before serving to allow excess liquid to boil away.

23. Horsetail Balls

Horsetail stems, cut ¼″
Whole wheat pastry flour
Oil for sauteing and deep frying

Clean horsetail stems as above and cut into ¼″ pieces. Saute as for nitsuke and cook 20 minutes. Mix with enough whole wheat pastry flour to form small balls ¾″ in diameter. Deep fry in tempura oil or a mixture of corn and safflower oil until crispy. Serve a couple of balls on a toothpick or on small wooden skewers. They make attractive hors d'oeuvres.

24. Horsetail Rolls

Horsetail nitsuke (#22)
Whole wheat pastry flour
Water
Salt
Oil for deep frying

Prepare horsetail nitsuke. Make a dough using whole wheat pastry flour and a small amount of water and salt. Knead dough until it is as soft as your ear lobe. Roll dough out to ⅛″ thickness and place on a sushi (bamboo) mat; spread a layer of nitsuke over the dough, leaving a one-inch border on two sides. Roll mat to form a jelly roll and seal ends of dough with a little water. Deep fry the whole roll in tempura oil. Drain and cut into ¾″ pieces.

Asters – Asters should be picked in the early spring when the plants are only three to four inches high. Both the leaves and the stems can be used. The flavor is milder than other wild vegetables.

25. Aster Nitsuke

Aster leaves and stems
Sesame Oil
Soy sauce for seasoning

Clean leaves and stems and cut into ¼ inch pieces. Saute in sesame oil. Season with soy sauce and cook until tender.

26. Onion Aster Boats

¼ lb. asters
2 med. onions, quartered
2 heaping Tbsp. roasted peanuts
1 Tbsp. soy sauce
¼ tsp. salt
1 Tbsp. sesame seeds, roasted

Cook asters in salted boiling water for three minutes. Remove asters and cook onions in this water for another three minutes. Drain onions, saving liquid.

Chop asters into one-inch pieces. Grind peanuts in a suribachi, add 2 Tbsp. of vegetable liquid, soy sauce and salt, and mix in aster leaves.

Separate the inside section of the onion pieces, leaving two layers of onion for the shells. Inside sections can be minced and sauteed in a little sesame oil and seasoned with miso to use as a garnish for the aster boats.

Fill the shells with a spoonful of aster mixture. Chop roasted sesame seeds with a knife and sprinkle over aster boats for decoration.

Dandelions – Dandelion greens should be picked only in the springtime while the leaves are still tender and before the flower develops. The roots may be used at any time during the growing season, but are best in spring when they are larger and contain more energy. The leaves become very bitter later in the season and contain much more potassium.

The leaves are also good in pressed salads. If you find a lot of leaves, those not used immediately in cooking can be pressed with salt for a few days. These leaves can then be used in cooking, served, or placed in a clean gauze sack and set on the bottom of a miso keg for pickling. They will keep a long period when prepared this way.

27. Dandelion Nitsuke

1 cup dandelion greens, chopped fine
1 Tbsp. soy sauce (or 1 Tbsp. miso,
    2 Tbsp. water)
1 Tbsp. sesame oil
Sesame seeds, toasted and chopped

Chop greens finely and saute in oil. After they have cooked 10 minutes in a covered pan, add soy sauce and cook until tender. Sprinkle with toasted sesame seeds that have been chopped with a knife.

28. Dandelion Roots

Dandelion roots
Oil
Soy sauce or miso for seasoning

Scrub roots thoroughly. Mince finely and saute in oil. Season with soy sauce or miso. If using miso, cover a few minutes. Saute another 7 minutes until fragrant and dry. Serve only 1 teaspoon per person or use as a condiment over rice. Very good for people suffering from arthritis.

If you want to keep dandelion roots as a condiment for a long time, prepare roots similar to thistle root condiment (#34).

29. Bracken Nitsuke————

1 handful bracken
1 Tbsp. sesame oil
¼ cup water
1 Tbsp. soy sauce

In the early spring, bracken can be found growing in open fields or on mountainsides. The plant should be used when the stems are about 8 to 10 inches high and before the leaves begin to grow. The top of the stem has a black, fist-shaped bud. When the bud opens, the stem becomes too hard to use for cooking. The brownish sections that appear on the stem should be trimmed.

Boil bracken in salted water for 5 minutes to remove excess potassium. Drain and cut into 1 inch pieces. Saute in oil. Cook in a covered pan about 15-20 minutes. Add soy sauce and cook until soft. Remove cover near end of cooking to remove excess liquid.

Variation: Carrot and age can be added to the above.

30. Chickweed————

Chickweed

Chickweed can be eaten at any time during its growing season because it is lower in potassium than other wild vegetables. It has a pleasant flavor, and is especially good for nursing mothers to take because it helps make good breast milk.

Prepare either as nitsuke or add to miso soup near the end of cooking, just before the miso is added.

31. Wild Scallion Nitsuke————

1 handful scallion leaves
1 Tbsp. sesame oil
1½ Tbsp. soy sauce
Egg (optional)

Wild scallions are fairly common and closely resemble the garden variety with leaves that are slightly flatter and thicker. Wild scallions are good for sexual appetite. In springtime, these can be harvested ½" from the ground; they will grow again and a month later they will be full grown. Discard the white blossoms – the stem will be hard.

Slice one handful scallion leaves into one inch pieces after washing. Saute in 1 Tbsp. sesame oil. When the color changes, add 1½ Tbsp. soy sauce and continue cooking until tender. A beaten egg can be added at the very end of cooking.

32. Wild Scallion in Soup————

¼ cup wild scallions, cut ⅓"

For vegetable miso soup or clear soup or in a kuzu sauce – at end of cooking, add scallions and bring slightly to a boil. When scallions change to a bright green color, then serve.

33. Thistle Nitsuke————

Thistle roots
Sesame oil
Soy sauce or miso for seasoning

Thistles should be eaten only in the early spring when the plant is just three or four inches high and the stem is still tender. The root can also be used. The leaves can be used in tempura, boiled in salted water (ohitashi style), or prepared with roasted peanuts, cashews, or sesame butter in salad (see #26). Thistle roots are good for people suffering from rheumatism and polio.

After cleaning the roots, mince and saute in sesame oil. Cover pan and cook for 20-30 minutes, or until tender. Season with soy sauce or miso during cooking. Use as a condiment for rice or cereals.

34. Thistle Root Condiment—

1½ cups thistle root, finely minced
2 Tbsp. sesame oil
1 cup mugi miso

Dig thistle roots in early spring. Wash carefully using a vegetable brush. Dry, and chop fine.

Heat 1 Tbsp. oil in a wok and saute root well, about 20 minutes, uncovered. Add the other tablespoon oil and saute well until tender. Add miso and mix with thistle root, always stirring. Cook about an hour over a low flame – until vegetable is almost dry and crumbly.

Stored in a glass jar, this condiment will keep a long time unrefrigerated.

Thistle root is good for rheumatism. George Ohsawa told me that one soldier who had a bullet pass through his spine was cured after 3 years of macrobiotic diet with thistle root.

35. Boiled Licorice—

Licorice leaves
Soy sauce or sesame butter miso

Licorice is best to use in the early spring when the tender leaves are still just three or four inches long. The plant's appearance resembles wild tiger lilies, with orange-colored flowers.

Cook leaves in salted boiling water for about 10 minutes or until soft. Season with soy sauce, or a mixture of sesame butter and miso. Serve only one tablespoon of cooked greens per person because the plant is very yin and high in potassium.

36. New Zealand Spinach—

New Zealand spinach
Seasonings

Slice thin. Good for miso soup or clear soup. Season with soy sauce or cook in salted water and mix with sesame butter.

This plant grows near the oceanside all year 'round. It fortifies the blood. Good for stomach cancer, and the juice is good for stomach ulcers.

37. Plantain—

Plantain

In Japan we usually use plantain for herb tea. But young plantain is tender and can be eaten as a vegetable. Saute as for nitsuke or cook as ohitashi or goma ai, and season with lemon juice.

For herb tea: Harvest in early July. The best time to pick it is before sunrise. Pick the whole plant, roots and all. Wash well and strain in a colander. Tie together at the roots with a string, and hang in a shed to dry. Cover with newspaper to keep dust off. After completely dry, cut with a scissors into small (1″) pieces. Boil a small handful of dried plantain in 5 cups of water. Good for strengthening digestive organs.

38. Pigweed—

Pigweed

Originally, it grew in India. Grows about 2-3 feet in the hills or in gardens.

Pick the soft stem and leaves. Saute. Season with miso or soy sauce. Also good in ohitashi and in miso soup.

Soups

39. Kombu Stock

3″ × 12″ piece dashi kombu,
   cut as shown
7 cups water

Place kombu in pot. Add water and cook about 10-15 minutes on medium low flame until kombu rises to surface. Strain and use stock.

40. Kombu Stock with Fish

3″ × 12″ piece dashi kombu
16 cups water
¾ cup chuba iriko (dried fish)

Place kombu in 8 cups water and bring to a boil. Add fish and bring to a boil, uncovered. Drain liquid off into a bowl. Reserve kombu and fish. Add 8 more cups water to kombu and fish, bring to boil and cook 30 minutes with cover. Drain and mix with first stock, or use separately, since they have a slightly different taste.

41. Bonita Stock

1 cup dried bonita (shaved fish)
3″ × 7″ piece dashi kombu
12 cups water

Place kombu in 6 cups water and bring to a boil. Remove kombu and add bonita. Bring to boil again and cook 10 seconds without a cover. Turn off heat and cool. Strain and reserve bonita. Add kombu and remaining water to bonita. Bring to boil and cook for 5 minutes with cover. Use separately or mix with first stock.

This stock is for special dishes only. It is not recommended as a daily food because bonita is not a whole fish like chuba iriko.

42. Fish Stock

1 lb. head and bones of flounder or
   1 lb. shrimp shells
½ onion, thinly sliced
1 small carrot, thinly sliced
⅓ cup chopped parsley
10 cups water

Do not mix red fish stock with white fish stock. Use liquid from either fish, but not both. Cut fish into 2″ squares. Put all ingredients in a pan and bring to a boil without cover, over medium flame. Lower flame and skim off bubbles gently. Cook on low flame 30-40 minutes. Strain and use stock for cooking.

43. Chicken Bouillon

Bones from 1 chicken
1 small onion, quartered
1 small carrot, 2-3 pieces
⅓ cup chopped parsley
10 cups water

Break or chop chicken bones into two to three inch pieces. Add water and bring to boil without cover. Lower flame, continue to boil, and skim off scum. When stock is clear, add carrot, onion, and parsley. Continue cooking about 3 hours until about 6 cups of stock remain. Strain and use stock for cooking.

Note: Any parts of vegetables normally thrown away, such as carrot tops, celery tops, scallion roots, etc., may be added when making stock.

44. Oyster Chowder

10 small oysters
1 small onion, minced large
1 med. carrot, diced
1 potato, ½″ quarter moons
1 Tbsp. sesame oil
2 Tbsp. whole wheat pastry flour
1 cup milk or soup stock (#39)
3 salty crackers
1½ tsp. salt
3 cups water

Wash oysters in salt water, shaking rapidly to remove salt, but don't soak them. Boil water, add oysters and return to boil with ¼ tsp. salt. Strain oysters through a cotton cloth, reserving the water for later use.

Heat oil and saute onion until brown. Add flour and saute for 5 minutes. Cool pan. Add water from cooking oysters. When it comes to a boil, add carrot and potato. Cook for 15 minutes, add remaining salt, and cook for 10 more minutes. Add milk (or stock) and oysters. Serve with a small amount of crushed crackers.

Wheat Gluten

> **Wheat gluten** is a valuable source of protein that has been used by people of many countries throughout history. Wheat products, including gluten and 'fu' (dried gluten), were known long before being introduced to the Japanese monks over 800 years ago when wheat was first brought to Japan from China. Gluten was traditionally prepared in the temples of Japan.

45. Wheat Gluten

10 cups whole wheat flour
4 cups unbleached flour
5 cups cold water
2 tsp. salt

Mix flours and add water in which the salt has been dissolved. Knead in a bowl. Continue kneading strongly until dough softens. (Note: this is best done by placing bowl on floor and kneading vigorously in a kneeling position.) The dough will not make good gluten unless it is well kneaded. Knead for 20 minutes or longer.

Set dough in a dry bowl and leave uncovered for 40 minutes. Add 8-10 cups cold water, knead vigorously to wring out all the cream-colored starch from dough. Change water, repeating this process 5-6 times, saving this rinse water to use in baking. Each time water is changed it will become less sedimented. When only slightly sedimented starch water is obtained, stop. Knead dough until it becomes rubbery. Place in a strainer. About 5 cups of gluten dough should remain.

In a separate pot bring 10-12 cups water to a boil. Pull the gluten with your fingers into thin one-inch pieces and drop into boiling water. Continue boiling until gluten rises to the top. (Note: when using 10 cups of water, remove gluten pieces from boiling water and repeat, cooking one more time.) Strain and retain this cooking water to use in baking. Wash the gluten in cold water one or two times until the gluten is cold. Gluten pieces *must be completely cold* before adding to the soy sauce mixture when making seitan.

Gluten is easy to digest, a good source of protein for sick people. It is eaten in all seasons, especially by vegetarian and non-meat-eating people. Not only is it very important as a source of protein, it is also very enjoyable and can be used in soups, stews, fried foods, etc. Seitan is made from wheat gluten.

Note: In using the rinse water, let settle overnight. The starch and water will separate. In the morning, pour off water and save the starch sediment. Should have about 5 cups. This sediment can be mixed with the cooking water for easiest use. Works well in bread (such as French Gluten Bread #87), pancakes, or puddings.

46. Seitan

1 Tbsp. sesame oil
1 Tbsp. minced ginger root
1-2 cups soy sauce
5 cups cold cooked gluten

Heat oil in a saucepan, add minced ginger (use only fresh ginger) and saute. Add soy sauce, bring to a boil, and drop in pieces of gluten. (The amount of soy sauce used depends upon how long you intend to store the seitan. Use a larger amount of soy sauce for longer storing and refrigeration.)

Cook on low heat about an hour or until liquid is almost absorbed, stirring frequently. Remove cover and continue cooking until excess liquid is absorbed and evaporated.

Seitan is ideal as a seasoning in noodles au gratin, stews, cooked with vegetables, etc. It will keep for long periods of time in the refrigerator.

47. Fresh Wheat Fu

5 cups wheat gluten, separated
    in 2 parts
3 cups sweet brown rice flour
3 cups whole wheat pastry flour
8 cups water

Knead one part of the wheat gluten with 3 cups rice flour. As the gluten is very sticky, kneading will be difficult at first, but after about 20 minutes of kneading, the dough will become smooth. Repeat as above for the remaining gluten and whole wheat pastry flour.

Pat out each section into a rectangle about 3 × 6 inches and 2 inches thick. Bring water to a boil and drop in one rectangle. Once the water comes to a boil again, lower flame and let simmer for 20 minutes. If using a steamer, cook gluten over a high flame for 30 minutes. Repeat for second rectangle.

Remove gluten with a ladle and place on a platter to cool. Cut into strips ½ inch wide. Reserve and store water in the refrigerator to use in cooking or baking.

48. Boiled Fu

Wheat fu made from either pastry
    or sweet brown rice flour
3 cups soup stock (see #39)
3 cups water
1 tsp. salt
3 Tbsp. soy sauce

Bring soup stock and water to a boil. Add salt and soy sauce. Drop in wheat fu and simmer over a medium flame for 30 minutes. Wheat fu will expand in size during cooking.

Cooked fu can be stored in a refrigerator for one week. Fu can be used in a variety of vegetable dishes or deep fried and served with noodles or stew.

49. Fried Fu (Gluten Cutlet)

5 strips boiled fu
1 cup whole wheat pastry flour
2 cups tempura batter (see #66)
2 cups cornmeal, bread crumbs, or cracked wheat
Tempura oil

Dust strips with pastry flour, then dip into tempura batter, cover with cornmeal and let sit on a plate for about 5 minutes.

Deep fry in hot oil (350 degrees), turning over once after strips rise to the top of oil. Cutlets take about 5 minutes to cook. Remove from oil with a strainer or slotted spoon and place in a strainer set inside another pan to catch excess oil before serving.

Serving suggestions: cut carrots and cabbage leaves into thin strips and saute in a small amount of oil with a pinch of salt over a high flame for about 5 minutes. Make a bed of the sauteed vegetables in the center of a serving dish and place cutlets on top. Garnish with red radishes cut into flower shapes. (See cutting diagrams, pp. 216-218.)

50. Shish Kebab

3 strips boiled fu
4 carrots, cut into logs
3 burdock roots, cut into logs
18 Brussels sprouts
1 cup whole wheat pastry flour
2 cups tempura batter (see #66)
2 cups cornmeal, bread crumbs, or cracked wheat
½ tsp. salt
Tempura oil

Cut each piece of fu into 6 pieces. Cut vegetables into logs 1½ inches long. Boil carrots and Brussels sprouts in just enough salted water to cover for 15 minutes. Carrots should be tender, but still firm. Use only the upper portion of burdock to maintain a diameter of about ¾ inch. Burdock may be pressure-cooked for 15 minutes in at least ¼″ water with ½ tsp. salt. If boiling, cook burdock for about 45 minutes in salted water.

Using the same amount of flour and tempura batter as for the gluten cutlet, dip vegetables first into flour, then batter, and finally into cornmeal or bread crumbs. Deep fry in oil. Repeat for the pieces of wheat fu.

Drain as for gluten cutlets, then alternate pieces of fu with vegetables on wooden skewers.

Serving suggestion: In the center of a platter, make a bed of string beans or snow peas that have been cooked in salted water. Surround with a layer of salad greens and arrange shish kebab on top of leaves.

Tofu

51. Tofu Making

3 cups green soybeans soaked in
  6 cups water
25 cups spring water
4½ tsp. liquid nigari (#53)

Soak soybeans overnight in water (figure 1). In summer, 7 hours is sufficient; in winter, if it is very cold, soak beans for 20 hours. To test, cut a bean in half; inside and outside should be the same color. Drain beans and discard water.

Blend beans in an electric blender or force through a food mill (figure 3), adding some water, if necessary, to make a paste. Bring 25 cups of water to a boil (figure 4), and add pureed beans immediately to avoid spoiling. Bring beans to a boil *without* cover and stir. Sprinkle cold water on beans to quiet bubbling. Repeat three times, always bringing the water back to a boil.

Place several cotton flour sacks in a wooden keg and pour bean mixture into a sack (figure 5), then place in keg to reserve liquid. Squeeze sack to remove water (figure 6). Sprinkle nigari over the water drained from the beans (figure 7). Note: Bean water must be hot in order for nigari to work. Let it rest 5 minutes. With a long handled wooden spoon, make 2 deep strokes into the water at right angles to each other (as though to form a cross). Make these strokes slowly as though you were going to lift the bottom matter up to the top of the keg – dipping in at the side of the keg and coming up again in the center.

Let rest again for 10 minutes, checking to see if liquid separated. If not, sprinkle another teaspoon of nigari over water. Let it stand 5 minutes and repeat 2 deep strokes with wooden spoon. Wait 5 minutes again. You will see a white thickened substance resembling scrambled eggs.

Line a slat-bottomed square box (figure 9) with a clean cotton cloth and spoon out the thick white substance into the towel. Cover the top of the container with a cloth and then a wooden lid. Place an empty quart jar on lid for pressure (figure 10). One hour later increase pressure by using a ½-gallon jug containing 4 cups water. About 1½ hours later, all water should be drained and tofu is ready to use. Place container in sink and slowly remove cover and towels. Cover tofu with cold water for 30 minutes before serving. Cut into pieces 3″ × 4½″ and one inch thick (figure 11) for 6 pieces of tofu.

Tofu will keep one week, covered in water and refrigerated. Change the water every two days to keep tofu fresh.

52. Quantity Tofu Preparation

10 lbs. soybeans
18 gallons water
1½ to 2 cups nigari

Proceed as for regular tofu. This amount makes 24 pieces of tofu 4″ × 4″.

Making Tofu (soybean curd) At Home

Making Nigari (gypsum) From Crude Salt

53. Nigari Making

5 lbs. crude sea salt
Clean linen cloth

To make nigari, use damp sea salt. If the sea salt is dry, sprinkle it with some water until fairly damp. Place salt in cloth and gather sides to make a sack. Hang sack in a cool, damp place to drain for several days. Collect the liquid that drips from the cloth sack into a pan or bucket – this liquid is nigari.

Variation: To use commercially available nigari powder, mix equal amounts of powder and water and let sit overnight or until clear. Skim and store clear liquid in a covered glass jar. Discard sediment.

54. Okara Vegetables

3 cups okara (residue from tofu making)
1 cup burdock, shaved
1 cup onion, crescents
1 cup carrot, shaved
½ cup green onions, cut in ¼" pieces
1 Tbsp. oil
1 tsp. salt
½ Tbsp. soy sauce

Saute burdock in oil until the smell is gone; add onion. When the onions become transparent, add carrots. Saute a few minutes and add salt and soy sauce. Cook with cover over medium flame for 30 minutes. When all vegetables are tender, add scallions and okara. If too dry, add ¼ cup water. Cook with cover over medium flame for 15 minutes, then mix from bottom to top. Cover and cook 5 more minutes, then mix again until hot.

Serve as a side dish with rice, or mix into rice, or press cooked rice into a casserole in a layer about 1½" thick. Spread okara vegetables on top about ½" thick. Cut into squares and serve.

Variation: Okara can be used in croquettes with pastry flour and minced vegetables. Okara is also good in clear soup. Yin, sick people should not eat okara dishes.

55. Tofu with Kuzu Sauce

1 lb. tofu
6 cups water
Parsley for garnish

Cut tofu into 2" squares. Bring water to a boil in pot and add tofu. Remove tofu with a slotted spoon and place on a plate that has been warmed in the oven.

Kuzu sauce

1 cup liquid – half soup stock (#39) and half water
2 Tbsp. soy sauce
1 tsp. kuzu

Bring liquid to a boil. Dissolve kuzu in a few spoonfuls of cold water and add to liquid along with soy sauce. Bring to a boil again and remove from heat. Pour over cooked tofu. Garnish the center of each tofu piece with a pinch of parsley.

56. Fried Tofu

Tofu cut into 2″ × ½″ × ½″ pieces
1 tsp. each: grated daikon and carrot
Soy sauce
Tempura oil or sesame oil

Place a clean towel over a wooden cutting board and set tofu on top. Cover with another towel and weigh down with another board, then telephone or heavy book. Set weighted board on an angle in the kitchen sink or dish drain. Let sit 30-60 minutes.

Heat oil to about 350° (just before smoking) on a high flame. If you have time, remove from heat and let cool for 5 minutes. Slide tofu into hot oil and return to flame. Fry until both sides are golden.

Drain by placing cooked tofu in a strainer set inside another pan for a few minutes. Remove and place on paper towels or serve immediately. Serve with grated daikon and carrots and soy sauce. (This aids in digesting oil.)

57. Fried Tofu with Buckwheat

1 lb. tofu
1 cup buckwheat flour
½ cup soup stock (#40)
3 Tbsp. soy sauce
4-5 scallions
Tempura oil

Dip pieces of tofu into buckwheat flour and deep-fry in hot (350°) oil until golden, or pan fry. If pan frying, cover the pan while cooking the first side of the tofu, then remove cover, turn tofu over, and fry other side.

While the tofu is cooking, bring soup stock water and soy sauce to a boil and simmer for just one minute. Remove from heat.

Serve sarashinegi scallions (see #205) as a garnish with the tofu and soup stock sauce.

58. Scrambled Tofu

5 med. shiitake mushrooms or
**   10 fresh mushrooms, sliced thin**
1 cup water
1 cup onion, minced
⅓ cup fresh green peas
½ cup carrot, minced
1 Tbsp. sesame oil
½ tsp. salt
1 Tbsp. soy sauce
1 lb. tofu, cut in half
¼ cup chopped parsley

Soak mushrooms (if dried) in 1 cup water for 20 minutes. Remove and reserve water; chop mushrooms fine, discarding hard stems. Heat oil in pan and saute onions, mushrooms, then peas and carrots. Add ⅓ cup reserved mushroom water and salt.

Cover pan and cook 20 minutes. Add 1 Tbsp. soy sauce halfway through cooking. In a separate pot, bring 6 cups water to boil. Add tofu; strain immediately. Puree tofu. Add puree to the cooked vegetables and stir with chopsticks until it resembles scrambled eggs. If desired, season with soy sauce to taste.

Add parsley and stir until parsley is bright green.

Note: Any combination of vegetables and mushrooms can be used in this preparation.

59. Tofu Rolled with Nori

1 lb. tofu
½ cup dried mushrooms or 1 cup
    fresh mushrooms, thinly sliced
⅓ cup string beans, thinly sliced
¼ cup carrots, minced large
½ cup chopped scallions
1 Tbsp. sesame oil
½ tsp. salt
1½ Tbsp. soy sauce
3 sheets nori seaweed
6 kampyo (gourd strips)

Mash the tofu in a suribachi and set aside. Heat oil and saute first the mushrooms (shiitake is best – soak and chop as in # 58), string beans, and finally the carrots. Add a small amount of water left over from soaking mushrooms, add salt, and cover pan. Cook 15 minutes. Remove cover, add soy sauce and continue cooking for another 5 minutes over a high flame to remove excess liquid.

Toast nori lightly and place on a sushi mat. Mix tofu thoroughly with vegetables. Spread a layer of tofu mixture ½″-thick over nori sheets, leaving a 1″ border on the two lengthwise sides of the nori.

Using the sushi mat, roll nori lengthwise. Wash gourd strips in warm water to soften, and tie at each end of nori rolls.

Place rolls in a vegetable steamer and steam uncovered for 10 minutes. Let cool. Slice into 1″ pieces and serve.

60. Stuffed Age

7 pieces age (available in Oriental
    stores)
Vegetable mixture, prepared
    as in #59
2 Tbsp. kuzu, 3 Tbsp. cold water
4 cups liquid (half soup stock,
    half water)
Soy sauce
Kampyo

Cut age in half. Open gently to make a pouch and stuff with vegetable mixture. Holding the stuffed age, tie each bundle with gourd strips that have been washed in warm water. Punch about 5 or 6 holes in sides of age with a toothpick and place them in a pan. Cover with soup stock and water.

Bring to a boil and simmer for 10 minutes. Add soy sauce and continue cooking for 10 minutes.

Turn age over gently and cook another 10 minutes. Remove age pouches. Add kuzu dissolved in cold water and bring to a boil. Remove from heat. Serve 1 Tbsp. of sauce over each age.

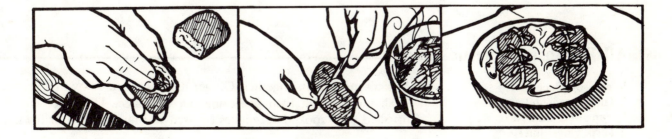

Special Dishes

> **Outdoor Barbecue –** Vegetables, fish, and chicken can all be easily prepared over an open fire, either at a campsite pit or on a hibachi. When constructing your own campfire pit in a stony area, first level the ground and make a circle around the area with stones. The diameter of the circle should be the same size as barbeque skewers. Then, pieces of food can be placed on the skewers and laid on top of the stones for uniform cooking. When using a hibachi or cooking over a grill, first heat the grating and then brush it with a little oil. This will allow easy cleaning afterwards.
> Vegetables such as yams, potatoes, tomatoes, green peppers, mushrooms, and corn on the cob can be wrapped in cornhusks and set in hot coals. You can leave them whole, or, for faster cooking, cut in halves or quarters.

61. Barbecued Chicken and Vegetables

5-6 chicken thighs
3 tomatoes, quartered, or
  12 cherry tomatoes
1 med. eggplant, quartered
  then sliced in 1″ strips
3 onions, quartered
3 bell peppers, quartered
Sesame oil
2 tsp. salt
Barbecue sauce (optional, #62)

After cutting eggplant, sprinkle with salt and let sit for 10 minutes. Pat dry.

If desired, marinate the chicken in sauce for 30 minutes. Chicken can either be placed directly over a grill or else cut into 1″ cubes and placed on skewers. Brush eggplant with oil and place on skewers, alternating with pieces of onion. Tomatoes and green peppers can be placed on the same skewer and put over fire last, as they take less time to cook. Brush cooked foods with sauce after cooking.

62. All-Purpose Barbecue Sauce

½ cup soy sauce
2 Tbsp. sesame oil
½ cup sweet wine (sake, etc.)
2 Tbsp. ginger juice

Mix all ingredients together. Ginger juice is prepared by first grating fresh ginger root, then squeezing out the juice. The sauce can be brushed over cooked vegetables or used to marinate fish or fowl.

63. Barbecued Fish

Fish
Oil for brushing
Salt and lemon juice
   for seasoning

Either fresh or salt water fish should be cleaned first, removing scales and internal organs and discarding them. Fresh shellfish need only to be washed; leave the shells on during cooking to enhance the flavor.

When barbecuing whole fish, clean and then take a metal skewer and insert it at the top of the head in the open space on the bone near the mouth. Push skewer through entire fish so the end of the skewer comes out near the tail. Move fish to center of skewer and brush with oil. Cook on both sides. Season with salt and lemon juice. Serve with rice balls, salad, bread, and grain coffee.

64. Sukiyaki

½ lb. chicken meat (or shrimp,
   flounder, or bass)
3 bunches scallions, 2″ rounds
½ Chinese cabbage, sliced 1″ strips
8oz. bean thread noodles (saifun)
10 shiitake mushrooms (halved) or
   15 fresh mushrooms (whole)
1 Tbsp. sesame or corn oil
1 lb. tofu, cut into bite-sized cubes
3 cups soup stock (#39)
⅓ cup soy sauce

Bring 7 cups water to a boil, add saifun, boil 5 minutes. Then cover and set aside. Strain in a colander. Cut into 3″ pieces, rinse in cold water.

Cut chicken or fish into thin pieces. Scallions should be cut on the diagonal into 2½″ pieces, but if thin, cut into 2″ rounds. If using dried mushrooms, soak in water, then cut into pie-shaped pieces. Cut tofu and arrange all items on a platter.

Preheat a heavy cast-iron pan. Heat oil. Saute vegetables, keeping each kind of vegetable in a separate section of the pan during cooking. Place chicken on top of vegetables. Pour soy sauce and soup stock over. Add bean threads and cook uncovered until tender. Serve at table directly from pan.

65. Thick Omelette

4 eggs
3 Tbsp. soup stock (#39)
½ Tbsp. soy sauce
½ tsp. salt
Oil

Beat eggs, add soup stock, salt, and soy sauce and mix well. Heat an oiled frying pan. Divide mixture into three parts. Pour a third of the mixture into pan and when eggs begin to cook, make a "Z" with chopsticks to insure even cooking. Omelette will bubble, but do not scramble it.

As the omelette sets, push it to the front of pan. Add more oil and pour in one more portion of mixture. Let some of the egg liquid slide under the cooked egg. Make more holes with chopsticks to insure even cooking. Fold egg when set, oil pan, pour in remaining mixture, letting some egg under as before. Fold again after it has cooked to a light brown color. Center of omelette will be soft.

Variation: Add ½ cup chopped mushrooms to egg mixture.

Deep Fried Foods

66. Tempura

1 cup whole wheat pastry flour
2 Tbsp. rice flour
1¼ cups water
1 tsp. salt
2 tsp. arrowroot

Tempura selections – see below

Mix salt and water. Cut flour in with two thick chopsticks. Batter may be left slightly lumpy.

Heat oil. Oil should be at least 3″ deep. Stir with chopsticks so temperature of oil is uniform. When oil is just beginning to smoke – about 330° – test it to see if a drop of batter rises to the top or if there is a 'sputter' sound when a bit of salt is added. If so, oil is ready to use. If oil is too shallow or too many pieces are dropped in at one time, temperature will fall quickly and tempura will be oily. Tempura which swims freely in oil will be crispy. Poor quality oil evaporates quickly and also gets burned (becomes dirty looking). When tempura turns light brown, turn over once and cook until both sides are same color.

Remove tempura to upright position in a strainer set in a pan to catch excess oil. Remove tempura from strainer to paper towels or brown paper before the next batch is ready to drain.

Grated ginger (for fish) and grated daikon are usually served with tempura. Daikon aids in digesting oily foods. Equal amounts of grated carrot and daikon mixed together pleases children as it is milder and more colorful.

Abalone – Pound gently and cut into slices ¼″ thick, 3″ wide.
Asparagus – Cut into pieces 3½″ long from tip to usable end.
Broccoli – Use flowers 3″ long.
Burdock – Cut on diagonal 3″ long, ¼″ thick. Precook in water, seasoned with soy sauce if desired.
Butternut Squash – Cut into strips 1″ × 3½″ × ¼″.
Carrots – Cut on diagonal into ¼″ thick rounds.
Carrot Greens – Use leafy section 5″ long. Dip only one side into batter.
Cauliflower – Cut as for broccoli.
Celery – Cut into 3″ lengths. Do leaves same way as carrot greens.
Eggplant – Slice into pieces ¼″ thick.
Green Peppers – De-seed and cut into rounds ¼″ thick.
Nori – Cut sheet in half lengthwise and then widthwise into 5 strips. Holding 2 strips together, dip halfway in batter.
Onions – Slice into rounds ¼″ thick.
Parsley – Hold 2 sprigs together at bloom end and dip into batter, covering stems and half of bloom.
Shiso Leaves – Same as for carrot greens.
Shrimp or Prawns – Remove skin, leave tail on. Slice across ends of tail and squeeze out water. Slit backs of prawns and remove intestines. Make 3 cuts in short side of prawns to straighten. Dip into batter, holding by tail.
Squid – Remove skin and cut into pieces 1½″ × 3½″.
Sweet Potatoes – Peel and cut into strips ½″ thick and steam. Cook until firm but not tender. Cool. Roll in pastry flour and dip into batter.

Tempura sauce——————
1 cup soup stock (#39)
¼ cup soy sauce

Bring these ingredients to a boil and cool. Serve in small individual dishes. Add grated daikon and/or ginger to individual dishes as desired.

67. Mock Goose (Ganmodoki)——————————————————

1 lb. tofu
5 shiitake or 10 fresh mushrooms, cut in ½″ chunks
1 med. carrot, minced
1 cup minced onions
½ cup scallion, thin rounds
1 egg or 1 heaping Tbsp. whole wheat pastry flour
1 tsp. salt

Squeeze water from tofu by placing in a strainer for 20-30 minutes. Remove and cover with a cotton cloth. Place between 2 boards weighted with a heavy book for 1 hour. Set board at an angle so that water drains off. Occasional pressing with your hands helps to drain off more water.

If using shiitake mushrooms, soak and cut into thin ½″ pieces.

Break pieces of tofu into a bowl. Knead by hand until well broken. Add egg (or flour), salt, carrot, onions, scallions, and mushrooms. Mix thoroughly. Makes 10 balls.

Fry at 350°. Place on paper towels to drain. Serve hot with mustard, soy sauce, daikon and soy sauce, or grated ginger and soy sauce.

68. Mock Chicken with Cream Sauce (Kashiwamodoki)——————————

3 cups burdock, minced
3 cups onion, minced
3 cups whole wheat pastry flour
3 tsp. salt
2-3 cups water
Parsley, minced

For chicken croquettes, mix ingredients together. Batter should have a heavier consistency than tempura batter. Drop by spoonfuls into hot corn oil.

Sauce——————
2½ cups whole wheat pastry flour
1 Tbsp. oil
4 tsp. salt
10 cups water

Heat oil in a frying pan. Saute flour until it has a nut-like fragrance. Cool. Add water and salt, bring to a boil, cook 15 minutes. Add croquettes, bring to a second boil and serve over rice, covering ½ of the portion of rice with sauce. Garnish with minced parsley.

Salads

69. Bean Sprout Miso Salad

5 cups bean sprouts
1-2 Tbsp. mixed soybean puree
  (half mugi and half kome miso)
2 Tbsp. lemon juice

Wash bean sprouts and place in a pot of hot salted water, bring to a boil and remove from heat. Strain quickly and cool with cold water so sprouts remain crisp. Refrigerate.

Grind miso in a suribachi, add lemon juice and grind together. When the sprouts are completely chilled, add dressing and toss together well. Or, top each serving of sprouts with dressing.

70. Cole Slaw with Bean Sprouts

2 med. sized carrots, matchsticks
1 head cabbage, shaved
2 cups fresh bean sprouts
Boiling salted water (1 tsp. salt
  to 5-6 cups water)

Dressing
½ cup chopped onions
Boiling salted water (¼ tsp. salt
  to 1 cup water)
4 umeboshi plums
1 cup water
1 Tbsp. fresh lemon juice,
  or rice vinegar
1 cup cooked grain (rice or
  rice cream)
1 Tbsp. sesame oil
3 Tbsp. minced parsley
3 Tbsp. minced watercress

Shred carrots and cabbage. Place in a strainer and pour boiling water over the vegetables. Place a pan under the strainer to catch the water, and repeat the process. Do not discard water – this is a very sweet liquid and can be saved for miso soup, etc. Set vegetables aside.

In a saucepan, bring 1 cup of water to a boil and add ¼ tsp. salt. Drop in bean sprouts that have been rinsed in cold water. Cook just one minute after water comes to a boil again. Drain and rinse sprouts with cold water. Set aside to cool. Place bean sprouts and cabbage and carrots in a large serving dish.

To prepare the dressing, boil onions in salted water for 3 minutes to remove excess acids and strong flavor. Drain. Boil umeboshi plums in 1 cup water in a covered pan for 5-10 minutes. Shred plums with chopsticks or your fingers and remove pits. Place umeboshi juice in a blender and add boiled onions. Blend at low speed until liquefied. Add lemon juice and the rice a little at a time until thoroughly blended. Slowly drizzle in oil, while blender is still running. Add minced greens and blend until the dressing is a light foamy green. Cool. Pour dressing over vegetables and toss lightly. Garnish if desired with small sprigs of fresh parsley or watercress. Soy sauce may be used as seasoning if dressing needs more salt.

71. Cucumber Carrot Salad

1 cup carrots (cut into thin
    matchstick pieces)
¼ tsp. salt
2 cups cucumber, thinly sliced
½ tsp. salt

Carrot dressing
2 tsp. rice vinegar
¼ tsp. salt
¼ tsp. soy sauce

Cucumber dressing
2 tsp. rice vinegar
¼ tsp. salt

Add ¼ tsp. salt to the carrot sticks. Add ½ tsp. salt to the cucumbers. Let each sit for 5-7 minutes. Squeeze gently to remove excess liquid. Keep each in separate bowls.

Combine ingredients for dressings. Pour on each vegetable and combine these two bowls just before serving. The cucumber color is retained best when prepared without soy sauce. That is why each vegetable is kept separate with separate dressing until serving time.

Note: Rice vinegar preparations are good for keeping the liver healthy. They are also good with oily or fried foods as the rice vinegar aids digestion.

72. Asparagus Sesame Salad

2 lbs. asparagus
1 Tbsp. whole wheat pastry flour
2 Tbsp. soy sauce
⅓ cup sesame seeds or 1 heaping
    Tbsp. sesame butter
1 Tbsp. lemon juice
1 tsp. salt

Add the flour to 5 cups cold water and bring to a boil. Add salt. Cook asparagus upright in this liquid uncovered until tender (the flour holds the color in the asparagus, dip in water to remove the flour). Drain and cut off the tough portion on the root end. Cut into one inch lengths from the tip to the root end. Wash sesame seeds and dry roast in a skillet until they are toasted and begin to pop. Grind seeds in a suribachi, and mix in lemon juice and soy sauce. Serve dressing over each portion of asparagus when serving.

If you use sesame butter, check to see how salty it is. If necessary, reduce amount of soy sauce.

73. Sour Cabbage

2 med. cabbage
1 Tbsp. salt
6-8 bay leaves
Japanese (or other) salad press

Quarter the cabbages. Wash and drain them half a day. Core, reserve cores for cooking, and slice cabbage as thinly as possible. Place 2 hand-fuls of cabbage in a suribachi or bowl and add ½ tsp. of salt. Knead the cabbage gently until it begins to soften. Place cabbage in the salad press along with 2 bay leaves. Press remainder of cabbage in the same way. Press this strongly at room temperature for a couple of days, or until a white bubbly fermentation appears.

Pressed cabbage can be packed tightly in a glass jar, or it can be kept in the salad press under a very light pressure. Store in the refrigerator. You can serve this up to 5 weeks or so.

74. Mustard Green Ohitashi

1 bunch mustard greens
1½ tsp. soy sauce
Bonita flakes or
    2 tsp. sesame seeds
2 tsp. salt

Bring 8-10 cups of water to a boil and add salt. Take off cover. Then place one bunch of mustard greens in a pot standing on end. Then bring to a boil over high flame uncovered, immerse greens and wait until it boils again. When the stem is soft it is done. Remove to a strainer with leaves hanging over the edge, and cool. When they are cool, squeeze out excess water. Slice greens straight across in 1″ wide strips. Then put these in a bowl, add soy sauce and mix well. Decorate with bonita flakes or kirigoma. This method is simple and good for any green such as Swiss chard, Chinese cabbage, romaine lettuce, watercress, etc. After roasting sesame seeds, sprinkle over greens.

Sauces and Dressings

75. Mayonnaise

1 egg yolk
2 tsp. salt
1 cup oil (corn, olive, or sesame),
    boiled and cooled
1½ Tbsp. lemon juice
Dash of white pepper for
    special occasions

Break egg and separate white and yolk. Keep only the yolk – take white out with a towel by moving the bowl. Beat, adding salt. Then drop in the oil by chopstick, drop by drop, beating with a wisk, about 3 Tbsp. Then add oil by the ¼ teaspoon and beat, until 2 Tbsp. oil is used. Then add by 1 tsp. until all the oil is used. As mixture hardens, add lemon juice to soften.

Your mayonnaise will be successful if the egg yolk is very fresh. Thick oil is better than thin. In warm weather, mixing bowl and beater should be refrigerated a few minutes prior to using, to help thicken ingredients. If the oil separates, sometimes ½ a beaten egg white beaten into the mayonnaise helps. If it is not successful, make a new batch adding the old batch to the egg yolk instead of fresh oil (using the same method).

More oil can be added if you desire a thicker mayonnaise to be used for decorating. (For a quicker mayonnaise, see #183.)

76. Tartar Sauce

1 hardboiled egg
8 Tbsp. mayonnaise
2 tsp. minced parsley
2 Tbsp. minced cucumber pickle

Mash egg and mix with other ingredients. Makes one cup. Good for fowl, fish, crab, shrimp.

77. French Dressing

3 Tbsp. rice vinegar or
   lemon or orange juice
1 Tbsp. salt
9 Tbsp. olive, corn, or sesame oil

Shake all ingredients well in a bottle. This dressing keeps well, but tastes best when fresh.
   Variation: Peel and de-seed tomato so that 3 Tbsp. of pulp remain. Cut into small pieces and mix with one cup French dressing. This dressing is served over fish. Or, mix 1 cup of French dressing with 1½ Tbsp. of grated horseradish. This dressing is good over grilled fish.

78. Other Dressings

Mix rice vinegar and soy sauce together in equal amounts. This is a good condiment for fish and shellfish. If you want to keep a light color in your food, add more salt and less soy sauce. If you find vinegar unappealing, add a little soup stock.

— Mix equal amounts of lemon or tangerine juice with soy sauce.

— Roast and grind 3 Tbsp. white sesame seeds. Mix with 2 Tbsp. rice vinegar, 1 tsp. salt, and 1 tsp. soy sauce. This is a good condiment for fresh mackerel, red snapper, cucumber, daikon, bean sprouts, or vegetables and age.

— See #69. Bring miso to a boil and cook until the miso smell is gone. Grind and cool and add rice vinegar. Good as a condiment for scallion, turnip, shingiku, celery, cooked squid.

— Pit 2 salt plums, grind well and mix with 1 tsp. soy sauce. For white fish, squid, scallops, cucumber.

— Mix together 3 Tbsp. rice vinegar, 1½ Tbsp. soy sauce, 1 tsp. salt, and 1 tsp. prepared mustard (see #83).

Pickles

To pickle usually means to mix a vegetable with salt under pressure for a given period of time.

Pickled vegetables contain vitamins and minerals. They are made with a variety of seasonings and accompaniments such as rice bran (nuka), miso, soy sauce, kombu, rice koji, amasake, and rice vinegar, all of which add to the nourishment and good taste of the vegetable being pickled. Pickles enhance your enjoyment of other foods.

When salt permeates a vegetable, the cells are broken down. Rice bran or other ingredients used for pickling, plus bacteria in the air, join with the broken-down vegetable cells to transmute into new components over a period of time.

Fresh young vegetables are best for making pickles. Examples: long white radishes, cucumbers, eggplant. If you use completely ripe vegetables, the skin becomes hard when pickled and the inside gets too soft rather than crispy. Vegetables should be thoroughly cleaned of bacteria and worms, and dried well.

The amount of salt used controls growth of bacteria from the air. For quick pickling (13 days) refined sea salt is best. For keeping pickles longer (one month, six months, or one year) use crude sea salt. Vegetables also contain pectin. Pectin plus crude salt makes long-keeping crispy pickles.

Pressure is important when making pickles. For root vegetables, 10 pounds of vegetables require 20-30 pounds of stone for pressure. When water comes to the top of vegetables, change pressure to 5 pounds. Then, when the water comes to the top again, leave the pressure the same until vegetables are eaten. Several stones can be used to make a 50-pound weight for easy lifting.

Accompaniments such as rice koji, rice bran, sake kasu, yinnie syrup, and amasake do not aid in fermentation, only in increasing flavor. Therefore, when using the above ingredients to make pickles, more salt and pressure are needed. Ingredients that aid fermentation are salt and rice vinegar.

Variety in flavor can be obtained by using red chili peppers, dry mustard, fresh ginger, and dried tangerine or orange skins.

Make pickles in wood or heavy porcelain containers. Wood reacts the least to changes in temperature and moisture. Wood is porous so it changes more slowly. Containers, wooden covers, and stones should be clean and dry.

Vegetables should be packed closely in layers with no spaces between pieces. Spaces should be filled with vegetables. If they are left open, the water comes up more slowly and the taste deteriorates.

The amount of salt determines how long a pickle will keep. Twenty-four-hour pickles require 3-5 percent salt. This means 3-5 percent of the vegetable's weight before washing. Pickles which take two weeks to one month require 8-12 percent salt. If you keep pickles over one year, use 18-20 percent salt. These are usually miso pickles, sake kasu pickles, or mustard pickles. These pickles can be used as a winter vegetable by washing thoroughly or soaking 2-3 hours in fresh water to remove some of the salt. If less salt is used, more pressure is needed and vice versa.

Check pickles 24 hours after making them. If the lid is uneven, level it. If you are making Chinese cabbage pickles (two week-one month variety), check to see if water is coming up after 48 hours. If not, reverse cabbage pieces, putting top on the bottom and bottom pieces on top. In 12 hours the water should be up to the top of the cabbage. Change to a lighter stone. If water leaked out, change to another container and cover cabbage with salt water, using about 5 percent salt. (Example: 10 cups water to ½ cup salt.) If about five days later white mold appears but the water is still clear, don't worry. If the water becomes dark, this means insufficient salt, so sprinkle a handful of salt into the water.

If the liquid is too sour, drain off and replace with salted water. If the odor is bad, wash the pickles and replace in salted water. Keep keg of pickles in a cool shady room.

When making nuka (rice bran) pickles (#79 and #203), occasionally worms may hatch out of the nuka paste. A cotton cloth cover placed under the wooden or other lid is desirable. Keep all edges and sides of cover and container absolutely clean.

When you are through making rice bran pickles, rice bran can be saved for the next batch of pickles by extracting as much water as possible. This can be done by pressing a strainer into the rice bran until water rises in the strainer. Then spoon water out. Re-used rice bran is more flavorful. When as much water as possible has been extracted, sprinkle 1½ cups of salt over the top of the rice bran. Place a wooden lid and small (5 lb.) stone on the rice bran for pressure, then place the keg cover on the container and seal the edges closed with self-adhesive tape. Rice bran thus sealed and kept in a cool place will remain usable for several months.

If you have to go on a trip for a week or two while making pickles, remove vegetables from paste and sprinkle a cup of salt over paste. Keep in a cool place.

When you return, mix salt into paste and add fresh vegetables.

This covers some basic general points about pickling. Pickles are made from many kinds of vegetables, harvested at different times of the year. Please experiment.

79. Rice Bran Pickles

5 lbs. (about 25 cups) rice bran
2-3 cups crude salt
5 cups water
Choice of vegetables: daikon, daikon leaves, turnip, turnip leaves, carrots, celery, cabbage, or cucumber

Roast rice bran (nuka) over medium heat until it changes color slightly. Let it cool.

Bring water to a boil, add salt and let it cool. Place rice bran in a porcelain or wood container and pour the cooled water over it. Mixture should be as soft as miso paste.

Turnips can be cut in quarters, daikon in half, about 6" long – or use whole. If cabbage is small, do not cut; leave it whole, but core it and pickle with core side up to catch liquid. Use one or two stalks of celery. Small carrots can be used whole. Chinese cabbage should be dried outside for 12 hours first. When pickling leafy green vegetables (Chinese cabbage, daikon or turnip greens) or watermelon rind, insert vegetables in cheese cloth or several folds of gauze first so they can be removed from nuka paste easily and without waste.

Layer vegetables in nuka paste: 2" layer of rice bran; layer of vegetables; rice bran; vegetables; rice bran on top. Cover container with cotton cloth, then wooden or other lid.

These vegetables can be eaten within 2-3 days. Always use the outside leaves of the whole cabbage first, as they soften and are ready. When vegetables change color slightly and have the flavor of rice bran, they are ready to eat. Remove ripe pickles from keg – taste of pickles will spoil if left in paste after they are ripe. Refrigerate in a covered container. Wash and slice just before serving.

Note: Every day, remove vegetables and stir nuka paste. (This is not necessary in the dry nuka recipe, #203.) As it becomes softer each day, roast more nuka occasionally and add with a little salt so batch maintains the same consistency. Maximum amount of salt is 2 Tbsp. to 2 cups rice bran. If vegetables get too salty, wash off rice bran and keep vegetables in container in refrigerator. For the first month no additional salt is needed, just vegetables. After one month, when adding vegetables rub a little salt into them before adding to the rice bran paste.

Variations: Empty egg shells placed in pickle container keep pickles from getting sour. One piece of kombu (4" × 10") added to the rice bran pickling mixture makes a delicious taste. When kombu becomes soft, eat it and put in more kombu.

Leftover food such as cooked rice, orange or tangerine skins, or cooked fish (bones and skin) can be mixed with nuka paste and left in container for two days. Then remove leftovers and wipe off excess nuka; excess nuka may be returned to the pickling mixture.

80. Chinese Cabbage Rice Bran Pickles

10 lbs. Chinese cabbage (6-7 heads)
2 cups salt
5 cups rice bran
3″ × 12″ piece dashi kombu

Wash cabbage and remove 2 or 3 leaves from each head. Quarter cabbage, leaving 3″ uncut at root. Break cabbage into quarters. Cut 2″ into each quarter at stem end. Then dry in the shade outside for one day.

Roast rice bran as in rice bran pickle recipe. When cool, mix in 1/3 cup salt and put rice bran mixture into bottom of keg. Cover with half of the green leaves. Rub each piece of cabbage with about 1 tsp. of salt on one side only and place snugly in keg, alternating direction of each layer. Place a few strips of kombu between layers. On top of the 4th layer, place second half of green leaves and remaining salt.

Use a 20-30 lb. stone weight on top of wooden cover until water comes up two or three days later, at which time change pressure to a 3-5 lb. stone.

You can eat this pickle in 5 days. These cabbage pickles need not be washed, as nuka is in contact with the green leaves only. Keep in a cool, shady place.

Green leaves can be eaten later. Wash nuka off, chop fine, and combine with raw chopped scallions, bonita flakes, and a bit of soy sauce. Mix thoroughly and sprinkle over rice. Cabbage prepared this way is delicious and rich in minerals.

81. Onion Pickles

1½ lbs. small onions
2 cups water
¼ cup salt

Wash onions and dry outside in a shady place for half a day. Remove skins and small portion of head and tail of onions. Rub onions with 3 Tbsp. salt. Mix remaining salt with water and bring to boil. Cool.

Place onions in a glass or china container and pour salted water over them. Instead of a rock for pressure, place a quart-size jar filled with water on top of a plate or wooden board on the onions. After two or three days, if bubbling fermentation is visible, mix onions thoroughly. Mix onions again when fermentation is visible. Fermentation ceases in 2-3 weeks, and then pickles can be eaten.

82. Onion Vinegar Pickles

1½ lb. small onions
2 cups natural rice vinegar
1 Tbsp. salt

Using onion pickles (#81), wash pickled onions and dry outside in a shady place for half a day.

Bring rice vinegar and salt to a boil in an enamel pan and stir until salt is dissolved. Cool. Place onion pickles in a glass jar and cover completely with rice vinegar mixture. Cover and keep in a cool place one month before serving. If liquid is insufficient to cover onions, add more vinegar.

83. Mustard Powder Pickles

36 pickling cucumbers
3-5 heaping Tbsp. salt
1½ Tbsp. green or bancha tea
3 Tbsp. powdered mustard
3 cups amasake (see #446)

After washing cucumbers, dry them and put in vegetable press with salt for 24 hours. Drain liquid and dry cucumbers.

Make about 1 cup of strong bancha tea. Place mustard in ovenproof bowl and add 1½ Tbsp. of hot tea. Stir quickly. Invert bowl over burner on low heat for about 5 minutes, until mustard mixture is slightly browned and there is a potent mustard fragrance. Add amasake to mustard mixture.

On the bottom of a clean porcelain or glass container, place about 3 Tbsp. of mustard mixture. Then add a layer of cucumbers. Alternate layers of cucumber and mustard until cucumbers are all used. Cover container and keep in refrigerator for one or one and a half months. These pickles will then be ready to eat and are delicious with fried foods.

Variation: After mustard and tea mixture has been fired, add a little soy sauce and blend. This is good on cooked vegetables. Note: Do not eat mustard if you are troubled with hemorrhoids.

Breads and Snacks

84. Rice Bread

4 cups cooked brown rice
8 cups whole wheat flour
2 cups millet flour
2 cups corn flour
3 tsp. salt
5 cups warm water

Combine rice and water and mix until large lumps are broken up. Add salt and flour and knead until all ingredients are well mixed. This dough is quite soft, somewhere between batter and bread dough. Cover with a wet towel and leave at room temperature 4-6 hours or overnight in a slightly cooler place. Knead dough and separate into loaves. Place in oiled bread pans, smooth top with wet hands or knife, and cut a slit ½″ deep lengthwise down middle of loaves. Let bread sit in a warm oven at low heat (150°) for 2 hours. Turn heat up to 350° and bake for 2 hours.

Variation: Substitute rice flour for millet. Or, omit millet and use 1 cup each buckwheat and rice flour, or 1 cup each rye and rice flour. If other cooked grains are added, use less rice and less water.

85. Ohsawa Bread

2 cups whole wheat flour
1 cup buckwheat flour
1½ tsp. cinnamon
1 tsp. salt
2 tsp. oil
1 cup water

Combine dry ingredients, mix oil and water, then knead together. Shape into loaves. Place in oiled pan and bake 1½ hours at 350°.

86. French Bread

4 cups unbleached white flour
3 cups whole wheat flour
½ tsp. dry yeast
2½ cups warm water
1 Tbsp. oil
1 Tbsp. salt
Cornmeal

Add yeast to warm (105°-115°) water. When completely dissolved, in about 5 minutes, add oil and salt. Add flour and make into a dough. Knead for 20 minutes. Dough should be earlobe-soft.

Cover with a wet cloth and let sit overnight until doubled in size. If you are in a hurry, keep dough on top of gas stove for 4-5 hours, or until doubled in size. Punch down, divide in half and shape into loaves 4 × 12 inches. Sprinkle a handful of cornmeal on a cookie sheet. Put loaves on cookie sheet and gently rub cornmeal over the loaves. Cover with a wet cloth and let rise about one hour or until doubled. With a sharp knife or razor, make 4 diagonal cuts ½″ deep in each loaf of bread. Bake at 450° for 30 minutes, or at 350° for 45 minutes.

87. Special French Bread

5 cups starch sediment
2 cups cooked gluten water
1 tsp. yeast
8 cups unbleached white flour
5 cups whole wheat flour
2 Tbsp. oil
2 Tbsp. salt
Cornmeal

This bread is made with the starch sediment left over from rinsing gluten, and the water left over from cooking the gluten. (Refer to #45.)

Bring gluten water to a boil. Mix with 3 cups of cold starch sediment. Add yeast to lukewarm mixture and let sit for 5 minutes until yeast dissolves. Add oil and salt. Add flour and make into dough. Mix in 2 more cups of starch water. Follow steps as for French bread (#86). This makes 4 loaves.

88. Gyoza

⅛ cup minced chicken or
   ⅓ cup minced seitan
¼ cup minced onion
¼ cup chopped scallion
½ cup minced Chinese cabbage
½ cup minced green cabbage
1 tsp. grated ginger juice
⅓ cup bread cubes or rolled oats
½ tsp. salt
1 Tbsp. soy sauce
1 tsp. oil

Dough

2 cups whole wheat pastry flour
1 cup unbleached white flour (or
   3 cups whole wheat flour)
¾ cup boiling water
1 tsp. oil

Lemon sauce

1 Tbsp. lemon juice
3 Tbsp. soy sauce

Squeeze excess water from vegetables by hand. Add ginger juice, soy sauce, and vegetables to chicken. Mix together. Add ⅓ cup bread cut into ⅓″ squares, or sauteed rolled oats. Mix together.

Add boiling water to flour and knead when comfortable to hands. Add oil after half kneading time. Cover with wet cloth for 30 minutes. Remove cloth, knead once more, roll into a 9″ long log with a 1½″ diameter, and cut into ½″-thick slices. Roll each piece into round shapes about 4″ in diameter. Add 1 tsp. of filling, leaving a ¾″ diameter on bottom. Flute dough on top into wonton or gyoza shape.

Heat fry pan, add 2 Tbsp. oil, heat oil, and reduce to medium heat. Place gyoza in pan and cover. Cook until browned, approximately 7 minutes. Remove cover, holding it in the left hand, and sprinkle ⅓ cup boiling water over gyozas and re-cover. Continue to cook until all water evaporates. Turn over, brown on other side, and serve.

Sprinkle lemon sauce on top of gyoza or serve with soy sauce alone or with a mixture of 1 Tbsp. soy sauce and 1 tsp. oil.

Gyoza may also be baked, steamed, deep-fried, or cooked in clear soup stock.

89. Vegetable Pancakes

3 cups whole wheat pastry flour
½ tsp. salt
3½ cups water
1½ cups scallions, ¼″ rounds
1 cup fresh mushrooms, sliced thin
½ cup bell peppers, sliced thin
Soy sauce and ginger juice
   for brushing
Oil for brushing

Mix the flour, salt, and water to a batter consistency, a little thicker than tempura batter. Spooning it from a height of about 5 inches it should run smoothly.

Combine the chopped vegetables with the batter, mix well. Brush heavy skillet with oil and pour in standard-sized pancakes – about 3″ in diameter. Cover and cook for 5-7 minutes – this will steam the vegetables. Turn when browned and cook uncovered on the other side awhile longer. Brush sauce on one side to serve. (Makes about 20 pancakes.)

Sauce variation: Mix ¼ tsp. mustard with 1 Tbsp. soy sauce and brush on pancakes. Avoid this sauce in case of hemorrhoids or yin sickness.

Desserts

90. Kanten Jello

2 bars kanten or 1 heaping
   Tbsp. kanten powder
2²/₃ cups water
4 cups fresh fruit
1 tsp. salt

Break kanten and rinse in cold water. Then soak in 2²/₃ cup water for 20 minutes. If using powder, rinsing and soaking is unnecessary. Cook regular kanten for 15 minutes before adding fruit and cook another 15 minutes with salt.

For powder, bring water and kanten to boil. Simmer a few minutes, skimming off any scum that comes to surface. Add fruit and cook as above.

Strawberries, cherries, melon, or any fruit in season may be used as well as dried apricots, apples, or raisins.

91. Whole Wheat Pudding

1 cup whole wheat flour
1 med. apple, chopped
3½ cups water
2 Tbsp. walnuts, chopped
2 Tbsp. raisins
1 tsp. salt
1 tsp. cinnamon

Heat a dry cast iron skillet. Pour in the flour and, using a wooden spoon, stir constantly until the flour is fragrant and nut brown in color. Put pan aside to cool. Then add chopped nuts, apple, raisins, water, and salt. Return to heat and cook uncovered over a low heat for about ½ hour, or until thick.

Cover skillet and simmer slowly for another ½ hour, stirring occasionally to prevent burning. During the last minutes of cooking time add cinnamon.

Serve hot, or pour mixture into a dessert mold or casserole that has been rinsed in cold water. Refrigerate for at least one hour. Unmold and serve.

92. Raisin Pie

Crust
½ cup pastry flour
2 Tbsp. oil
2 Tbsp. cold water
Pinch of salt

Filling
1 heaping Tbsp. kuzu
2 eggs
¼ tsp. vanilla
¼ cup oil
½ tsp. salt
1 cup raisins
1 cup chopped roasted walnuts

For crust, mix salt, flour, and oil lightly with a fork. Sprinkle in water and mix lightly again. Press dough into a 9″ pie pan.

For filling, dilute kuzu (arrowroot may be substituted) in ¼ cup cold water and mix well. Add oil, salt, vanilla, and eggs and beat 1 minute with a hand or electric mixer or a wire whisk. Add ¼-⅛ tsp. salt. Pour mixture over raisins and nuts in unbaked pie shell.

Bake in a 350° oven for 30 minutes, or until a knife inserted in center comes out clean.

93. Apple Chestnut Twist

1 cup dried chestnuts
1 cups water
4 cups sliced apples
¾ tsp. salt
1 Tbsp. grain coffee

Dough
5 cups flour
5 Tbsp. oil
1 tsp. salt
2 cups water

Pressure-cook chestnuts in water for 45 minutes. Remove cover, add salt, and cook until remaining liquid is reduced. Mash chestnuts and mix in apples and yannoh (grain coffee).

Mix flour, salt, and oil together. Add water and mix again to form dough. Separate dough into 2 balls. Roll out dough into rectangles. Spread half of filling over each rectangle and sprinkle dough with a little water, then form into jelly rolls so dough will stick.

Place the 2 rolls in a 'V' shape, attach and braid. Brush with a beaten egg yolk for a golden color, or a little oil for extra crispness. Bake in a 350 degree oven for 45 minutes.

Beverages

94. Bancha (Twig) Tea

¼ cup bancha tea
4-5 cups boiling water

Bancha is a three-year-old green tea that contains the leaves and small twigs of the tea bush. It helps to remove toxins from the body in the case of people who have taken drugs. Also, it helps to make vitamin C in the body. It is perfectly safe for children and contains almost no caffeine.

To prepare, dry roast the leaves in a pan over a medium high flame for a few minutes. Stir constantly to prevent burning. Then pick out the twigs and pour the leaves into a clean glass jar. Dry roast the twigs a second time, until they turn brown. Add to leaves in jar.

Add ¼ cup tea to 4-5 cups boiling water. Shut off flame and let steep a few minutes before serving. When the liquid has all been served, add more water and boil for ten minutes. Add a teaspoon of fresh tea and let steep. This process can be repeated until the leaves form a layer 1″ deep in the bottom of the pot.

Note: When making all teas, glass or porcelain pots should be used for best results. Old leaves can be used for compost, or saved for making koi koku (carp soup).

95. Mu Tea

1 package mu tea
4 cups water

Mu tea is a sixteen-herb tea which is very yang. When served as a beverage after dinner, it should be made fairly weak because strong mu tea can induce vomiting when served after dinner. Drink strong mu tea at least 30 minutes before dinner.

Preparation: Bring 4 cups of cold water to a boil with one package of mu tea. Simmer 10-15 minutes. Grounds can be used a second time.

Medicinal preparation: Bring 2 cups of cold water and one package mu tea to a boil and cook ten minutes. Add 2 cups of water and boil until liquid is reduced to 1 cup. To make another pot the next day, leave old grounds in pot, add a new package and more water, and prepare as above.

96. Ohsawa Coffee (Yannoh)

1 heaping tsp. grain coffee
2 cups boiling water
Few grains of salt
1 level tsp. kuzu (optional)

Simmer coffee 20 minutes with a few grains of salt. Add 1 level tsp. kuzu near the end of cooking if a thick beverage is desired. This preparation makes an excellent breakfast drink. If you don't have much appetite in the morning, this beverage will give you a lot of energy. More kuzu can be added if desired.

97. Pearled Barley Tea (Hatocha)

1 heaping Tbsp. hatocha
5 cups boiling water

This beverage is prepared in Japan. It makes a rich, stimulating drink that is very good for removing excess animal protein from the body. It also helps to clean the blood, and is good for internal female ailments.

Pre-roasted barley (hatocha) is available in Japanese stores, or you can roast pearled barley in a dry pan until dark brown.

Preparation: Add 1 heaping Tbsp. hatocha to 5 cups boiling water. Simmer 5 minutes. For a second pot, add more water and a generous pinch of tea. Simmer again for 5 minutes.

98. Dandelion Coffee (Tan Po Po)

1 level Tbsp. dried dandelion root
2 cups water
Pinch of salt

Dig dandelion roots in early spring because then the roots are biggest. Later on, all the energy goes up into the leaves and the root shrinks and turns very bitter. After washing with scrub brush, cut thin and dry in a shady place. When completely dry, keep in a glass jar or covered container. To make coffee, roast dried dandelion until dark brown, not burned, and add 1 level tablespoon to 2 cups of water. Bring to a boil for 20 minutes, and serve with a pinch of salt.

Summer

#149 – Fresh Corn Potage. #110 – Fresh Corn Tortillas. a. Crispy scallions and oily miso sauce.
#302 – Chili Beans (and Cornmeal Pan Bread, #332). #223 – Kanten.

Grains

99. Double Pot Pressure Cooked Rice
100. Azuki Bean Rice
101. Bulghur
102. Barley Kayu
103. Cornmeal Cereal
104. Grain Milk Cereal
105. Ohagi

Grains with Vegetables

106. Norimaki Sushi
107. Rice Salad
108. Rice Salad (Cooked Vegetables)
109. Cracked Wheat with Onions
110. Fresh Corn Tortillas
111. Tostadas
112. Torta Rustica
113. Mock Mashed Potatoes with Gravy
114. Green Corn Tamale Casserole

Noodles

115. Spaghetti with Tomato Sauce
116. Roman Style Noodles
117. Homemade Noodles with Soup
118. Macaroni Salad
119. Udon Salad
120. Five Color Somen

Vegetables

121. Broccoli Nitsuke
122. Summer Squash Nitsuke
123. Tofu Stuffed Cabbage
124. Vegetable Kabobs
125. Chinese Vegetables Supreme
126. Grated Zucchini Nitsuke
127. Baked Zucchini
128. Zucchini Spread
129. Stuffed Cucumbers
130. Vegetables with Miso Sauce
131. Pan Fried Eggplant
132. Fried Eggplant with Miso
133. Green Pepper with Miso
134. Vegetable Curry with Fish

Wild Vegetables

135. Purslane
136. Goosefoot
137. Wood Sorrel
138. Beefsteak Leaves
139. Wild Ginger

Seaweeds

140. Toasted Nori
141. Nori with Soy Sauce *(Nori Nitsuke)*
142. Kombu Maki (Kombu Roll)
143. Kombu in Soy Sauce *(Shio Kombu)*
144. Wakame Salad
145. Wakame Cucumber Sesame Salad
146. Hijiki Tofu Salad

Soups

147. Cold Miso Soup
148. Split Pea Miso Soup
149. Fresh Corn Potage
150. Wakame Miso Soup
151. Wakame Onion Soup

Beans

152. Black Beans Mexicana
153. Soybean Surprise
154. Chick Pea Pie
155. Chick Peas with Soba
156. Chick Peas with Vegetables
157. Chick Pea Party Dip
158. Cooked Salad with Bean Dressing
159. Bean Salad
160. Lentil Salad Sandwich

Tofu

161. Cold Tofu *(Hiya Yako)*
162. Kanten Tofu (Tofu Aspic)
163. Tofu Kuzu Vegetables
164. Tofu Vegetable Saute
165. Fried Tofu with Nori
166. Tofu Salad Sandwich

Fried Foods

167. Rice Croquettes
168. Bulghur Croquettes
169. Fried Eggplant with Sesame Sauce
170. Breaded Eggplant
171. Corncob Tempura
172. Mock Egg Roll
173. Deep Fried Miso Balls

Salads

174. Bean Thread Salad
175. Vegetable Salad (Cooked)
176. Party Ohitashi
177. Konnyaku Carrot Shiro Ai
178. Vegetable Fruit Salad
179. String Bean Goma Ai
180. String Bean Aemono

Sauces and Dressings

181. Salad Dressing
182. Italian Style Salad Dressing
183. Quick Mayonnaise
184. Eggless Mayonnaise
185. Lyonnaise Sauce
186. Green Sauce
187. Bechamel Sauce
188. Gravy
189. Mushroom Gravy for Pasta
190. Tomato Sauce
191. Onion Sauce
192. Tahini Soy Sauce with Onion
193. Vegetable Curry Sauce
194. Scallop Cucumber Sauce

Pickles

195. Rolled Cabbage Pickles
196. Cabbage Oil Pickles
197. Cabbage Cucumber Pickles
198. Bright Green Cucumber Pickles
199. Instant Cucumber Pickles
200. Spicy Cucumber Pickles
201. Dill Pickles
202. Russian Cucumber Pickles
203. Rice Bran Pickles (Nuka Pickles)

Condiments

204. Gomashio
205. Sarashinegi (Washed Scallion)
206. Daikon Leaf Furikake
207. Wakame Furikake
208. Shiso Furikake
209. Sesame Shiso
210. Scallion Shiso Ai
211. Cucumber Onion Shiso Ai
212. Burdock Condiment
213. Umeboshi Tempura
214. Umeboshi Soy Sauce

Breads

215. Unyeasted Bread
216. Sourdough Starter
217. Sourdough Bread
218. Corn Bread
219. Light Party Rolls
220. Cream Puffs
221. Rice Muffins

Desserts

222. Kanten Noodles *(Tokoroten)*
223. Canteloupe Strawberry Kanten
224. Dessert Kanten or Cake Frosting
225. Party Cake
226. Rice Cream Pie
227. Lemon Meringue Pie
228. Yam Karinto
229. Sweet Potato Senbei
230. The Best Simple Donuts
231. Fig Newtons
232. Apple Oatmeal Cookies
233. Granola Cookies
234. Fresh Fruit Sherbet
235. Lemon Sherbet

Beverages

236. Umeboshi Beverage
237. Umesho Bancha
238. Barley Tea *(Mugicha)*

Summer Cooking

In this country, the same vegetables are available all year around because of modern transportation and hothouse cultivation. Cucumber, eggplant, corn, and stringbeans are summer vegetables, so they taste really good during this season. They are also inexpensive at this time because they are so plentiful. All summer cooking should be lighter than during other seasons. The taste should be less salty. Saute less often. Too much heavy cooking makes us lose our appetite. So you must cook cooler, more brightly colored vegetables to make them more appealing to the eye. For example, after a very hot day, a dinnertime menu might be cold noodles placed in a big glass salad bowl with cold water covering the noodles, and several ice cubes floating among thinly-sliced green cucumbers with red radishes cut in flower shapes, served with cold sauce in small bowls. A condiment of green scallion or green shiso really refreshes your eyes and appetite. You can also serve this on green vegetable leaves such as lettuce, romaine, cabbage, etc. Macaroni salad or rice salad can also be served on fresh green leaves. Cookies or other desserts can also be served on green leaves or bamboo leaves to give a cooler feeling. Kanten jello served in glass bowls looks delicious.

We present to you many summer recipes, but urge everyone to please study and try to bring to your table new and attractive recipes which will create a cool atmosphere for summer. Food is not tasted by tongue alone, but by the eyes too. Balanced and harmonious cooking should be beautifully displayed.

In Japan in the country, cucumbers are plentiful, so all children keep cucumbers cool in well water. Then they put miso or salt in one hand and take a cucumber and dip it in the salt or miso. This makes a good snack – better than fruit, and it cools the body. At your table you can serve fresh raw cucumber cut in ½″-thick slices with miso served in side dishes, or serve fresh slices lightly sprinkled with salt before dinner as an appetizer. The taste of fresh cucumbers is most delicious in hot summer.

In summer we usually like a plain or light taste in most cooking, such as noodles, salads, or pickles. However, in summer we also sweat, which takes oil and salt out of the body. So sometimes we should replace it with fried foods. A Japanese custom in the hottest period of summer, around August, is to take eel kabayaki (like shish-kebab – sliced and baked with soy sauce). Eel is very oily. Japanese eat very simple, light food all summer. This makes them feel weak sometimes in the heat, so they recommend eel. Also eels are yin, unlike most ocean fish, and have a very strong life power.

In summertime, hot drinks are better than cold drinks, even though it may be very hot outside. So serve hot amasake or light kuzu-yu sometimes, to make sudden sweat come out. After you sweat, you will feel very comfortable. To 1½ Tbsp. of kuzu add 1 cup of cold water and mix together. Add 1 tsp. raisin, yinnie, or malt syrup. Bring to a boil and cook for 5 minutes, then serve immediately. I still remember how good this tasted in my childhood. During summer we eat much cold food. The heat causes less appetite, so the stomach and intestines become weak; this kuzu drink helps make your stomach strong. The Japanese say kuzu makes all digestive organs strong.

In the hot Japanese summer all the farmers go to the rice fields at four or five o'clock, bend down, and pull wild grass and weeds by hand from among the rice plants. The rice plants have pointed leaves which prick your skin or scratch your eyes, so it is very hard work. Sweat comes out like running water. After lunch they nap for a couple of hours, then return to weeding again. So a Japanese song says we must give thanks to the hot sun which makes us sweat because it also makes the rice plants multiply two or three times in number. Rice would not grow in abundance without a hot summer. Please train your body not to be defeated by the heat. If you take too little salt and your condition is yin, it is very hard to pass through the hot season.

If you take too much animal food in fall and winter and become too yang, you can have a very uncomfortable summer. Vegetables (yin) and salt (yang) balance each other. Such balanced cooking allows you to enjoy the hot summer easily everywhere – at the ocean, in the mountains, near the rivers, camping, hiking, or on picnics – if your condition is 'salt-yang' instead of 'animal food-yang.' If your body is very uncomfortable in hot sunshine, you must discover whether your condition is too yin or too yang. So you balance yourself by changing your cooking. Also we must be careful of the quality of seasonings we use. Miso, soy sauce, salt, sesame oil, and other oils should be naturally produced. We don't need any MSG or other commercial seasonings for tasteful cooking.

All vegetables taste different. This difference we realize by our cooking. This is macrobiotic cooking. So don't take off skins, don't soak fresh vegetables in water, and save water from boiling.

All vegetables contain yin and yang qualities. Cooking creates a harmonious blend of yin and yang, and also gives vegetables a more delicious taste. Whole vegetables have a life power, so we should not waste any part. That life power gives us blood and body cells and thinking ability. Therefore, we should give thanks to nature.

Please make your cooking fit the season. As the summer gets hotter and hotter, you need more yin food. During summer, yin food tastes especially good. But be very careful and be moderate. When you take yin food in the summer it doesn't affect you. But three months later the colder season comes, and most people catch cold very easily. If you drink less, you will very quickly become yang in the summer. So we can be thankful for summer.

Also, everyone has less appetite. This is normal because we take energy from the sun. Early mornings are usually cool, so if you work outside in the mornings you will build a good appetite. This will make you feel energy throughout the day. Walking with bare feet during summertime improves blood circulation. It also helps the body make vitamin B. Women's diseases and men's sexual troubles are also cured very

easily by walking barefoot on green grass during the summer in the early morning, when the grass is wet. At first, walk for 5-10 minutes because the feet are tender. Then after one month, walk for 20 minutes. At first the feet are tender and may hurt, but they later become strong.

During the hot season, food spoils very quickly. If you cook in the morning and have leftovers, wait until they cool, then keep them in the refrigerator. When you serve food later, you must heat it up first before serving, because the refrigerator makes food very yin. You must make it more yang by heating it – steaming, baking, or warming it in the oven. It is all right, however, to serve salads and pickles straight from the refrigerator.

A friend of mine working in Belgium, a macrobiotic nurse who has experience curing sick people, said to me, "Cornellia, if you give refrigerated food to sick people, you will never cure them." So she never uses a refrigerator. Therefore, if you take care of sick people, use the refrigerator only when necessary. When you have leftover food, heat it up again in the evening. (A good technique to keep food fresh.) Keep it in a cool place and cover it with a strainer, bamboo mat, or sushi roller. This helps keep it from spoiling because the air circulation is good. Tightly covered food spoils quickly. Brown rice spoils more quickly than white rice because it contains more vitamins. So if there is a lot of leftover brown rice and it has begun to spoil, make flattened rice balls and toast them on the stove with a Japanese metal toaster. Make both sides slightly brown in color. Then brush both sides with miso or soy sauce and toast again. You will really be surprised how good they taste, with their delicious crunchiness. They stimulate your appetite. Even when cold they taste good. If you don't have a metal toaster, use an oven rack on top of the stove. To keep them from sticking, first heat up the rack, and then toast the cold rice balls.

If you have a lot of leftover rice such as after a party, please don't throw it away. Wash it in water, then dry it on a cutting board. This rice can then be roasted in a dry pan (good for croutons) or deep-fried and stored in a glass jar. If you have children, mix a little yinnie syrup or amasake with it; this is a really sweet treat.

Please enjoy the hot season. It will make you more yang. I hope you all have a nice summer, cooking meals and enjoying your family and your table.

Grains

99. Double Pot Pressure Cooked Rice

2 cups brown rice
3 cups water
½ tsp. salt

After washing rice, soak in 3 cups of water for 1 hour in a 6″-diameter stainless steel mixing bowl or any kind of pan that will fit in a 4-quart pressure cooker. Add the salt, then put 2 cups of water into a 4-quart pressure cooker. Place the mixing bowl in the pressure cooker. Lock the cover on, and bring to a boil over high flame. After 3 minutes, when pressure comes up to full, continue cooking over high flame for 15 minutes. Then cook 20 minutes more over a medium flame. Shut off flame and let sit for 20 minutes and take off the cover and serve. This rice is not so sticky – good for summer.

100. Azuki Bean Rice

1⅔ cups brown rice
⅓ cup azuki beans
¼-½ tsp. salt
3 cups water

Wash azuki beans and rice until water drains clear. Soak for 2 hours in 3 cups water before cooking, then cook as in recipe #99. Many people say that 2 cups of regular rice does not cook well in a 4-quart pressure cooker, but this combination comes out really well. This is a good way to cook a small amount of rice.

101. Bulghur

3 cups bulghur
6 cups cold water
½ tsp. salt

Wash the bulghur and let drain until dry. Roast it in a dry pan until fragrant. Add water and bring to boil. Add salt and cook on a low flame for 1 hour. Note: If you use boiling water, you only need to cook the bulghur 20 minutes.

Kuzu or curry sauces combine well with this grain. (See #193.) Bulghur is a light grain, it digests fast and is good for summer meals.

102. Barley Kayu

1 cup pressed barley
1 onion, minced
5 cups water
1 tsp. salt

Wash the pressed barley, put in a saucepan, add water and bring to a boil. Turn flame down and simmer for 4 hours or overnight. Saute onion in 1 tsp. oil and add to barley kayu. Add salt and cook for 30 minutes more. When you make barley or rice kayu, don't stir while it is cooking. After you have shut off the flame, then you can stir it.

103. Cornmeal Cereal

1 cup cornmeal
¼ tsp. salt
3-4 cups boiling water
⅛ tsp. oil

Saute cornmeal in oil. Add salt and boiling water. Cook 30-35 minutes or until well done. Add soy sauce to taste.

104. Grain Milk Cereal

1 cup grain milk powder (kokkoh, available in stores selling macrobiotic products)
5 cups water
¼ tsp. salt
½ tsp. oil

Saute grain milk powder in oil until there is a nutlike fragrance. Cool. Add water gradually to prevent lumping. Bring to a boil on medium flame, stirring continuously from side to side to keep from sticking. (Don't use the highest flame until you get the knack of cooking cereal.) Add salt. Lower the flame and simmer until thickened. Cook about 30-45 minutes. Serve with sesame salt and/or soy sauce.

105. Ohagi

3 cups sweet brown rice, cooked in 3 cups water
1 cup azuki beans
5 Tbsp. yinnie syrup
½ tsp. salt
½ cup sesame seeds
1 Tbsp. soy sauce
3 sheets of nori

Wash azuki beans, place in a pan with 1½ cups water to soak overnight. Bring the beans to a boil in the pot, then add ½ cup of water. Bring to another boil. Add another ½ cup of water, bring to boil (three times in all). Then cook for 1 hour in a covered pot. (Azuki beans are yang, so it is better to cook them in a pot than in a pressure cooker. Cooked in a pressure cooker, they become bitter.) After 1 hour add the yinnie syrup to the azuki beans, uncover and cook for 20 minutes, add ½ tsp. salt and cook for 5-10 minutes more. If you don't want a sweet taste, add salt only. Wash the sesame seeds and strain them. Put a sponge under the strainer to absorb the excess water. Roast the sesame seeds in a dry pan until they are golden brown. Put them in a suribachi, add soy sauce and grind until about half the seeds are ground. Put 2 sheets of nori together and roast on both sides over the flame on the kitchen stove and crush the sheets in your hands.

Soak the sweet brown rice in the water overnight. Cook the rice using a flame a little higher than medium; it takes about 30 minutes to come up to pressure. The top on the pressure cooker will not jiggle a lot. Cook for 20 minutes on a low flame. Let the pressure come down, take off the cover and pound with a wooden pestle until half of the grains have been mashed. Wet your hands and form 2″ long rectangles from the rice. These are then covered with the sesame seeds, nori, or azuki beans, so that you will have red, brown, and black ohagi. For the azuki bean covering, the ohagi should be a little smaller, since this is a thicker covering.

Grains with Vegetables

106. Norimaki Sushi

5 cups brown rice, cooked in
    6½ cups water
2 carrots, cut in half
1 head romaine lettuce, quartered
1 onion, crescents
3 umeboshi, pitted and minced
½ tsp. grated fresh ginger
Oil for brushing
1 package nori
½ lemon
1 tsp. soy sauce
1½ tsp. salt

Cook rice as in #1. Let cool.

Bring 1½ cups water to a boil, add ½ tsp. salt and the carrots. Cook covered 20 minutes until soft but not completely. Let cool, then cut lengthwise into ⅓″ squared strips.

Bring 5 cups water to a boil with 1 tsp. salt, add washed lettuce standing up, bring to a boil uncovered. Immerse leaves and bring to boil again, then remove and strain. Let cool. Squeeze out excess liquid and sprinkle with ½ tsp. soy sauce.

Brush a pan with oil and saute onion, covered, until transparent. Add umeboshi and mix, adding ½ tsp. soy sauce. Cook 10 minutes – until onion is slightly soft. Add grated ginger and mix. Put into bowl and cool.

On a clean bamboo sushi mat lay 1 sheet of nori. Wet hands with lemon and spread rice over nori to within 1″ of the edge. Two inches from the bottom edge place a layer of carrot strips, then small pieces of onion on top of carrot (not too much), then a layer of romaine lettuce. Then roll up the sushi with the bamboo mat like a cigarette, pressing firmly all the time to keep a uniform shape. Wet knife with lemon and cut a ¼″ slice off each end. Then slice roll into 8 pieces, wetting knife with lemon each time to prevent sticking. Repeat for remaining ingredients.

This recipe, using umeboshi, can keep for one day – or two days if refrigerated. Good for summer picnic or travelling.

107. Rice Salad

4 cups cooked rice
2 small carrots, uncooked
1 small cucumber, uncooked
½ bunch radishes, uncooked
⅓ green pepper, uncooked
1-2 med. beets, precooked, diced,
    and chilled
4 scallions, uncooked

Dressing
Diced raw onion
Umeboshi juice or meat
Dash of oil
Dash of soy sauce
Lemon juice (optional)
Tahini (optional)

Dice and cut all vegetables being added to salad. Blend into chilled, cooked rice by hand. If rice is glutinous, break by hand and/or rinse in cold water to make rice more separate.

Heat oil and cool. Place diced onion and umeboshi meat in suribachi and grind together, add oil and soy sauce gradually to taste. Pour on top of salad and mix by hand. Place salad in refrigerator for several hours before serving. Chill thoroughly and serve immediately. This makes a delightful salad, nice for picnics. Be sure to keep it chilled until just before serving as it does turn quickly when it warms up to room temperature.

Stir thoroughly just before serving, as dressing goes to the bottom while it is chilling and more salt may be needed after chilling to bring out flavors.

108. Rice Salad (Cooked Vegetables)

1 cup cooked brown rice
½ small cauliflower cut
    into small flowerettes
10 string beans, ½″ diagonals
¼ cup carrot, ¼″ diced
½ cup onion, minced
1 cucumber, ¼″ diced
5 red radishes, cut into flower shapes
    and kept in cold water
1-3 Tbsp. sesame oil, to taste
1½ tsp. salt
Juice of ½ lemon

Bring 1 quart of water to a boil with 1 heaping tsp. salt. Cook the cauliflower, string beans, then carrots in this water separately until they are soft. Heat the oil, then let it cool. Add the onion and let it sit 5 minutes, then add the lemon juice. Take ¼ cup of the water left from cooking the vegetables and pour it over the rice to separate it into individual grains. Mix in the onion/oil mixture, slowly mix in the carrot, string beans, cucumber, and cauliflower. Place radishes for decoration. Minced parsley can also be used for a garnish. If you wish, you can increase the quantity of rice in this recipe, since there are so many vegetables.

109. Cracked Wheat with Onions

2 cups cracked wheat
2 onions, chopped
1 tsp. oil
½ tsp. salt
6 cups boiling water

Brown wheat in dry frying pan until slightly colored and fragrant. Saute onions in a separate pan. When onions are done, add them to the wheat with salt and boiling water. Cover and let simmer for 1 hour, stirring occasionally. Add more water if necessary. (A pinch of thyme, basil, or garlic can be added to enhance flavor.)

110. Fresh Corn Tortillas

3 ears corn
2 cups whole wheat flour
½ tsp. salt
15 scallions (white part only)
⅓ cup mugi miso
2-3 Tbsp. water
4 Tbsp. sesame oil

Take off corn husks, then scrape off kernels with a knife. Rub off the remaining parts of the kernels with the back of the knife. Grind kernels in a suribachi or blender. Add flour and ½ tsp. salt, mix, and knead into a stiff dough of earlobe consistency. Roll into ¼″ thick 4″-diameter tortillas. Heat up frying pan, add sesame oil, and fry tortillas over a medium flame until both sides are golden brown. Keep warm in the oven in a covered dish. Cut white scallions 2″ long matchstick style, and soak in cold water until scallions get crispy and cold. Then drain off the water. Heat up a pan, add 4 Tbsp. oil and miso, and saute until a fragrant smell is given off. Dilute with 2-3 Tbsp. water to soften. Around the edge of a big plate arrange the tortillas and put scallions in the center. Serve miso to each person in small bowls. Each person should put one tortilla on his plate, add scallions and miso, and roll up. Eat them either with your fingers or chopsticks. These are really good as a summer food. You can substitute them for rice at dinner, or use them as an afternoon snack.

111. Tostadas

2 cups cooked brown rice
2 cups cooked pinto beans
(or other beans)
3 Tbsp. tahini
4-6 Tbsp. soy sauce
Corn tortillas
1 head lettuce
2 tomatoes
1 bunch scallions

Cook the rice and beans as usual – the beans should be creamy, not dry. Make a tahini soy sauce by adding water to tahini until it is the consistency of cream. Add soy sauce to taste. Bring almost to a boil, stirring constantly. It will thicken. Deep fry or pan fry the tortillas until crisp. (You can make your own by mixing 3 parts corn flour with 1 part whole wheat pastry flour. Add salt and enough water until doughy. Roll out and cut into circles 6″ in diameter, then pan fry.) To assemble, lay a tortilla on the plate and cover with rice, then a layer of beans. Sprinkle with shredded lettuce and pour a tahini or goma sauce over it. Sprinkle with chopped scallions and garnish with ½ cherry tomato or a small wedge of regular tomato. It is best if the tortilla, rice, beans, and sauce are piping hot and the lettuce and scallions are crispy cold. Serve immediately.

112. Torta Rustica

Step #1:
1½ cup lukewarm water
1 tsp. yeast
1 Tbsp. honey, yinnie syrup, or
barley malt
2 cups whole wheat flour
1 egg

Step #2:
1 tsp. salt
3 Tbsp. oil
2 cups unbleached white flour
Additional flour for kneading dough
(¼ to ½ cup)

Filling
3 small tomatoes
1 onion, minced
2 cups cabbage, chopped
½ cup grated cheese or ½ lb. tofu,
press out water and crumble
1 sheet nori, toasted and cut
in 1″ squares

To make bread: mix #1 as a sponge, beat 100 times. Cover and let rise 30 minutes. Add #2, mix, knead, and let rise 60 minutes. Punch down and let rise another 20 minutes.

To make filling: slice the tomatoes thin and simmer in ½ cup water for 40 minutes with a lid. Puree; this will make almost 1 cup of tomatoes. Saute onion and cabbage and add salt with a little water for 20 minutes.

After the last rising of the dough, take about ⅓ of the dough and roll it out in a ⅜″ thick round and put it in a 10″ pie pan like a crust. Arrange the filling in layers: on the bottom the cabbage and onion, then the tomato puree, nori, cheese or tofu. Roll out another round of dough, about ⅓ again, roll to a ⅜″ thickness, cut in 1″ strips, make a lattice-work top, tucking the extra edges under. (Make rolls with the leftover dough.) Brush with egg wash (one egg beaten in 1 Tbsp. water), let rise for 15 minutes covered, and bake in a 350° oven for 30-40 minutes. Serve warm, cut in wedges.

113. Mock Mashed Potatoes with Gravy

3 cups uncooked millet
1 head cauliflower
6 cups boiling water or soup stock
½ cup fresh peas
1 tsp. salt

Pressure cook millet and cauliflower together with 6 cups boiling water or soup stock and 1 tsp. salt for 45 minutes. Put through a Foley food mill, add fresh peas and bake for 30 minutes in preheated 350° oven.

Gravy

½ cup sweet brown rice flour
1½ cup whole wheat pastry flour
2 Tbsp. oil
3 tsp. salt
1 Tbsp. soy sauce

Brown flours in oil, add water or soup stock until desired consistency is obtained, stirring continuously over medium-high heat. Season with remaining salt and soy sauce (or moromi). Pour gravy on top of a scoop of millet 'mashed potatoes' and serve immediately.

114. Green Corn Tamale Casserole

8 or 9 ears of corn
2 tsp. salt
3 Tbsp. corn oil
1-1½ cups cornmeal
Sharp cheddar cheese or
    tofu or tahini
1 green pepper (this is usually
    enough for flavor)

Shuck corn, reserving husks, and cut kernels from cobs. Grind corn or blend in blender until enough mush to make 3 cups. Add salt, corn oil, and enough cornmeal to make a thick spreading consistency. Cut cheese into thin strips. Remove seeds and cut green pepper into thin strips. Rinse and drain corn husks, then spread flat. Line bottom and sides of greased casserole with husks. Place thin layer of corn mush into dish, pressing down to hold husks in place. Next put in a layer of cheese (or tofu) and green pepper strips. Repeat these two layers and finish off with remaining mush, spreading to edges of casserole. Fold corn husk ends over top of 2 tamales. Cover with foil and bake at 350° for 1 hour. Serve hot.

Noodles

115. Spaghetti with Tomato Sauce

1½ lbs. whole wheat spaghetti
4 Tbsp. sesame oil
2 tsp. salt
Grated cheese (optional)

Tomato sauce
½ lb. tomatoes
⅓ cup seitan or ½ lb.
    minced chicken
2 Tbsp. sesame oil
1 onion, thin crescents
½ lb. fresh mushrooms, thin sliced
2 inches of carrot, minced
1 stalk celery, cut in half
3 Tbsp. applesauce
1 tsp. salt
1 Tbsp. parsley
Pinch of white or black pepper
2 Tbsp. arrowroot

Dip tomatoes in boiling water, then remove their skins. Cover seitan with 2 Tbsp. arrowroot flour, let sit for 5 minutes – the seitan will absorb the flour. Heat 1 Tbsp. oil in a stewing pot, fry the seitan or chicken in this oil so it is browned on both sides, and take it out of the pan. Add another tablespoon oil, then saute the onion, mushroom, and carrot. Add one vegetable at a time. Add tomatoes which have been cut into ½″ squares. After the tomatoes become softened, add 3½ cups water, celery, 1 tsp. salt, parsley, and seitan. Bring to a boil, turn flame down and cook for 1 hour without a cover. The sauce will thicken and the color will darken. Remove the celery, then add the applesauce and a pinch of pepper.

Cook the spaghetti in 10 cups of water with 1 heaping Tbsp. of salt. Bring to a boil, add cold water and bring to another boil. Shut off the flame and let the noodles sit for a few minutes. Taste a noodle to see if it is thoroughly cooked. Strain off the water, wash in cold water and strain again. Heat 4 Tbsp. oil and add the cooked spaghetti. Turn over just a few times so that the noodles don't break. Sprinkle 2 tsp. salt over the noodles. To serve, put ⅓ of the tomato sauce in a warmed-up serving dish, place the noodles on top of this, and pour the rest of the tomato sauce over the noodles. Garnish with grated cheese if desired. The longer the tomato sauce cooks the better the taste, so simmer it as long as possible.

116. Roman Style Noodles

1½ lbs. whole wheat spaghetti
2 small cloves garlic, minced finely
⅓ cup seitan
2 Tbsp. arrowroot
½ cup olive oil

Cook the spaghetti as in recipe #115. Cover the seitan with 2 Tbsp. arrowroot flour, let sit for 5 minutes. Heat 2 Tbsp. oil, add seitan and fry on both sides. Remove from pan. Add remaining olive oil, heat, put garlic in pan and saute. Later add cooked noodles and seitan. Serve by placing in a heated serving dish.

117. Homemade Noodles with Soup

5 cups whole wheat flour
1 tsp. salt
1⅓ cups water
½ cup sesame seeds or
    2 Tbsp. sesame butter
Soy sauce to taste

Sift whole wheat flour with a fine strainer. (Keep bran and use in bread.) Mix flour, salt, and water, and knead very thoroughly for 20 minutes. Roll ⅛″ thin, then slice ⅓″ wide. Bring 8 cups of water to a boil. Add noodles, bring to a boil, add 1 cup of cold water and bring to a boil once again. Repeat two more times, then shut off flame. Allow to sit for 2 minutes, then strain, washing with cold water until noodles are completely cold. Wash sesame seeds and roast them, as in recipe #204. Then grind firmly in a suribachi until oil comes out. Add soy sauce to taste and some of the vegetable soup stock to make a sauce.

Soup

1 carrot, thin matchsticks
1 onion, minced
2 cabbage leaves, matchsticks
3 cups water
2 Tbsp. soy sauce

Cook vegetables in 3 cups of water for 30 minutes. Then strain. This is vegetable soup stock. Puree vegetables, add 2 Tbsp. soy sauce, mix together, and add to soup stock until thick and creamy. Serve noodles in a big bowl. Give each person a small bowl of sesame sauce. For condiments serve grated daikon, sarashinegi scallions (#205), and roasted nori in three separate bowls, each bowl containing the different condiments. If you have fresh shiso leaves available, slice very thin after washing and use as a condiment on noodles. They taste very good, they stimulate the appetite, and look really summer-like. Cold noodles keep you cool in summer. If you don't have the time to make your own noodles, you can use commercial whole wheat spaghetti.

118. Macaroni Salad

1 lb. macaroni, white or
    whole wheat
1 bunch scallions
Several pieces celery
Several sprigs parsley
Several cucumber pickles (#198, #199)
1 cup mayonnaise (see #183 or #75)
Salt and soy sauce
Oil

Boil macaroni in salted water, drain and let cool. Saute chopped scallions in a little oil. When cool, mix with chopped parsley, celery, and pickles. Add mayonnaise and stir the dressing into the macaroni, adding salt and soy sauce. Refrigerate.

119. Udon Salad

1 lb. whole wheat udon noodles
    or spaghetti
2 onions, diced
1 carrot, matchsticks
1 small cabbage, matchsticks
2 Tbsp. oil
Sesame shiso

Break noodles into 3 pieces, bring to boil in salted water and simmer until tender. Wash in cold water and strain. Saute onions, carrot, and cabbage over high flame for a few minutes until the vegetables change color slightly. Cool. Add sesame shiso (#209) and mix with cooked noodles. If you need a more salty taste, add umeboshi shoyu sauce (use #214).

120. Five Color Somen

1½ boxes of somen (about 1½ lbs.)
2 med. sized carrots (about ¼ lb.),
  matchsticks
2 handfuls of green beans
1 handful (¼ cup) wakame dried
  seaweed (about 1 oz.)
3 squares of age (deep fried tofu)
2 Tbsp. soy sauce
½ tsp. salt

Sauce
1½ cup soup stock (#39)
5 Tbsp. soy sauce

Take strings off beans and wash, then cook in salted water (1 quart water, 1 heaping tsp. salt). Bring water to a boil with cover. After boiling take off cover, add string beans, and bring to a boil on high heat. Cook for 5 minutes, then remove beans to a strainer and cool. Then cut them in very thin matchsticks. Slice age the same way. Bring ½ cup of water to a boil, add age, and cover. Bring to a boil again and cook for a few minutes. Add 1 Tbsp. soy sauce. Cook 15-20 minutes with cover. Then take off cover and cook until all the juice is gone. Saute carrots for a few minutes, cover and let them steam-cook for a few more minutes, adding no water. Add ½ tsp. salt, sprinkling it on top of the carrots. Then sprinkle 2 tsp. soy sauce around, mix, cover, and cook for 5 minutes. Take off cover after carrots are tender. Sprinkle with 1 tsp. soy sauce. Shut off heat and shake the pan until soy sauce flavor covers all the carrots. Soak wakame in 2 cups of water for 20 minutes. Save soaking water because it contains many minerals. Wash wakame carefully to take off sand. Cut matchstick style, 1″ long and as thin as possible. Bring ½ cup of soaking water to a boil, and put in wakame. Cover and cook for 20 minutes with 1 tsp. soy sauce until tender.

Separate somen and drop separately into 10 cups boiling water. Bring to a boil again and add ½ cup of cold water. Bring to a boil again, then turn off heat, strain in a colander, and wash under cold water until all noodles are completely cold. Put the noodles in a large bowl. Take the vegetables and arrange beautifully on top. Bring sauce ingredients to a boil, cool, pour over noodles and serve immediately.

Vegetables

121. Broccoli Nitsuke

1 bunch broccoli
½ tsp. salt
1-2 tsp. soy sauce
3 Tbsp. sesame seeds, roasted

Separate the broccoli, saving the very hard parts for soup stock. Peel the medium hard parts and cut in ¼″ rounds. Cut the stems the same and the leaves into 1″ pieces. Separate the flowerettes and their stems into 1″ lengths.

Place stem parts and leaves in a pot, add ½ cup water and ½ tsp. salt. Bring to boil with cover and cook for 5 minutes on medium high flame. Add flowerettes and sprinkle in soy sauce. Continue to cook, uncovered, for 10 minutes or until soft. Mix in roasted sesame seeds and serve.

122. Summer Squash Nitsuke

1 lb. summer squash, ½″ diagonals
¼ tsp. salt
2 tsp. soy sauce
¼ tsp. grated ginger

Place sliced squash in a pot, add ¼ cup water and sprinkle with salt. Bring to a boil. Add soy sauce and cook on a medium flame for 10-15 minutes, stirring occasionally. Take off cover and add grated ginger. Cook a few more minutes.

123. Tofu Stuffed Cabbage

10 cabbage leaves
½ med. carrot, matchsticks
3 med. onions, ⅛″ crescents
½ lb. tofu
2 Tbsp. seitan, minced
1 piece kombu 3″ × 4″
1 heaping Tbsp. unbleached white or whole wheat pastry flour
1 tsp. salt
2 Tbsp. oil

Cook cabbage leaves in salted water until soft. Press water from tofu and crumble.

Heat 1 Tbsp. oil in pan and saute onions, carrot, tofu, and seitan in that order. When the vegetables begin to soften, add 1 tsp. salt and continue to cook until vegetables are half done. Remove the hard part near the core of the already cooked cabbage. Place a leaf of cooked cabbage on a cutting board. Inside the leaf put 2 Tbsp. of the vegetable mixture. Roll the cabbage lengthwise so it looks like a roll, place a toothpick at each end to prevent the mixture from falling out and also place a toothpick in the middle. Do this with all the cabbage leaves, until you have used up the vegetable mixture. Cut the kombu at ½″ intervals, but do not cut through; it will resemble a comb. Place this on the bottom of pan. On top place the cabbage rolls, add water to cover, and bring to a boil with a cover. Add ½ tsp. salt and 1 tsp. soy sauce and cook for 20 minutes. When the cabbage rolls are done, remove and slice each roll into 3 pieces. Serve these by standing them up on the cut end and cover with a white sauce.

Roast unbleached flour in 1 Tbsp. oil, add leftover water from cooking the cabbage (approximately ¾ cup), bring to boil, and pour over the cabbage.

124. Vegetable Kabobs

1 small cauliflower
10 string beans or 1 bunch broccoli
2 carrots
3 stalks celery
1 Tbsp. salt

Lemon miso sauce
1 heaping Tbsp. rice miso
1 heaping Tbsp. barley miso
⅔ cup water from the cooked
   vegetables
1 tsp. lemon rind, grated
1 Tbsp. lemon juice

Cook the vegetables whole, separately, in 8 cups salted boiling water in an uncovered pot on a high flame. Cook the cauliflower about 7 minutes, the other vegetables until they are tender. Remove from the water and let them cool. Separate the cauliflower and broccoli into flowerettes. Cut the string beans in half and cut the celery and carrots into 1½″ pieces.

On a bamboo skewer place pieces of carrot, celery, string bean, and cauliflower. Place the cauliflower so that it covers the skewer point. It will look like a flower on the end of the skewer. Top kabobs with lemon miso sauce.

Sauce variations: Mix 3 Tbsp. mayonnaise and 1 Tbsp. soy sauce or 1 Tbsp. sesame butter, ½ Tbsp. soy sauce, and 2 Tbsp. boiling water (enough to make a creamy consistency).

125. Chinese Vegetables Supreme

½ lb. tofu, cut in ½″ squares
1 onion, sliced fine
3 stalks celery, sliced fine
2 cups finely cut Chinese or
   regular cabbage
3 cups mung bean sprouts
4 shiitake mushrooms, soaked
   and thinly sliced
1 tsp. salt
2 Tbsp. oil
3 Tbsp. arrowroot
3 Tbsp. soy sauce

Brown tofu well on all sides, until it slides around in the pan. Add mushrooms and salt and brown some more. Saute onion, celery, cabbage, and sprouts in a wok. Add water enough to cover. When it boils, add diluted arrowroot to thicken. Let cook for 3 or 4 minutes. Add soy sauce to taste, mix in tofu and mushrooms and pour immediately into serving dish. Serve with soba, whole wheat noodles, or fried noodles and roasted nori.

126. Grated Zucchini Nitsuke

1 med. onion, minced
3 cups grated zucchini
1 tsp. oil
1 tsp. salt
½ tsp. lemon or orange peel, grated
   fine, or 1 tsp. lemon juice

Saute minced onion with cover until transparent. Add grated zucchini and salt and saute without cover for 10 minutes. Serve with finely grated citrus peel or juice.

127. Baked Zucchini

Large zucchini
Cooked bulghur
Chick pea sauce (#156)

Cut large zucchini squash in half, lengthwise. Stuff with cooked bulghur that has been seasoned with chick peas and vegetables sauce (see #156), keeping extra sauce to serve on top of the zucchini at meal time. Bake in 400° preheated oven 1 hour or longer, until tender and golden brown.

128. Zucchini Spread

Large zucchini (3-4 lbs.)
Whole wheat flour
Oil for pan frying
2-3 small umeboshi plums

Cut zucchini into rounds ½″ thick. Take out large seeds (you may use them in your garden next spring). Coat zucchini with whole wheat flour. Pan fry in ¼″ oil until they get walnut brown. Drain on paper towels. Place zucchini in pan with ½ cup water and 2-3 small umeboshi plums or 1-2 larger ones. Cook for about 1½ hours, mashing the zucchini and adding water if necessary. Put through a food mill. Serve on bread, karinto, etc.

129. Stuffed Cucumbers

3 cucumbers
3 prawns, minced
2 onions, crescents
1-2 med. zucchini, quarter moons
1 Tbsp. oil
1 tsp. salt
3 Tbsp. mayonnaise

Cut off ½″ piece of cucumber from the top. Salt it and replace it snugly against the cut edge of the remaining cucumber (this helps to eliminate any bitter taste cucumber may have). After 20 minutes, rinse salt from cucumber and discard the small ½″ piece (this is the most bitter part of the cucumber). Remove pulp of cucumber with a spoon, scooping out all the seeds and pulp. Saute onions and zucchini. Add minced prawn. Continue cooking until ready to eat. Season with salt lightly. Chill. Add to this some homemade mayonnaise (#183) seasoned with minced onion and/or garlic. Chill the mixture completely. Turn cucumber upside-down to drain out any liquid portion from the pulpy center that remains. Stuff compactly with the vegetable mixture which has been thoroughly chilled. Place wax paper over top of cucumber and refrigerate 2 hours before serving. Cut into ¾″ or ½″ slices and serve 2-3 slices per person. Makes a delightful hors d'oeuvre, or may be served in place of a salad on special occasions.

130. Vegetables with Miso Sauce

1 med. eggplant, ⅓″ thick ×1″ wide
    flat rectangles
2 carrots, ¼″ diagonals
2 cucumbers, ½″ rounds
2 zucchini squash, 1″ rounds
1 handful of green vegetable ohitashi
    (see #74), cut 2″ long
2½ tsp. salt
Oil for deep frying

Sesame miso
1 cup sesame seeds
½ cup mugi miso
3 Tbsp. cooking water

Slice eggplant and deep fry until slightly brown. Cut carrots and deep fry until tender. Cut zucchini and cook with ½ tsp. salt in small amount of water. Cut cucumbers, toss, and mix with 2 tsp. salt.

Arrange all vegetables on a big plate. Serve with sesame miso made in the following way:

After roasting sesame seeds, grind strongly. Add miso and a little bit (3 Tbsp.) of water left from cooking zucchini and grind well (until creamy).

131. Pan Fried Eggplant

1 large or 5 small eggplants
3 Tbsp. mugi miso
1 tsp. orange or tangerine rind,
    grated
2 tsp. salt
Oil for frying

Remove the head of the eggplant, cut each eggplant in ½″ pieces lengthwise. Score each piece diagonally, so it resembles basket weaving. Sprinkle with 2 tsp. of salt. Let the eggplant sit for 30 minutes. Remove the surface moisture with a paper towel. Heat up a cast iron frying pan, add 2-3 Tbsp. of oil, place a layer of eggplant in the frying pan, cover. On a flame slightly higher than medium, fry for 1 minute. Turn the eggplant over, press slightly with a spatula, and fry again for 5 minutes. Take off the cover, turn again, and cook until the eggplant is soft. The eggplant will have a transparent color. In another pan, heat 1 Tbsp. of oil, add the miso, and cook until it smells fragrant. Add 5 Tbsp. of boiling water to make it creamy, bring to a boil, add the orange or tangerine rind, and pour as a sauce over the eggplant. Serve immediately. Eggplant is more delicious served hot.

132. Fried Eggplant with Miso

1 large eggplant
5 Tbsp. oil
1 tsp. rice miso mixed with
    1 tsp. mugi miso
1 Tbsp. sake (optional)

Remove the head of the eggplant, cut remainder into bite size pieces. Heat up a frying pan, add the oil, and then the eggplant. Saute with a cover until the eggplant is done, add miso mixture, bring to a boil, and serve.

133. Green Pepper with Miso

1 green pepper
½ Tbsp. oil
½ Tbsp. mugi miso
3 Tbsp. soup stock (see #40)

Cut the pepper in half lengthwise and remove the seeds. Cut each half into 3 pieces lengthwise. Dilute the miso with the soup stock. Heat up a frying pan. Add oil and saute the green pepper until the color changes. Then add the diluted miso, cooking for 5 minutes more. Serve.

134. Vegetable Curry with Fish

7 pieces fish, cut in 2″ squares
1 tsp. ginger juice
Flour and oil for frying
3 small onions, ½″ crescents
1 handful string beans, cut in thirds
    widthwise
1 small carrot, ¼″ diagonals
2 tsp. salt
1 tsp. oil
5 cups water

Curry sauce
  1 tsp. curry powder
  1 cup whole wheat pastry flour
  1 Tbsp. oil
  2 cups water

Saute curry powder in 1 Tbsp. oil a few minutes, then add pastry flour and saute 5-7 minutes on a low to medium flame. Set aside to cool in a bowl. Add 2 cups water and blend until smooth.

    Marinate fish in ginger juice. Saute vegetables with 1 tsp. salt in 1 tsp. oil (onions, beans, then carrot). Add 5 cups water and simmer 30 minutes with 1 tsp. salt added. Dip fish in whole wheat flour and fry in 1″ oil. Add fish to vegetables. At the end, add curry sauce and boil 5 minutes.

    Note: This recipe is also good without the fish.

Wild Vegetables

135. Purslane

2 cups purslane
1 Tbsp. oil
1 Tbsp. miso

Summer vegetable. Slightly acid or sour taste. If eaten during the summer, you never get tired. Tastes good with miso. Good for acne and freckles.

After washing, cut in 1″ strips and saute well. Add miso. Cover and cook over medium flame for 20 minutes.

Purslane is good for miso pickles (see #263 in *Calendar Cookbook).*

136. Goosefoot

2 cups goosefoot
1 Tbsp. oil
1 Tbsp. soy sauce
2 Tbsp. water
1 Tbsp. roasted and ground
    sesame seeds

Leaves are very good for strokes and high blood pressure. Juice is good for toothaches and bug-bites. If you pick too much, you can shade-dry and keep it for a long time. According to Japanese tradition, if you cook the dried goosefoot (soaked overnight first) and eat it in the winter, you are completely protected from a stroke during the year.

After washing, cut in 1″ strips. Saute well. Add soy sauce and water simultaneously. Cook 20 minutes until tender. Add sesame seeds. Cook 5 more minutes. (It is all right to use sesame butter instead of seeds.)

Goosefoot is good for ohitashi (#176) and/or goma-ai (#179).

137. Wood Sorrel

Slightly acid or sour. Good for women's diseases. Wash. Mix with tossed salad or mix with salt in pressed salad. Or pickle.

138. Beefsteak Leaves

Shiso leaves
Oil for sauteing
Miso for seasoning

There are two kinds of shiso: green and purple. Green shiso is used for a condiment, cooking, and pickles. Purple shiso is used for umeboshi coloring. The purple has more iron and minerals. If you are not able to purchase it in a store, it is best to plant. You can buy the seeds in Japanese stores. Shiso is good for anemia, and aids in the quick manufacture of hemoglobin.

Pick young leaves, wash, and saute in oil. Season with miso. Good in building summer appetites. Slice green and purple leaves very thin. Use as a condiment for noodles – a very beautiful color.

At the beginning of autumn (end of Sept.), little flowers blossom. At this time, remove seeds and wash them. Mix with salt (2 cups seeds to 1 heaping Tbsp. salt) and put in pressed salad. It keeps a long time. Or, put seeds in cotton gauze bag and put them in the bottom of a miso container. In 6 months you'll have great pickles. A good condiment.

Shiso seeds can also be sauteed. Season with soy sauce. A good condiment for nitsuke.

139. Wild Ginger

Wild ginger
Soy sauce

Use the root. Wash gently. Grate. Mix with a little soy sauce. It is a good condiment with raw or broiled fish. Also good as a condiment pickle. Builds good summer appetites.

Seaweeds

140. Toasted Nori

Nori Seaweed

Roast nori until crisp by taking 1 piece or sheet, unfolding it and passing it over the flame quickly until it changes from its original color to an iridescent green and is no longer smooth but coarse-looking. Roast only on 1 side – if both sides are done then the nori loses its nutritional value. Nori can be crushed in your hands or it can be crushed between the layers of a cotton cloth. This method produces a fine powder. Use nori as a garnish on rice, vegetables, soups, etc.

141. Nori with Soy Sauce *(Nori Nitsuke)*

1 pkg. nori seaweed
2 cups water
3 Tbsp. soy sauce

Break nori into 1″ squares. Soak in water for 20 minutes. Cook in the same water for 30 minutes in covered sauce pan. The water should be all absorbed. Add soy sauce, cover and simmer 30 minutes longer. Stored in refrigerator, this will keep for a week or more.

142. Kombu Maki (Kombu Roll)

2 pieces kombu, 4″ × 4″
1 small carrot, cut lengthwise and
    cut each half into 3 long pieces
1 small burdock, cut like carrot
Kampyo
Soy sauce

Soak kombu. Reserve the water. Place 2 pieces of carrot and 2 pieces of burdock in the kombu. Roll the kombu up, tie with kampyo at each end and at the center. Put the kombu rolls in a pan, add water reserved from soaking the kombu, strain with a cotton cloth to filter the dust. Add enough water to cover the kombu, bring to a boil, then turn down flame to medium. Cook until tender, season to taste. This dish can be pressure cooked for 20 minutes. Run cold water over the pressure cooker to bring down the pressure, add soy sauce and cook for 10 minutes more. When the kombu is completely soft, slice it into 3 parts. Serve with the sliced part up, showing the burdock and carrot.

143. Kombu in Soy Sauce *(Shio Kombu)*

8oz. kombu
1 pt. soy sauce

Clean kombu by running a damp cloth over it and cut into ½″ squares. Allow to dry on absorbent paper. Soak in bowl overnight with soy sauce to cover. Put kombu and soy sauce into a pot, cover, bring to a boil, lower flame and simmer about 3 hours, stirring occasionally. Remove cover and mix thoroughly. Continue cooking and stirring until soy sauce is absorbed. These are extremely salty and only 2 or 3 pieces should be eaten at any one meal. It can be stored in a covered container for many years. Good to use inside of musubi (rice balls) as a condiment.

When George Ohsawa came to the U.S. the second time, he stayed with us in our New York apartment. One day I served him this shio kombu, and he said it tasted really good. If you are tired, try 2-3 pieces of shio kombu inside a cup of bancha tea.

144. Wakame Salad

2 cups wakame
1½ cucumbers
2 oranges
1 tsp. salt

Wash wakame and soak in water for 20 minutes. Cut soft leaves from the stems. Cut in ½″ pieces. Slice cucumber very thin and mix with 1 tsp. salt. Let sit for 20 minutes and mix with wakame. Remove skin of orange; remove also the white inner skin, separating each wedge if you wish. Mix with other ingredients. Serve 1 heaping Tbsp. per person.

145. Wakame Cucumber Sesame Salad

2 cucumbers, irregular wedges
  (if waxed, remove outer skin)
⅓ cup wakame
1 tsp. salt
1 Tbsp. sesame butter
1 tsp. soy sauce

Soak wakame in water for 20 minutes, wash and cut in ½″ lengths. Mix 1 tsp. salt with the cucumbers. Keep under slight pressure for 10 minutes (use a bowl with water and place it over the cucumbers to create pressure). Squeeze off the excess water and mix the cucumbers with the wakame. Mix the sesame butter and soy sauce thoroughly. If the sauce is too thick, add a little more water to make it creamy. Mix in the cucumber and wakame.

146. Hijiki Tofu Salad

1 lb. tofu
⅓ cup dry hijiki
1 med. carrot, matchsticks
1 tsp. sesame oil
3-4 Tbsp. rice miso
½ cup sesame seeds

Wash hijiki and soak for 10 minutes. Strain and reserve water. Cut hijiki in 1″ lengths. Wash sesame seeds and roast in a dry pan. Grind in a suribachi and set aside. Heat 1 tsp. oil and saute carrots in covered pan, stirring several times. After slightly soft, add hijiki and saute for 5-7 minutes. Add soaking water to cover vegetables, cover pan and cook for 30 minutes or until tender. Strain and set aside to cool.

Bring 4 cups of water to a boil, add tofu to the water, bring to a boil again and strain. Squeeze any excess water from the tofu, add it to the suribachi with the sesame seeds and mash the tofu. Add miso at this time. After the hijiki and carrot have cooled, combine with the tofu mixture. Mix well and serve cold.

Soups

147. Cold Miso Soup

1 cucumber, ¼″ matchsticks
1 sheet toasted nori, crushed
5 Tbsp. mugi miso
2 scallions, sarashinegi (see #205)
4 cups cool soup stock (#39)

Form miso into small ball 1½″ diameter and ½″ thick (similar to a rice ball). Heat up a metal toaster on a gas burner or use an oven rack slightly oiled. Toast miso ball on both sides. When a pleasant smell comes, it is done. Mix ⅓ of miso ball with the cool soup stock. Put the cucumbers and scallions in each soup bowl, pour the soup stock in each bowl, sprinkle with nori and serve immediately. Tofu can be substituted for the cucumber. Baked miso is also a good condiment for rice.

148. Split Pea Miso Soup

2 cups split peas
1 piece of kombu, 4″ × 4″
8 cups of water
2 large onions, chopped
1 cup chopped celery
1 cup chopped carrots
1 tsp. fish shavings (optional)
2 Tbsp. rice flour
⅓-½ cup mugi miso
1 Tbsp. oil

Wash split peas and soak in 4 cups of water one hour. Boil in 8 cups of water with strip of kombu until split peas are tender. Remove kombu. Saute onions, fish shavings, celery and carrots in oil; add to soup and simmer until done. Saute flour in oil. Add soup to flour, then put in with rest of soup. (Mix some of soup in blender if creamy style is preferred.) Add miso to taste.

149. Fresh Corn Potage

3 ears corn
1 onion, large minced
1 Tbsp. kuzu
4 cups water
1 tsp. salt
1 tsp. sesame oil
½ tsp. soy sauce

Shave corn kernels. With the back of the knife scrape the cob to remove all the juice. Saute onion covered until transparent and add ½ tsp. salt. Add the corn and the pulp and saute a few minutes. Add ½ tsp. salt and water. Bring to a boil, then lower flame and cook 20 minutes.

Dilute kuzu in 3 Tbsp. water, add to soup and boil 5 minutes. Add soy sauce to your taste. This potage has a beautiful yellow color.

150. Wakame Miso Soup

1 large handful of wakame
5 cups boiling water from
    soaking the wakame
1 Tbsp. mugi miso

Soak wakame until soft. Wash well. Chop, add to boiling water and cook until tender. Put miso in a bamboo strainer and with a spoon mash it while holding the strainer in the soup. Note: Before adding miso, turn off the flame. If there is any miso holding onto the strainer, keep dipping it into the soup until it is all removed. Serve immediately.

151. Wakame Onion Soup

1 cup wakame
1 onion, chopped
5 cups water from soaking
  the wakame
7 tsp. mugi miso
1 tsp. oil

Soak wakame until it is soft, cut in ½″ pieces. Saute onions, add water from soaked wakame, bring to a boil, add the wakame, and cook until it is tender. Add miso as in #150.

Beans

Azuki beans, black beans, and chick peas all follow a general rule for cooking: cook beans in 2½-3 times the amount of water for pressure cooking, 4 times the amount of water for regular cooking. Black beans should be soaked 1 hour. Salt should be added only after cooking; if added in the beginning, the beans do not become tender.

Chick peas grow in India, South Asia, and Africa. These beans are quite yang. People who work hard live on chick pea flour alone in these countries. Chick peas are yang enough to be used as a staple. When George Ohsawa came to Chico in 1962 for a macrobiotic summer camp, he told me, "Chico is very hot, and Mexican people eat beans every day, so we can eat them frequently also." Before that he didn't recommend so many beans in the macrobiotic diet.

For pressure cooking: Place beans and water in pressure cooker. Bring to full pressure and cook 45 minutes. Allow pressure to reduce to normal. Remove cover, add salt and soy sauce if desired, and cook slowly until liquid is almost evaporated. Adjust seasoning to taste. Note: If using beans for a salad, pressure-cook only 30 minutes, let stand 10 minutes. Then remove pressure top.

For regular cooking: Bring to boil and cook on very low flame for about 2 hours. Remove cover, add salt and continue to cook without cover on low flame until liquid boils off.

152. Black Beans Mexicana

2 cups black beans
5 cups water
1 med. onion, diced
1 tsp. salt
1 tsp. cumin seeds

Wash and soak beans for 4-6 hours before cooking. Pressure-cook for 45 minutes, or boil and simmer for 1-2 hours. Saute onion and add. Continue to cook on low flame for 1-2 hours. Add salt 30-45 minutes before serving. Add cumin near end of cooking. Good also chilled and served as a side dish or when added to salad.

153. Soybean Surprise

2 cups soybeans
5-6 cups water
2 cups onion, minced
1 cup carrots, minced
Parsley, minced

Sauce
4 Tbsp. tahini
4 Tbsp. water
Miso to taste
Green scallions (optional)

Soak soybeans for 6 hours or overnight. Place in pressure cooker, bring to full pressure, reduce flame and cook for 45 minutes. Watch soybeans so that liquid does not clog air vent. Saute onions and carrots. Place tahini and water in a saucepan, stir constantly while cooking on a medium flame until it has a creamy consistency. Add onions and carrots and simmer 10-15 minutes until flavors mingle. Blend in miso until desired taste is obtained. May need to add a little more water for desired consistency. When using scallions, add them to the sauce just before serving, so that they are heated through but not well cooked. Place soybeans in serving bowls, pour sauce over and sprinkle parsley on top.

154. Chick Pea Pie

1 cup cooked mashed chick peas
3 cups sliced apples
1 tsp. cinnamon
½ tsp. salt

Crust
3 cups whole wheat pastry flour
3 Tbsp. oil
½ tsp. salt
1¼ cups cold water

Mix flour, salt, and oil by hand. Add cold water and mix with wooden spoon. Mix dough gently. Separate into 2 parts and roll out 1 part ¼″ thick and place in an oiled pie pan. Mix chick peas with salt. Place in pie dough. Mix apple and cinnamon together and spread over chick peas. Then cover with rolled-out pie dough. In center of pie shell cut a 2″ cross. Brush with egg yolk. Bake in 450° oven for 30 minutes.

155. Chick Peas with Soba

2 cups dry chick peas
   (soak 4-5 hours)
5 cups water
1 med. onion, crescents
2 tsp. oil
2 tsp. salt
1 cup scallion, ¼″ rounds
1 lb. soba (see #9)
Nori for garnish

Saute onion in a pressure cooker with 2 tsp. oil until slightly brown. Add chick peas and water, and cover. Bring pressure up over high flame. After pressure is up, turn the flame down to low and cook for 45 minutes. Shut off heat until pressure returns to normal. Add 2 tsp. salt and cook for 15 more minutes. Mix evenly every few minutes. Then take off the cover and mash with a wooden spoon for 15 minutes until one-third of the peas are mashed. Then fold scallions into chick peas. This will change scallions to a bright green color. Cover cooked cold soba with this sauce. Roast and crush nori and sprinkle it on the sauce. You can serve this sauce either cold or hot.

156. Chick Peas with Vegetables

1 cup chick peas
2 med. onions, 1 minced, the
    other ¼″ crescents
1 med. carrot, ¼″ diced
10 cabbage leaves, cut into
    1″ squares
1 stalk of celery, ¼″ diagonals
2 tsp. salt
1 Tbsp. sesame butter
1 tsp. sesame oil

Wash and soak the chick peas in 2 cups of water overnight or at least 5 hours, in a pressure cooker. Bring to pressure and cook 45 minutes on a low flame. Let pressure come down to normal and remove the cover.

Heat the oil in another pan, saute the minced onions until they are slightly brown in color, then add the other onions and saute until they are transparent. Add the cabbage, celery and then the carrots, sauteing each until the color changes before adding the next vegetable. Add boiling water to cover vegetables and bring them to a boil on a high flame. Cook 20 minutes on a medium flame.

Add the chick peas without stirring. Sprinkle in the salt and continue to cook until everything is tender. Stir and add the sesame butter, which has been diluted with some of the liquid from the cooking vegetables. Cook for 5 minutes more. If more salt is needed, add soy sauce to taste.

157. Chick Pea Party Dip

1 cup chick peas
1 onion, minced
1 tsp. oil
½ tsp. salt
1 Tbsp. soy sauce
1 Tbsp. tahini

Wash and soak the chick peas in 2½ cups water as in #156.

In a pressure cooker, saute onion in oil until transparent. Add the soaked chick peas and water and pressure cook for 45 minutes. Remove from heat. Reduce pressure. Uncover, add salt and cook 15 minutes more. Blend in a blender or through a food mill until thick and creamy. Blend with soy sauce and tahini.

158. Cooked Salad with Bean Dressing

6 cups cooked vegetables
2 cups cooked pinto, kidney, or
    red beans
4 umeboshi
1 small onion, diced
½ cup oil

Arrange any combination of the following vegetables in a serving dish: carrots, broccoli, cauliflower, onions, Brussels sprouts, or zucchini. Vegetables should be cooked but firm. Blend umeboshi, beans, onion, and oil to a smooth paste. Add enough water to make a dressing thin enough to pour over vegetables.

159. Bean Salad

1 cup black beans
1 cup chick peas
2 cups green beans, cut in
    ¾″ pieces diagonally
1½ cups whole wheat macaroni
2 cups fresh peas
2 cups wax beans
1 tsp. salt

Cook but do not overcook black beans, chick peas, and macaroni. Cut fresh green beans in ¾″ diagonal slices and saute. Saute fresh peas, add a little water and ½ tsp. salt and cook uncovered until tender. Cook wax beans same as peas.

Mix all precooked ingredients into a large bowl. Mix in dressing of your choice (see #181-194). Be careful not to break up anything, or it will look like mush. This salad tastes just as good the second day.

160. Lentil Salad Sandwich

1 cup lentils
3 cups water
1 small onion, large minced
1" carrot, matchsticks
2" stalk celery, ¼" diced
2 bay leaves
½ tsp. salt
1 tsp. soy sauce
1 head lettuce, cut thin
Sesame oil for brushing
Sliced bread

Soak lentils in 2 cups water, at least two hours. Brush a pot with oil and saute onions until transparent. Add celery and carrot. Add the soaked beans with soaking water. Add one more cup water. Bring to boil with bay leaves and cook until lentils are tender, about one hour. Add more water if necessary. Add salt, cook another 20 minutes, then add soy sauce to taste. Remove bay leaves. Slightly mash, then cool lentils.

Slice lettuce leaves. Mix with French dressing (#77) or leave plain. On bread, first place salad leaves, then mashed lentils, then salad leaves, then bread. Apply slight pressure and slice.

Tofu

161. Cold Tofu (Hiya Yako)

Tofu
Ginger soy sauce or
    lemon soy sauce

Hiya yako (cold, uncooked tofu) tastes very good in summer. Slice tofu and serve on a glass plate. Tofu is quite watery, so tilt plate to one side and drain off excess water. Serve with ginger soy sauce (5 Tbsp. soy sauce and 1 tsp. grated fresh ginger, mixed together) or lemon sauce (1 Tbsp. soy sauce and 1 Tbsp. lemon juice). Use whichever you like.

Tofu spoils very quickly, so cover with cold water and keep in the refrigerator. Change water every 2 days. It can keep for about one week. If tofu floats on the surface, this means it is spoiling. Do not use it. (See #51, for instructions on how to make tofu.)

162. Kanten Tofu (Tofu Aspic)

1 lb. fresh tofu
1 kanten bar, soaked and cooked in
    2 cups water
7 young string beans, boiled and
    cut thin
5 scallions, sarashinegi (#205)

Slice tofu into 6 pieces and add it to 8 cups of boiling water. Then bring to a boil again. Pour off liquid and save. Mash tofu in suribachi. Soak kanten in 2 cups of water for 20 minutes, breaking it into small pieces. Bring to a boil and cook for 20 minutes. Remove pan from the heat and set aside to cool without cover. After it is lukewarm, add it to the tofu in the suribachi and grind well. Repeat a few times adding liquid and grinding until all the liquid is used. Then pour it into a mold and place in the refrigerator. After it hardens, take it out of the mold and cut it into 4″ long thin matchstick strips. Then serve on a glass plate and decorate with boiled string beans cut thin.

Serve sarashinegi (washed scallions, #205) as a condiment for cold, sliced tofu, along with a dipping sauce made by combining ½ cup soup stock (#39 or #40) with 2 Tbsp. soy sauce, or a vinegar sauce made by mixing 5 Tbsp. rice vinegar, 2 Tbsp. soy sauce, and 1 Tbsp. mirin.

163. Tofu Kuzu Vegetables

1 lb. tofu, wedges as described
2 med. cucumbers, ½″ rounds
    (peel if waxed)
Handful string beans, ½″ diagonals
½ small carrot, ¼″ half moons
1 Tbsp. parsley, minced
3 cups soup stock (#39)
½ tsp. salt
2 Tbsp. soy sauce
1 heaping Tbsp. kuzu or 3 Tbsp.
    arrowroot (diluted in 3 times
    water)

Hold block of tofu in hand and slice away from you, thin to thick wedges, starting 2″ from far right corner. Alternate cuts toward far left and far right corners. The resulting pieces are irregular trianglar shapes.

In a dry pan arrange cucumber, string beans, and carrot. Add soup stock. Add ½ tsp. salt and cover. Bring to boil, lower flame, and cook 20 minutes. Add tofu and 1 Tbsp. soy sauce and bring to boil. Dilute kuzu and add. Slowly mix. Bring to boil again and cook a few minutes. Season with 1 Tbsp. soy sauce, then shut off flame. Serve with sprinkled parsley or chopped scallions.

This is a very quick dish, good for the hot weather when you don't want to cook.

164. Tofu Vegetable Saute

1 lb. tofu
3 stalks celery, ¼″ thin diagonals
½ lb. fresh mushrooms, sliced thin
3 stalks bok choy, thin diagonals or
    5 cabbage leaves, thin matchsticks
5 scallions, chopped
1 Tbsp. sesame oil
1 tsp. salt
1 Tbsp. soy sauce

Strain tofu in a colander and break by hand into large pieces, not completely mashed. Heat oil in a heavy pot. Saute mushrooms, add salt and let cook a few minutes. Add bok choy or cabbage and cook until color changes. Add celery, then the tofu. After tofu is completely hot, add the scallions. Season with soy sauce.

Note: The white part of bok choy can be thick, so cut very thin on the diagonal.

165. Fried Tofu with Nori

1 lb. tofu (prepare as in #162)
½ tsp. salt
½ cup whole wheat pastry flour
1 sheet nori seaweed
Oil for deep frying
Small knob of fresh ginger root
1 Tbsp. soy sauce

Mash tofu in a suribachi. If you don't have the time to prepare it as in #162, then place tofu in a clean cloth and squeeze over a sink to remove excess liquid. Add flour and salt to mashed tofu and mix well. Cut nori into 4 pieces and place on a flat surface. Cover each piece of nori with a ⅓″ thick layer of tofu mixture. Heat oil to 350°. Deep fry tofu pieces for only a few minutes with the nori side down. Remove when tofu is still light in color. Do not brown. When tofu is done, drain. To prepare ginger, peel if the outside skin is hard, then grate with a fine grater. Squeeze out ginger juice. Mix 1 tsp. ginger juice with soy sauce. Then pierce each piece of tofu with 2 skewers and brush with ginger soy sauce. Serve immediately.

166. Tofu Salad Sandwich

1 lb. tofu cut into 8 pieces
1 heaping Tbsp. sesame butter
1-2 Tbsp. lemon juice
1-2 tsp. soy sauce
1 head lettuce, cut thin
Sliced bread

Boil tofu in 5 cups water for 5 minutes, then strain. Mash tofu in a cotton cloth and place in a suribachi. Add sesame butter, lemon juice, and soy sauce to suribachi and grind well. Cool.

On bread place lettuce, then spread mashed tofu, then lettuce, and bread. Slightly press, then slice.

Fried Foods

167. Rice Croquettes

4 cups leftover rice
2 onions, minced
1 carrot, minced
Salt to taste
Whole wheat pastry flour
Tempura batter
Bread crumbs
Oil for deep frying

To leftover cold rice add a little bit of cold water and separate the cooked rice grains. Add minced onions and minced carrot to the rice. Add a little bit of salt. Add whole wheat pastry flour until the mixture sticks together. Make croquette shapes, dip into tempura batter, roll in bread crumbs and deep fry. Serve with green vegetable ohitashi (see #176) or serve with a tossed salad.

168. Bulghur Croquettes

3 cups cooked bulghur
1 med. onion, minced
½ carrot, minced
½ block tofu
1 Tbsp. sesame oil for sauteing
2 Tbsp. corn oil for frying
⅓ cup whole wheat pastry flour
1 tsp. salt
1 heaping Tbsp. minced parsley

Saute the onion until it is transparent. Add the carrot and saute it 5 minutes. Squeeze excess water from tofu using a cotton cloth. Add the tofu, salt, and cooked bulghur and mix thoroughly. Remove from heat and let the mixture cool to body temperature. Mix in the pastry flour.

Make patties about 1" thick. Heat a frying pan, add 2 Tbsp. oil and place the patties in the pan. Cover and cook them for 7 minutes on each side over a medium flame.

Use the leftover oil in the pan to make a bechamel sauce (as in #187). Cover the croquettes with bechamel sauce and minced parsley.

169. Fried Eggplant with Sesame Sauce

1 large eggplant, quarter moons
3 Tbsp. sesame butter
1 cup soup stock (#39)
1 Tbsp. soy sauce
Oil for deep frying

Remove the head of the eggplant. Cut in quarters lengthwise, then widthwise strips. Deep fry, set on a strainer. Heat up the soup stock and soy sauce, add the eggplant and cook on a medium flame in a covered pot for 20 minutes, turning the eggplant so that both sides cook evenly. Remove the eggplant from the soup stock and mix in the sesame butter so that it is creamy. Cover the eggplant with the sauce, garnish with parsley and serve.

170. Breaded Eggplant

1 large eggplant
½ cup whole wheat pastry flour
1 egg
1 cup bread crumbs
2 tsp. salt
Oil for deep frying

Remove the head of the eggplant. Cut in half lengthwise, then in half widthwise, then twice lengthwise (3 pieces). Sprinkle with salt, let sit for 10 minutes, wiping off excess moisture with a paper towel. Beat the egg and add a small amount of water – approximately 3 tablespoons. Roll the eggplant in the flour, egg, and bread crumbs. Put into hot oil and deep fry until done. Remove from oil. Drain and serve.

171. Corncob Tempura

2 ears baby corn
Tempura oil

Tempura batter
1 cup whole wheat pastry flour
1¼ cup cold water
1 heaping tsp. arrowroot or
    sweet brown rice flour
½ tsp. salt

This is for baby corn, not the large commercial ones. Husk corn and cut whole cob into 1″ pieces. Dip in tempura batter and deep fry.

172. Mock Egg Roll

2oz. saifun
2 med. onions, minced
1 carrot, thin quarter moons
½ cup sliced white mushrooms
1 stalk celery, cut in thirds
    lengthwise then thin rounds
3 cups whole wheat flour
¾ cup cold water
2 Tbsp. oil
2 tsp. salt
Oil for deep frying

Boil saifun 5 minutes. Drain and cut into 1″ strips.

Heat pan, add 1 Tbsp. oil, and saute onions. Add salt and carrot and saute a short time. Add mushroom and celery. When the celery changes color, add the saifun. Remove from heat.

To make dough, mix 3 cups flour, 1 Tbsp. oil, 1 tsp. salt. Add water and knead to earlobe consistency. Roll dough thin. Cut into 3″ × 5″ pieces. Place vegetables on the pieces and roll up. Fold in at both ends and deep fry until crispy. Slice rolls into 4-5 pieces per roll and serve.

173. Deep Fried Miso Balls

1 cup whole wheat flour
½ to ¾ cup water
1 onion, minced
1 Tbsp. miso
⅛ tsp. salt

Add salt to flour and mix well. Add water to onion and miso, then add flour mixture. The dough should be fairly dry. Drop by spoonfuls into deep oil until they turn a dark golden color. Drain in a strainer, then lay on a platter covered with absorbent paper to take off the excess oil.

Salads

174. Bean Thread Salad

2 oz. saifun (bean threads)
¼ head cabbage, cut in 1″ pieces
   (core removed)
1 med. carrot, thin diagonals
1 med. cucumber
1 peach, 1 apple, cut into 8 pieces
   each, sliced ¼″ thick fan shape
   (optional)
2 heaping tsp. salt

Onion mayonnaise
1 egg, beaten
1 onion, minced
2 tsp. salt
½ cup oil
3 Tbsp. orange juice
1 Tbsp. lemon juice

Boil 3 cups of water, add the saifun and cook it for 5 minutes. Strain it and set it aside to cool. Cook the cabbage in 5 cups water with salt. Bring it to a boil in an uncovered pot. Cook until slightly tender, then set it aside to cool. Cook the carrot in the same water until it is slightly tender. Strain and set aside to cool. The remainder of the water can be reserved for clear soup.

Cut about ½″ off the stem part of the cucumber and rub it with salt. This will remove some of the bitterness. Cut it in half lengthwise, then cut it thinly in fan shapes. Place in a salad press, sprinkle with ½ tsp. salt, and press for 10 minutes. Form into fan shapes by pushing down the cut edges.

Add the 2 tsp. salt to the beaten egg and continue beating as you add the oil by drops (using a chopstick) until one third of the oil is used. Add a further third of the oil by using a teaspoon, and the remaining third by tablespoon. Continue beating until it is creamy. When it becomes thick, add the lemon juice and the orange juice. Add the minced onion and let this sit for 20 minutes.

Cut the cold saifun in 2″ lengths. When all the vegetables are completely cooled, mix with the fruit and the mayonnaise dressing. Use fan-shaped cucumbers to decorate, opened so that their point is away from the center.

175. Vegetable Salad (Cooked)

2 med. onions, minced
1 small cabbage, matchsticks
2 med. carrots, matchsticks
2 partly peeled cucumbers, thin rounds
⅓ cup whole wheat pastry flour
1 Tbsp. umeboshi juice
3 Tbsp. sesame oil
1 tsp. salt

Sprinkle salt on sliced cucumbers, let sit until moisture is released (about 10 minutes), then squeeze slightly. Keep ¼ of the cabbage and onions in a separate bowl. Heat 1 Tbsp. oil and saute the rest of the onions and cabbage and all of the carrot for a few minutes over a high flame until cabbage turns a bright green color. Set aside to cool. Heat up 2 Tbsp. sesame oil in another pan. Add flour and saute over a medium flame until slightly brown in color. Set aside to cool. After completely cold, add water, bring to a boil and make bechamel sauce. When this sauce gets cold, mix with salted plum juice. Mix cold sauteed vegetables with the ¼ cabbage and onions and mix in squeezed cucumbers. Then add cold bechamel sauce and mix well. Keep in the refrigerator for awhile before serving.

176. Party Ohitashi

2 bunches spinach
2 tsp. salt
1½ tsp. soy sauce
2 tsp. sesame seeds or bonita flakes

Bring 8-10 cups of water to a boil. After boiling add 2 heaping tsp. salt. Take off cover. Then place 1 bunch of spinach in the pot, standing on end. Then bring to a boil over high flame, immerse and wait until it boils again. When the stem is soft it is done. Remove to a strainer with leaves hanging over the edge, and cool. Repeat with the second bunch. When they are cool, squeeze out excess water and take off pink roots and save for miso soup.

Sprinkle with 1 tsp. soy sauce and set on bamboo mats, alternating root and leaves until forming a cluster 1½″ in diameter. Roll up sushi mat and squeeze gently. Save liquid for soup stock. Cut rolled spinach in 1½″ thick slices. Serve them on a flat plate, laid on side, and sprinkle with soy sauce. Top with roasted sesame seeds or bonita flakes on each center.

Konnyaku – Konnyaku yams grow wild in India, Ceylon, Indonesia, Burma, and South China. Konnyaku came to Japan with the Buddhist religion imported from China. Konnyaku is not digested by the enzymes in saliva or stomach juice, but by the bacteria in the intestines. So it does not feel heavy in the stomach. Pieces of konnyaku are rubbery and help sweep out intestinal deposits and stones. This helps stimulate intestinal peristalsis. Therefore, it helps cure constipation. And it also helps soften hardened arteries. Its alkalinity helps balance acid blood. Konnyaku is very yin, because enzymes cannot digest it. Only very yang intestinal bacteria can.

When you cook konnyaku, cut it with a sake cup or break it apart with your fingers. You can use a knife, but it will taste better if you use your fingers or a sake cup.

An old Japanese traditional belief was that konnyaku takes away sexual appetite. So George Ohsawa said to give konnyaku to overactive bachelors.

Though konnyaku comes originally from the hot South Eastern Asian climate, it grows in the more temperate climate of California, and is cooked with salt which makes it more yang. You must try to determine whether your own condition is yin or yang to decide how much is right for you.

---

177. Konnyaku Carrot Shiro Ai

1 lb. tofu
2 blocks konnyaku, flat
    rectangles ½″ × 1″
1 med. carrot, flat rectangles ½″ × 1″
1 cup soup stock (#39)
2 Tbsp. and 1 tsp. soy sauce
½ tsp. salt

To 2 cups boiling water add konnyaku and cook for 5 minutes. Then strain. Bring to boil 1 cup soup stock, 1 tsp. soy sauce, ½ tsp. salt, and carrots. Cook until tender but still firm. Strain and save juices. Cover tofu with a cotton cloth and place between 2 cutting boards. For pressure use a heavy object (like a telephone book) for about 1 hour, then grind in a suribachi. Add a little bit of soup stock until creamy. Then add 2 Tbsp. soy sauce, and mix with cooked konnyaku and carrot. This salad spoils quickly, so if you are going to keep it for awhile, boil tofu for a few minutes, then allow it to cool and squeeze out the water. For variety, add 1 Tbsp. of ground roasted sesame seeds to the tofu and for soy sauce substitute white miso. Or, substitute cooked daikon, summer squash, broccoli, cauliflower, or celery instead of carrot. Note: In Japanese, shiro means 'white,' and ai means 'mix.'

178. Vegetable Fruit Salad

1 small cabbage, shredded
1 cauliflower, small pieces
1 large carrot, shredded
2 apples, cored, ¼″ pieces

Cut cauliflower and apples into small pieces. Put aside. Prepare salad dressing (see #181). Pour boiling water over cabbage and carrot. Boil cauliflower. Soak apples in salted water. Mix cooled vegetables with salt and dressing and mound attractively on a large platter lined with lettuce.

179. String Bean Goma Ai

1 lb. young string beans
2 Tbsp. soy sauce
3 Tbsp. sesame seeds

'Goma-ai' is roasted and ground sesame seeds mixed with soy sauce or miso. It has a very elegant taste. To make really good goma-ai, it is very important to roast and grind the sesame seeds properly. Parsley, celery, summer squash, eggplant, spinach, or Swiss chard are good to use in goma-ai.

Remove strings from string beans. Bring 6 cups of water and 1 tsp. salt to a boil. Without cover, boil string beans until tender, then strain and set aside to cool. Cut string beans diagonally into 2 or 3 pieces and remove to a bowl. Roast and grind sesame seeds and mix with 2 Tbsp. soy sauce and add with string beans. (See #204 for instructions on how to roast seeds.)

180. String Bean Aemono

½ lb. string beans
2 Tbsp. mayonnaise (#75, #183, or #184)
1 Tbsp. soy sauce

Cook string beans in salted water without cover until tender, drain and set aside to cool. Then cut each bean diagonally into 2-3 pieces. Mix mayonnaise and soy sauce well with string beans.

Sauces and Dressings

181. Salad Dressing

1 bell pepper cut into 8-10 slices
2-3 Tbsp. sesame oil
1-2 umeboshi, pitted
2-3 Tbsp. rice vinegar or
    lemon juice (optional)
⅓ cup (approx.) pumpkin
    or sesame seeds
Dash of salt or soy sauce

Blend all ingredients in blender until well mixed, thick and creamy.

182. Italian Style Salad Dressing

½ small onion, minced
2 umeboshi, pitted
1 small clove garlic
3 Tbsp. oil, olive oil best
2 Tbsp. red wine

Rub bottom of suribachi with garlic. Add onion, umeboshi, and blend. Add oil and mix well, then add wine. Toss dressing with green salad.

183. Quick Mayonnaise

1 cup oil (corn, sesame, or olive)
1 egg
2 Tbsp. lemon juice
1-2 tsp. salt

Blend egg and salt together at low speed in a blender. Drop ⅓ of the oil in by chopstick, with blender on low. Then add ⅓ of the oil by teaspoon. Mayonnaise will begin to thicken. Then add the last ⅓ cup oil by tablespoon. If mayonnaise is very thick, soften by adding lemon juice. Increase speed if necessary. Add a pinch of white pepper if you like.
    Variation: Add a little orange juice for flavor.

184. Eggless Mayonnaise

2 Tbsp. soy flour
3 Tbsp. water
1 cup oil
½ tsp. salt or minced salted plum
Juice of ½ lemon
3 Tbsp. parsley, minced (optional)
Grated garlic or onion to taste
    (optional)
¼ tsp. basil (optional)

Brown flour in a dry pan and cool. Blend flour and water. Using the double boiler method, heat over hot water. Gradually beat in oil with a rotary beater. Add salt and lemon juice. Other seasonings are added last.

185. Lyonnaise Sauce

1 small onion, minced
1 Tbsp. white wine
3 Tbsp. bechamel sauce (#187)
¼ tsp. oil

Prepare bechamel sauce (#187). Saute minced onion in ¼ tsp. oil. Add wine and mix with bechamel sauce. This is delicious served with grilled fish.

186. Green Sauce

2 umeboshi, pitted
1 bunch scallions, chopped
1 bunch parsley, chopped
Oil and water

Place umeboshi plum meat, minced scallions, and parsley in a suribachi. Stir until it becomes a thick green creamy mixture. Add water and heated oil spoonful by spoonful, mixing them into it well and checking taste from time to time so that not too much oil is used. Delicious on salads or spread on bread.

187. Bechamel Sauce

White bechamel sauce
1 cup unbleached white flour
1-2 Tbsp. oil
1 tsp. salt
7-8 cups water

Bechamel sauce can be prepared with either 2 parts flour to 1 part oil, or 3 parts flour to 1 part oil. The former is more delicious, but you may not want to use so much oil in one dish. The amount of water or soup stock used depends upon desired thickness of sauce. Heat the oil slightly and add flour, roasting and stirring gently. Do not roast too long – only until lumps are smoothed out. Color should remain unchanged and the flour a powdery white. For the best result, cool before adding soup stock or water. Note: After roasting the flour, cool pan by setting in cold water and adding cold liquid to the flour, mixing very rapidly. A wire wisk is quite helpful. The difficulty in making this type of sauce is that it lumps easily. In an emergency, use a blender to smooth out lumps. Bring to a boil, add salt and simmer 20 minutes without cover, stirring occasionally. Add salt to taste and simmer a few minutes. Keep hot until serving time or sauce will harden.

Light bechamel sauce
1 cup whole wheat pastry flour
1-2 Tbsp. oil
1 tsp. salt
7-8 cups water

Prepare as in white sauce for making light bechamel. Allow the flour to turn slightly brown as you roast it in an oiled pan. Finish process as above.

Brown bechamel sauce
1 cup whole wheat flour
1-2 Tbsp. oil
1 tsp. salt
7-8 cups water

For brown sauce, roast flour until brown but not burned, stirring constantly. About 15-20 minutes is sufficient. It should have a nut-like fragrance. Finish as above.

188. Gravy

Prepare as directed

After cooking any kind of fish or sauteing vegetables, remove food and add flour to pan. Use 3 times as much flour as oil. Roast the flour a little. Finish as in the white sauce recipe. The various flavors are delicious. No waste of precious nutrients, either.

189. Mushroom Gravy for Pasta

2 onions, chopped
3 cloves garlic
½ lb. fresh mushrooms, sliced
Several crookneck or zucchini
  squash, chopped
1-2 Tbsp. oil
1 bay leaf
1 tsp. salt
2 Tbsp. miso (approx.)

Saute chopped onions in oil, add whole garlic cloves, then sliced mushrooms, then chopped squash. When browned, add bay leaf, salt, and small amount of water. Simmer until cooked, then remove garlic. Add miso and let stand a few minutes. Serve over spaghetti.

190. Tomato Sauce

6 large tomatoes
1-2 cloves garlic, minced
1-2 onions, diced or minced
½ green pepper, minced
2 tsp. bonita flakes
Salt to taste
Dash of cinnamon (optional)

Skin tomatoes and puree them. Saute garlic, onions, and green pepper, and add to paste. Add bonita flakes, salt, and a dash of cinnamon. Cook for 6 hours on a low flame with cover about three-quarters on. Mix into cooked noodles. Sprinkle a little cheddar cheese and parsley on top if desired.

191. Onion Sauce

1 med. onion, crescents
1 tsp. oil
2 Tbsp. light bechamel sauce (#187)
1 cup water
¼ tsp. salt
2 tsp. soy sauce

Heat 1 tsp. oil. Saute onion until golden. Add ½ cup water and ¼ tsp. salt and cook 15 minutes. Gradually add ½ cup cold water to bechamel sauce, stirring constantly. When blended, add to cooked onions. Bring to boil, lower flame and simmer 10 minutes. Add soy sauce to taste and simmer a few minutes longer. Delicious served with buckwheat groats or noodles.

192. Tahini Soy Sauce with Onion

1 Tbsp. tahini or sesame butter
3 Tbsp. soy sauce
1 cup water
1 onion, minced
1 tsp. corn oil

Saute onion in oil until transparent. Add water. Cover and simmer about 20 minutes. Add tahini or sesame butter and soy sauce, cover and cook 5 minutes.

193. Vegetable Curry Sauce

2 onions, thin crescents
1 carrot, matchsticks
⅓ lb. string beans, cut in 1″ pieces
1 cup whole wheat pastry flour
3 Tbsp. oil
7 cups water
½ tsp. curry powder
2 tsp. salt
Soy sauce

Saute onions until browned. Add carrot and saute a few minutes, covered. Uncover, add curry powder and flour. Saute 7 minutes. Set aside to cool.

In another pan, boil 5 cups water or soup stock with the salt. Add string beans and cook uncovered until tender and bright green. Remove beans and reserve liquid.

Blend 2 cups cold water with the onions, carrot, flour, and curry powder. Then add string bean liquid. Bring to boil and cook on low flame for 30 minutes. Mix with string beans. Add soy sauce to taste.

194. Scallop Cucumber Sauce

20 scallops (1 lb.)
1½ cucumbers, sliced in thin rounds
    (skin if waxed)
4 cups water – use scallop juice
2 Tbsp. kuzu arrowroot, diluted
    in a little water
4 tsp. soy sauce
1 Tbsp. parsley

Boil scallops about 3 minutes uncovered, in salted water. Drain, reserving liquid for sauce. Add scallop juice and water to cucumbers (to make 4 cups) and boil about 15 minutes. Add soy sauce. Boil 5 minutes longer. Add kuzu arrowroot. Boil a few minutes longer, adding scallops last. (If cooked too long, scallops become tough.) Garnish with parsley.

Pickles

195. Rolled Cabbage Pickles

10 cabbage leaves
1 cup celery, matchsticks
½ cup carrot, matchsticks
2 Tbsp. rice vinegar or
    3 Tbsp. lemon juice
1 tsp. salt

Cut away hard central part from cabbage leaves. Place leaves in boiling water, bring to a boil again and boil until leaves turn soft. Then drain and set leaves aside to cool. Mix celery and carrot, place on cabbage leaves near the thickest lower end, and roll them up. Place these rolls in a porcelain or glass bowl in one layer.

Bring rice vinegar and salt to a boil, and set aside to cool. After it cools, sprinkle on cabbage leaves and cover with cellophane. Apply pressure (a rock or bottle, etc.) for over 2 hours. When you serve, cut rolls in 1″ lengths and stand them on ends showing the spiral pattern. Sprinkle with soy sauce.

196. Cabbage Oil Pickles

1 small cabbage, cut in 1″ squares
1 carrot, thin half moons
3 Tbsp. olive oil
1 Tbsp. rice vinegar or lemon juice
1 tsp. salt

Mix cabbage with salt. Heat oil and add rice vinegar. Bring to a boil. Place cabbage and carrot in a salad press. Cover vegetables with hot oil and apply pressure. After 2 hours apply more pressure again. The next day you can serve. Good with bread or with beer.

197. Cabbage Cucumber Pickles

1 small cabbage, 8 crescents
5 cucumbers, irregular wedges
¼ lb. whole wheat bread
2 cups rice bran
¼ cup (or 5% of the vegetable weight) salt

Cut cabbage, wash, drain, and let sit until soft (about 2 hours). Sprinkle 2 tsp. salt in the bottom of a salad press. Place 2 cabbage sections in the bottom of the jar. Cut cucumber in irregular slices and put 1 layer of cucumber slices on top of the cabbage. Break bread into small pieces and mix with salt and rice bran. Take 2 handfuls and cover cucumbers. Then repeat by placing 2 more cabbage sections next, then a layer of cucumbers, then bread mixture. Repeat until full. Then apply pressure. After half a day water will come to the top. After the water comes out, relax the pressure but keep the water covering the vegetables. After a few days they can be served. If you keep them in the refrigerator they will keep for one month. You can substitute ½″ daikon slices instead of cucumbers.

198. Bright Green Cucumber Pickles

15 pickling cucumbers
⅓ cup crude salt
1½ cups water

Bring water to a boil and add salt. Set aside to cool. Wash cucumbers, dry and place in a porcelain or wooden keg and pour in the cold salty water. Apply light pressure with a stone. Seven days later you can use these. Cut into slices before serving. These can be used in salad as well.

199. Instant Cucumber Pickles

10-12 pickling cucumbers
¼ cup salt

Wash cucumbers, strain, and rub each cucumber with 1 tsp. salt. Place in a wooden keg or big porcelain jar and sprinkle with leftover salt. Apply pressure. These are ready in a couple of days. These are quick because a lot of salt is used. Water is released the next day.

200. Spicy Cucumber Pickles

10-12 pickling cucumbers
½ cup salt
¼ cup fresh minced ginger
1 clove minced garlic
3 med. scallions, 1½" rounds
½ tsp. red pepper powder

Prepare cucumbers with salt as in #199. After 2 days, remove cucumbers and place on a cutting board. Make 3 or 4 slits lengthwise about ½" deep. Keep these cucumbers in a covered porcelain jar. Mix ginger, garlic, scallions, and red chili pepper powder, and cover the cucumbers. Pour in cold salted water until they are covered. The salted water is made by boiling 1 Tbsp. salt in 2 cups of water and setting it aside to cool. Cover with a small plate or wooden cover and place a rock on top. After one night these have a delicious spicy taste which stimulates the appetite. After cucumbers are finished, strain off spices. Bring the salty liquid to a boil and use this liquid and spices 1 or 2 more times for more pickles.

201. Dill Pickles

50 pickling cucumbers
3 stalks dill
6 bay leaves
2 onions, quartered
6 cloves garlic
½ cup salt
3 quarts water

Wash the cucumbers, drain and dry. Place in layers standing up in a large jar: 2 rows of cucumbers, then 3-4 blossom ends of dill, then onions, adding garlic and bay leaf at the top. Repeat until full. Boil the salt and the water until the salt is dissolved. Cool. Pour over the pickles. Let stand in warm room for a few days, skimming the top when the ferment rises. Place under refrigeration after a few days.

202. Russian Cucumber Pickles

30 pickling cucumbers
1 cup crude salt
8 cups water
7-8 celery leaves, minced
7-8 dried red chili peppers, minced
2 cloves garlic, minced
1 tsp. cinnamon powder
1 stalk of dill

After washing cucumbers, dry outside in the shade for ½ day. Bring water to a boil, add salt, bring to a boil again, and allow to cool completely. Mix celery, garlic, pepper, cinnamon, and dill in the water. After cucumbers are dry, bring inside and let sit until heat is gone. Place them in a glass jar or porcelain pickle jar on end and pack in close together. Pour in salted spiced water and cover cucumbers. If they are packed tight, they will not rise out of the water. Then seal cover with tape. You can serve after 10 days. If you want to keep these for a long time, you must completely clean the jar out first by sterilizing it with boiling water and drying in a low oven. This kills all bacteria. Then, if they are sealed well, they will keep through winter. The longer you keep them, the better they will taste, as the spices mellow with time.

> **Rice Bran Pickles –** Many American friends make rice bran pickles but most people don't succeed because my recipe was not completely explained. People don't understand that pickles must be stirred once a day or they will spoil. This new recipe, without water, should succeed. This recipe is quite salty, so it will keep longer. When vegetables slightly change color, then they are ready to eat. Some friends have tried wheat bran and various mixtures of grain bran with salt and other ingredients; please be creative and invent your own pickles.
>
> I took these pickles on our summer tour; they lasted 1½ months. I served them at each cooking class and people enjoyed them. When pickling mixture is new, it is especially salty – later it will become more balanced from the vegetable juices. Be sure and remove pickles when the color changes, and push down the rice bran to keep it airtight.

203. Rice Bran Pickles (Nuka Pickles)

10 cups rice bran (nuka, available at Japanese stores)
2 cups sea salt (crude salt okay)
1 heaping Tbsp. red chili powder (optional)
8"-10" diameter ceramic crock with cover

Mix rice bran and salt and dry roast over a medium flame, constantly stirring, about 10 minutes. The color will slightly change and mixture will smell very fragrant. Turn off heat and mix in chili powder. Cover and let sit one hour. Spread on a cookie sheet and let cool.

After completely cold, place about 2" of the mixture into crock (after pushing down). Then add a layer of vegetables. Cover with the rest of the rice bran. If you wish, you can do 2 or 3 layers of vegetables. Then cover with a cotton towel, then the clay cover. The towel protects from insect eggs. Keep in a cool place.

The vegetables will release their juices, slowly making the dry mixture into a paste. Celery takes about 8 hours; 1½"-diameter daikon takes one or two days; skinned cucumbers take 6 to 8 hours; skinned watermelon rind, 2-3 hours. For small whole cabbage, take out the core and pickle whole with the cored end up so the juice doesn't go into the nuka mixture. Discard this excess liquid. Remove 4-5 leaves every day as they pickle. It should take from 3-5 days to pickle the whole cabbage. Remove pickled vegetables into a storage container and keep in refrigerator. Wash the nuka paste off and dry pickles before slicing and serving.

After you have used all the pickles, mix the rice bran to keep the moisture even. After about one month the rice bran paste becomes very wet. So, roast 2 new cups of rice bran and ⅓ cup salt and add 1 tsp. chili powder. When completely cold, add to the rice bran paste. If you go on vacation, remove all vegetables from crock, push down the rice bran, and use a stone on a board for pressure. Cover with cotton cloth and clay top, and store in a cool place while away.

Condiments

204. Gomashio (Sesame Salt)

10 parts sesame seeds (10 Tbsp.)
1 part sea salt (1 Tbsp.)

Fill a bowl with cold water, add sesame seeds and stir until half the seeds float on top of the water. Pour the floating seeds into a fine mesh strainer. Add more cold water to the sesame seeds remaining in the bowl, stir and strain again. Repeat this step until all sesame seeds are washed and strained, and only sand and dirt remain in the bottom of the washing bowl. Drain the seeds in the strainer for 30 minutes, placing a sponge or toweling underneath to catch the water that drips down from the strainer. If you have time, let them dry for half a day. Heat a dry frying pan and roast the salt, stirring constantly until the acid smell is gone. Place the roasted salt in a suribachi and grind it very fine. Roast the sesame seeds (see below) and add them to the ground salt in the suribachi. Grind evenly until most of the sesame seeds are crushed and ground. Don't grind too forcefully – stop just before oil comes out. This gives the best taste. If you grind too much, it will not taste as good. Cool completely and place in a glass or porcelain jar that has a cover. Keep tightly covered when not using.

Gomashio – If you roast too much or too little, the taste is not good. It is very important not to roast unevenly. To avoid this, roast on a medium flame, stirring constantly until all seeds are equally roasted. A very high or very low flame is not good for roasting evenly. Brown sesame seeds become very fragrant and taste good when roasted dark. Black sesame seeds are more yang, thus over-roasting makes them taste bitter. Roast the sesame seeds until your thumb and fourth finger can crush the seeds (your other fingers are too strong). When the roasted seeds crush easily, they are done. Another test is to eat a few of the roasted seeds. Raw seeds have a green taste which means they are not done. If they have a good taste they are done.

It is best to grind hot sesame seeds; cold seeds do not grind smoothly. Sesame seeds are most important in our daily food. So please cook them with your whole heart. Lima Ohsawa said, "If you cannot make good gomashio or good rice you are not yet a good macrobiotic cook." Cooking rice and preparing gomashio is simple but the most important part of the macrobiotic diet.

Sesame seeds have a very high quality oil and a good ratio of calcium and phosphorous which aid development of the nervous system and bone formation. The lecithin in sesame seeds dissolves cholesterol which accumulates on the walls of the veins and arteries, helping to eliminate the possibility of heart attack or high blood pressure. They are high in minerals and they are the only vegetable food which contains all the essential amino acids. Grind and roast them often and use a little sometimes when you cook vegetables.

205. Sarashinegi (Washed Scallion)

Scallions

Wash in cold water, then chop scallions fine. Use all the white part, 2″ into the green sections, reserving tops for use in other dishes. Place in a cotton cloth or cotton bag. Tie so that scallions do not fall out. Run cold water at sink over cotton cloth, wringing it by hand. The water coming from the bag will turn green from the potassium in the scallions. Rinse and wring, repeating until the water is clear and no longer green. Wring cloth dry. Remove scallions from cloth and flake with a pair of chopsticks.

206. Daikon Leaf Furikake

1 daikon leaf
1 tsp. ginger, minced
1 tsp. salt

After washing 1 daikon leaf, pass it through boiling water and set it aside to cool. Squeeze out water and cut in small pieces. Then again squeeze out water. Mix minced ginger with salt. Mix this with the daikon leaf.

207. Wakame Furikake

1 bag (2oz.) wakame
1½ cups dry chuba iriko
20 shelled peanuts
1 Tbsp. salt

Clean sand, dust, etc. off dry wakame and roast in a dry frying pan until it breaks easily when folded. Place in a suribachi and grind into small pieces. If pieces remain and cannot be ground up, roast them again in the pan until they can be ground in the suribachi. Choose small chuba iriko and roast them in a dry frying pan. Then grind them in a suribachi or electric blender until powdered. Roast peanuts, take off red skins and discard, and mince peanuts. Roast 1 Tbsp. salt in a dry frying pan until acid smell is gone and grind in a suribachi. Mix chuba iriko, wakame, peanuts, and salt well and keep in a glass jar. Good for weak-boned people, as it is high in calcium and other bone-building minerals. It also contains iodine and oil – very nutritious.

208. Shiso Furikake

Shiso leaves from umeboshi

Dry the salted shiso leaves from umeboshi outside in the sun. When they are completely dry, rub them into small pieces between your fingers and palms and keep them in a glass or porcelain jar and sprinkle on rice. Very good for summertime.

Shiso has a lot of iron and calcium. It builds blood hemoglobin. So please plant shiso bushes in your backyard so you can have fresh shiso leaves all summer. Fresh shiso leaves make a good condiment for all year. There are 2 kinds: green and purple. Green shiso has more flavor, but purple shiso has more iron, so plant either one.

209. Sesame Shiso

Sesame seeds
Shiso leaves, powdered

Take the shiso leaves from the salted plums, squeeze out the juice and dry in the sun on a sushi mat. When completely dry, rub in your hand and make into a powder. After washing seeds, roast as in #204. Then grind and mix with the powdered shiso leaves. This is especially good as a summer condiment for rice or other cooked grains.

210. Scallion Shiso Ai

3 Tbsp. chopped salted shiso leaves
2 Tbsp. white sesame seeds
3 bunches of scallions
2 tsp. sesame oil

Roast and grind sesame seeds. Add chopped shiso and grind well in a suribachi. Wash scallions, cut 1″ long and saute in a little bit of oil until tender. Set aside to cool and mix with sesame shiso. Any kind of ohitashi (see #176) goes with this condiment.

211. Cucumber Onion Shiso Ai

2 cucumbers, thick rounds
1 tsp. salt
3 onions, crescents
2 tsp. sesame oil
Sesame shiso

Slice cucumbers (half-peel if desired) and add salt. Slice onions. Heat up sesame oil and add onions. Saute until transparent. After onions are completely cool, mix with sesame shiso (#209) and cucumber.

212. Burdock Condiment

3 burdock, thin diagonals
1 Tbsp. oil
½ cup water
2 tsp. soy sauce
2 salt plums or 1 tsp. chopped shiso
   leaf and 1 tsp. soy sauce

After washing burdock, cut into thin long diagonal strips and saute in sesame oil. Just before becoming too brown, add a little water. Bring to a boil without cover. When the burdock begins to smell sweet, add a little soy sauce and salt plum, or 2 or 3 pieces of salty shiso leaves. Continue to cook until tender. When you serve, take out salt plums. Serve cool.

213. Umeboshi Tempura

Umeboshi plums
Tempura batter

Use 1 small plum or slice a big one in half. Dip in tempura batter (see #66) and deep fry. Don't fry too many at one time. Don't allow them to burn or get too crispy. This would spoil the good taste. Use as an hors d'oeuvre or serve with rice.

214. Umeboshi Soy Sauce

Umeboshi plums
Soy sauce to cover

If you have umeboshi that are too salty, set them in a bamboo strainer and pour boiling water over them. Save the water for a refreshing summer drink and dry the plums in the sun. Then remove them to a covered porcelain container or a glass jar and cover with soy sauce. Serve them as a condiment for rice. Especially good for breakfast. Some people don't like umeboshi, but these taste very good. You can use umeboshi soy sauce for ohitashi, or add a couple of drops to noodle sauce.

During the hot summer, everyone's stomach gets weaker. This sauce and the plums are very yangizing and will strengthen the stomach. So keep them on your table all summer. Old Japanese people say if you eat umeboshi every day you will never catch contagious diseases, because the strong acid and salt of umeboshi kill bad bacteria very quickly. If you are traveling on a long journey, take umeboshi every morning and you will never have an accident.

Breads

215. Unyeasted Bread

5 lbs. stoneground whole wheat flour
6 cups water (will vary with variety
    of flour; use as little water as
    possible)
¼-½ tsp. salt to each cup flour

Smaller proportions
3 cups whole wheat flour or
    2 cups whole wheat and
    1 cup brown rice flour
¼-½ tsp. salt per cup of flour
1½ cup water

This is a basic recipe. Use combinations of flour for different tasting loaves. Mix flour and salt thoroughly. Add water gradually, stirring from the center until all water is absorbed. Use your hands if necessary. Knead well. Cover and let stand overnight. Divide dough into 3 parts. The dough should feel pliable and be the consistency of the lobe of your ear. Knead each part into a well-shaped loaf. Place in oiled bread pans. Let rise for several hours, the longer the better. Cut a vertical slit on top of each loaf before baking. This will allow for expansion and keep the bread from splitting on the sides. Place in preheated oven at about 350° depending upon individual oven (they differ greatly). Since no two ovens are alike, experiment until you find the temperature best suited. Bake 1 to 1¼ hours, depending upon how crusty you like your bread. Turn out immediately on cooling racks. Let cool before slicing. Store bread in wrappers only after it has cooled completely. It will mellow and soften the second and third days, as you are using it. After that it may mold due to its natural inclinations.

Any combination of flours may be used. It's up to you.

216. Sourdough Starter

1 Tbsp. dry yeast
2½ cups warm water
2½ cups flour
2 tsp. raisin syrup or
    yinnie syrup

Combine all ingredients and cover top of container with a mesh cloth or take several layers of cheesecloth to make a cover. Good to use a jar such as a mason jar, then mesh cover can be sealed over top with a rubber band. Uncover and stir daily for 5 days. Keep in a warm, dry place. Then refrigerate your starter and stir daily. Add flour and water each time you remove starter to bake bread. Must keep refrigerated after the 5-day period in which starter is beginning to ferment.

217. Sourdough Bread

1 cup sourdough starter
2 cups water
3 cups flour
1 tsp. salt
Sesame or caraway seeds, roasted

Combine all ingredients. Cover with a damp cloth and raise in a warm spot for 12-24 hours. Add roasted sesame seeds or caraway seeds and make into loaves. Raise in a warm oven (100-150°) 1 to 2½ hours. Bake in preheated oven at 325° for 55 minutes. Add a combination of flours when first beginning to mix ingredients. Add only whole wheat flour when more flour is added to dough to obtain desired consistency for loaves.

218. Corn Bread

1½ cups cornmeal
1½ cups whole wheat or
    pastry flour
½ tsp. yeast
¾ tsp. salt
1½ cups grain milk
1 Tbsp. oil
1 egg (optional)

Put yeast in ¼ cup warm water and let activate. Roast cornmeal in small amount of oil. Add flour and salt. Separately, mix grain milk, oil, and egg and add to dry ingredients. Add yeast and mix well. Let sit in bowl in warm place until it rises, 1 or 2 hours. Pour into 9″ oiled pan and let rise again. Bake at 375° for 45 minutes or 1 hour.

219. Light Party Rolls

1 tsp. yeast diluted in ½ cup
    warmed water
1 cup soba water (ferment several
    days before using if possible)
4-4½ cups unbleached white flour
    or blend of flours
⅓ cup corn or safflower oil
2 tsp. salt

This recipe uses water reserved from cooking buckwheat noodles.
    Combine all ingredients. Set in refrigerator overnight. Stand at room temperature ½ hour before using next day. Knead well, roll into desired shapes and let rise for 1 hour. Bake 15-20 minutes at 375-400° in a preheated oven.

220. Cream Puffs

1 cup whole wheat pastry flour
1 egg
½ cup corn oil
1¼ cups boiling water
⅛ tsp. salt

Sift flour and add salt. Boil water and oil and add to flour all at once. Beat well. Add egg. Drop from tablespoon about 2″ apart on oiled sheet. Bake in hot oven 400° for 10 minutes. Then 300° for 20 minutes.

221. Rice Muffins

1 cup cooked rice
¾ cup rice flour
2¼ cups whole wheat flour
3 tsp. corn oil
¾ tsp. salt

Puree cooked rice in 1½ cups water. Put rice flour and whole wheat flour in bowl. Add oil, mixing in with fingers. To this, add pureed rice plus 1 cup more of water in which salt has been dissolved. Spoon dough in oiled muffin tins and bake for 45 minutes in a 350° oven. Makes approximately 1½ dozen muffins.

Desserts

> **Kanten** (sea gelatin) is made from a variety of Japanese seaweed called 'ten gusa.' It has no calories, but is high in minerals. Thus it cools the body but is a much better form of yin than fruits. This makes it excellent for summertime. Being low in calories, it is good for overweight people to help them lose weight. The minerals also help low or high blood pressure and help relieve constipation.

222. Kanten Noodles *(Tokoroten)*

1 heaping Tbsp. kanten powder with 5 cups water or 2 kanten bars with 4 cups water

Mix kanten with cold water. Bring to a boil without cover. After boiling, continue cooking for 15 minutes. The foam that forms around the edge should be skimmed off. Pour into a mold and chill. Then cut into thin noodles with a knife or with a wooden plunger device called a tentuki which cuts kanten into uniform strips. Serve with a sauce made of 1 part rice vinegar to 3 parts soy sauce (not for yin people). If your body is very hot and uncomfortable or you feel tired and exhausted, this recipe will make you feel cool and comfortable very quickly.

You can also serve this cut into ½″ cubes with watermelon balls, cantaloupe or other melon balls, fresh strawberries, or any fruit in season. Mixture should be ⅔ kanten cubes and ⅓ fruit, or add 1 Tbsp. applesauce or raisin syrup (see #233). You can also serve kanten as a salad with boiled green peas, red beans, or azuki beans.

223. Cantaloupe Strawberry Kanten

1 cantaloupe
3 small boxes strawberries
6 cups water
2 cups apple juice or apple cider
5 bars kanten
Mint tea (optional)

Make cantaloupe into balls and reserve juice to add to kanten. Add water to juices. Break kanten into pieces and soak for 20 minutes in this liquid. Bring mixture to a boil and simmer for 20-30 minutes. Pour through a strainer. Partially chill, add cantaloupe balls and strawberries. Refrigerate and chill until completely firm. When using mint tea, add the mint leaves to the water and juice mixture and cook together. Then strain out the mint leaves, add the kanten and proceed as above.

224. Dessert Kanten or Cake Frosting

2 cups oat milk
2 cups apple cider
2 tsp. lemon rind, grated
2 tsp. lemon juice
¼ cup kuzu, arrowroot, or
    1½ bars kanten

Oat milk: Pressure cook 1 cup oat groats in 5 cups water for 45 minutes. Reduce pressure to normal, uncover, strain and reserve cooked groats to use in baking or in casseroles, etc. Oat milk is good to use in place of milk in baking or in soups, sauces, etc.

Blend ingredients together. Place in a saucepan and bring to a boil. When using kanten, follow usual directions for making kanten gelatin (see #222). When using kuzu or arrowroot, be sure to reserve some of the uncooked blended liquid mixture with which to dissolve the kuzu/arrowroot before adding it to the heated mixture. If you dissolve the kuzu/arrowroot in water, this dilutes the flavor of the mixture very much and it does not come out as well. For variety, slice and roast ½ cup of almonds and simmer them with the cooking mixture to add the natural almond flavor, or add a piece of vanilla bean that has been split open and simmer it with the mixture for 15-20 minutes. Vary the texture of the mixture by letting it set until almost completely firm. Then beat with an egg beater or electric beater and re-chill in the refrigerator. This makes an airy, light-textured mixture. This makes a good frosting that can be spread over a cake or served as an individual dessert by itself. Resembles a lemon meringue filling.

225. Party Cake

1 cup fermented plum mash
1¾ cups whole wheat pastry flour
1¾ cups unbleached white flour or
    blend of flours
1 tsp. salt
1 tsp. cinnamon
½ cup chopped, cooked raisins
1 cup roasted, chopped walnuts
½ cup raisin water (see #233)
1 med. fertile egg, beaten
½ cup corn or safflower oil

Make plum mash from fresh plums that have been cooked, pureed, and fermented for several weeks.

Combine dry ingredients. Blend in oil with fingers. Add plum mash, raisins, raisin water, and egg. Mix together well. Add walnuts last. Cover with damp cloth and let rise for several hours. The fermented fruit acts like a leavening agent, and makes a very light cake. For cake icing see #224.

226. Rice Cream Pie

1 cup brown rice
3 cups apple juice
1 cup raisins
2 Tbsp. tahini
½ cup rolled oats
1 Tbsp. wheat germ
1 egg
½ cup finely chopped nuts
½ tsp. cinnamon
1 tsp. salt
Pie crust (refer to #92)

Pressure cook rice in apple juice. Cook ¾ cup raisins in ¾ cup water for 5 minutes. Add raisin water to rice and set aside raisins. Blend rice, raisin water and tahini in blender. Then fold in the raisins. Cook oats, wheat germ, and ¼ cup raisins in 1½ cups water for 10 minutes. Blend with egg in blender. Add to rice mixture. Add spices.

Crust: Regular pie crust – I use whole wheat flour, sesame oil, salt, and a little orange rind.

Put filling in crust and sprinkle chopped nuts over the top. Bake 35 minutes about 350°. Cool and refrigerate before serving.

227. Lemon Meringue Pie

Filling
3 or 4 Tbsp. arrowroot
4 Tbsp. pastry flour
½ cup cold water
Pinch of salt
½ cup yinnie syrup
1 cup boiling water
2 or 3 egg yolks
2 tsp. corn oil
Rind and juice of 2 lemons,
    at least ⅓ cup juice

Meringue
2 or 3 egg whites
¼ cup yinnie syrup

Pie crust (#92)

Make pie crust, bottom shell only. Prebake at 350° until partially done, but not browned. While crust bakes, mix arrowroot and pastry flour in ½ cup cold water. Add with a pinch of salt and ½ cup yinnie syrup to boiling water, mix well with wisk and cook for 10 minutes over double boiler. Beat egg yolks, stir *rapidly* into mixture in double boiler. Add oil, grated lemon rind and juice. Let crust and filling cool separately while you beat egg whites for meringue. Add ¼ cup yinnie syrup to egg white mixture. When cool, pour lemon mixture into crust, top with meringue, return to oven to brown.

228. Yam Karinto

2 lbs. yams
1 Tbsp. arrowroot
Oil for deep frying
1 Tbsp. salt
⅓ cup yinnie syrup
    with 1 cup water

Wash yams, cut into ¼″ squares or 3″ long matchsticks. Soak in salted water for 1 hour (helps remove excess potassium), then strain off water and leave yams in a shady place until dry. Heat up tempura oil to 350°. Add dry yams – 1 layer thick – and fry until they come to the surface and turn light brown. Drain on towel. Mix yinnie (or malt) syrup and 1 cup water. Bring to a boil and put all the fried yams in the syrup at one time. While still cooking, mix until completely coated with syrup. Then sprinkle 1 Tbsp. arrowroot starch over the yams. Mix well by tossing in the pan until all pieces are separate and coated, then remove from the heat.

229. Sweet Potato Senbei

1 lb. sweet potatoes, ½″ thick
2 Tbsp. whole wheat pastry flour
2 tsp. cinnamon
1 tsp. salt

Remove potato skins. Slice ½″ thick. Soak in salted water for a few hours. Then steam, drain, and mash. Mix mashed potato with flour. Bring it to a boil, add cinnamon, and salt, and stir until it gets thick. Pour into a mold and press down with fingers until 1″ thick. Then let sit in a cool place until top starts getting hard. Then cut into 2″ long by 1″ wide pieces ½″ thick. Then place in a 200° oven and bake until slightly browned (1 hour). These keep about 1 week. The center is soft and creamy and the outside is hard.

230. The Best Simple Donuts

4 parts pastry flour
½ part corn flour
½ part rice flour
¼ tsp. salt for each cup flour
Apple cider
Oil for deep frying

Combine all ingredients to make a moist, bread-like dough. Let sit to rise overnight, or longer, as for bread. Form into donuts and deep fry.

231. Fig Newtons

1 cup dried figs or
    4 cups fresh figs
¼-½ tsp. salt

For dried figs: Soak figs in 2 cups hot water 2-3 hours. Squeeze water out, reserve. Chop figs, return to water, add salt. Simmer 2-3 hours till they become a medium thick paste. Mash with fork.

    For fresh figs: Quarter and put in a saucepan with lid, adding ¼ to ½ tsp. salt. Cook on low heat ½ hour until water comes out. Then cook on medium heat without lid, mashing with fork until a paste is formed.

Dough

1¾ cups unbleached white flour
¾ cup sweet brown rice flour
2 Tbsp. oil
¼ cup oat flakes, roasted in
    1 Tbsp. oil
1 tsp. salt
½ cup water (approximately)

Mix unbleached flour, rice flour, salt, and oil with fork, adding cold water and mixing lightly – dough should be like pie dough – partly sticky and partly crumbly. Pat ⅔ of dough onto an oiled standard size cookie sheet (about 10½ by 15½). Spread warm fig mixture on dough. Sprinkle the rest of the dough on top, filling in spaces with oat flakes. Flatten with rolling pin. Bake at 350° for ½ hour. Cut in bars and serve.

232. Apple Oatmeal Cookies

3 cups whole wheat flour or 2 cups
    whole wheat and 1 cup rye
3 cups oatmeal
1 cup sesame seeds
2 eggs, optional but better
2 or 3 apples, chopped
1-2 cups chopped nuts
1-2 cups raisins (currants, prunes,
    or other dried fruit)
1 cup soba water, or liquid from
    carrots or squash, or apple juice
1 tsp. salt
⅔ cup sesame oil

Simmer chopped apples and raisins (or dried fruit) until apples are medium soft – not mushy. Let stand while preparing batter and chopped nuts. Preheat oven to 350°. Beat oil, liquid, and eggs in large bowl. Then add raisin-apple mixture. Add salt, flour, oatmeal, sesame seeds, and nuts. Mix together and press together with your hands where necessary so the mixture doesn't fall apart. Roll in ½″ balls and flatten out on cookie sheet. Bake approximately 30 minutes. Makes approximately 4½ dozen cookies.

233. Granola Cookies

2 cups unsweetened granola mix
1 cup whole wheat pastry flour
½ cup unbleached white flour or other flour
¾ cup soba water
¾ cup raisin syrup
1 tsp. salt
½ cup roasted sunflower seeds
½ cup cooked raisins or currants (optional)

Combine granola, salt, and flour. Add sunflower seeds. Gradually mix in soba water (leftover from cooking buckwheat noodles) and raisin syrup. Preheat oven to 350°. Bake on preheated, oiled cookie sheet for 30 minutes. Turn cookies over and brown bottom side. Cool and serve.

Note: When placing cookie batter on cookie sheet, spoon batter on sheet, take chopsticks and dot down batter so that cookies are evenly spread in shape. This makes for an attractive appearing cookie that bakes evenly and is very crunchy.

Raisin syrup

⅓ cup raisins
1½ cups water

Bring raisins to a boil and simmer for 20 minutes. Strain and reserve raisins for baking and cooking. Syrup can be used as a sweetener in baking, etc.

234. Fresh Fruit Sherbet

2 cups melon, apple, peach, watermelon, or any kind of fresh fruit juice
⅓ cup yinnie syrup
½ egg white

Bring fruit juice to a boil and add yinnie syrup. Set aside to cool in ice cube trays. Then place in freezer compartment. After 20 minutes, it will begin to freeze. When half frozen, beat the egg white until stiff and mix this with the fruit juice and return to the freezer. After 30 minutes, again take it out and mix with a spoon. Then return to the freezer. About 30 minutes later, again take it out and mix until it is like sherbet. Then you can serve.

235. Lemon Sherbet

1½ cups apple juice or cider
½ tsp. lemon juice
2½ cups water
¼ cup kuzu or arrowroot

Dilute apple juice or cider more than half and half with water until very little apple taste remains and it tastes only slightly sweet. Add lemon juice. Reserve 1 cup of this liquid to dilute kuzu or arrowroot. Boil liquid and simmer 15-20 minutes. Add diluted kuzu and stir until it becomes transparent. Chill in freezer section of refrigerator. Good served with 1 or 2 sliced green grapes per person and 2 or 3 small cantaloupe or other melon balls.

Beverages

236. Umeboshi Beverage

5 salted plums (umeboshi)
2 cups water

Boil water and plums together for 30 minutes, and strain. Keep juice in a glass jar in the refrigerator. Add a teaspoon plum juice to ½ cup cold water, mix and serve. This is very refreshing for hot days – quenches thirst better than lemonade. After cooking plums, remove the seeds, dry, and save in a glass jar. Grind the meat in a suribachi. Add sesame oil or miso to make a delicious salad dressing.

237. Umesho Bancha

¼-½ salted plum
Pinch of fresh grated ginger
½ tsp. soy sauce
⅔ cup boiling bancha tea

In summer, wake up early to enjoy some outdoor work. After hard work, umesho bancha – which is made by mixing the ingredients listed – tastes especially good. It has a bracing effect and is very good for blood circulation and anemia. It also will soothe a stomachache and strengthen the stomach and intestines. In Japan this drink is called furo choju, which means 'never grow old.'

238. Barley Tea (Mugicha)

Handful of mugicha
6 cups water

Mugicha can be purchased already prepared, or it can be made at home. Use only unhulled barley. Dry roast in a skillet over medium flame until dark brown, almost black, or spread grain on a cookie sheet and roast in a slow oven.

Preparation: Bring 6 cups cold water and a handful of mugicha to a boil and cook 5 minutes. Makes a good summer drink when served chilled and has a cooling effect on the body.

Autumn

#66 – Tempura, grated daikon and carrot, tempura sauce. #453 – Amasake Cake. #58 – Scrambled Tofu.
#203 – Daikon and daikon top pickles. #9 – Soba Roll. #284 – Chinese Cabbage Roll.

Grains

239. Chestnut Rice
240. Tendon
241. Walnut Rice
242. Bancha Rice, Pressure Cooked
243. Rice Balls *(Musubi)*
244. Shiso Musubi
245. Whole Oat Groats
246. Buckwheat Groats
247. Thick Buckwheat Cream
248. Millet
249. Millet Kayu

Noodles and Sauces

250. Buckwheat Noodles with Goma Sauce
251. Homemade Buckwheat Noodles
252. Chow Mein Noodles
253. Vegetable Hoto
254. Udon with Azuki
255. Broccoli Shrimp Sauce with Noodles
256. Mock Meat Sauce for Noodles
257. Tahini Soy Sauce
258. Thick Soy Sauce

Casseroles

259. Oat Groats with Brussels Sprouts
260. Barley Cabbage Casserole
261. Parsnip Rice Cream Casserole
262. Ryeberry Casserole with Purple Cabbage Nitsuke
263. Autumn Casserole
264. Polenta Casserole
265. Vegetable Pie
266. Onion Strudel

Vegetables and Seaweeds

267. Celery with Scallions
268. Carrots and Onions Miso
269. Vegetables with Miso
270. Kinpira
271. Boiled Vegetables
272. Watercress
273. Oriental Style Vegetables
274. Dried Daikon *(Sengiri Daikon)*
275. Fu Vegetable Cream
276. Vegetable Rolls
277. Jerusalem Artichokes
278. Sliced Kombu Nitsuke
279. Mekabu Nitsuke

Cooked Salads

280. Broccoli Salad
281. Cauliflower Salad
282. Cauliflower Carrot Salad
283. Watercress Sesame Salad
284. Chinese Cabbage Roll

Stews and Soups

285. Onion Squash Stew
286. Vegetable Stew with Kuzu
287. White Oyster Stew
288. Vegetable Stew with Sesame Rounds
289. Buffalo Stew
290. Oatmeal Potage
291. French Onion Soup
292. Egg Drop Soup
293. Buckwheat Cream Soup
294. Azuki Bean Soup
295. Vegetable Soup Au Polenta
296. Creamed Miso Soup
297. Carp Soup *(Koi Koku)*
298. Kenchin Soup
299. Daikon Bechamel Soup or Sauce
300. Metropolitan Soup

Beans

301. Split Pea Potage
302. Chili Beans
303. Soy Burgers
304. Baked Chick Peas
305. Hummus
306. Homemade Natto
307. Scrambled Natto

Special Holiday Dishes

308. Stuffed Turkey
309. Whole Wheat Bread for Stuffing
310. Turkey Dressing
311. Russian Soup
312. Gefilte Fish (Japanese Style)
313. Glazed Mackerel Nitsuke
314. Prawns with Cauliflower and Onion
315. Shrimp Curry
316. Scallops Gratin
317. Azuki Chestnut Kanten

Fried Foods

318. Buckwheat Croquettes
319. Yam Croquettes
320. Lotus Root Balls
321. Seasoned Tempura
322. Collard Green Tempura with Tofu
323. Burdock Roll
324. Deep Fried Kombu
325. Tofu Raft
326. Split Burdock Logs

Pickles

327. Cabbage Salt Pickles
328. Chinese Cabbage Salt Pickles
329. Fresh Daikon Nuka Pickles
330. Eggplant Mustard Pickles

Breads and Desserts

331. Pressure Cooked Bread
332. Cornmeal Pan Bread
333. Corn Popovers
334. Toren's Cake
335. Loaf Cake
336. Cake Icing
337. Muffin or Cookie Icing
338. Tahini Custard
339. Raised Donuts
340. Carrot Macaroons
341. Ladyfingers
342. Persimmon Pudding
343. Plum Pudding
344. Vanilla Sauce

Autumn Cooking

In October when the weather starts getting cool, you should start drinking less and using a little more salt. In Japan there is a folk saying which goes: 'In autumn the sky is high and clear and horses get fat.' (Ten takaku uma koeru aki.) Food tastes very good in this season because the summer is past, when your stomach is weaker. In autumn the stomach and intestines become very active. This is the time of the new rice harvest. But be careful not to overeat because the new rice tastes so good.

If your body feels cold in autumn and winter, take a two-inch square piece of brown rice mochi in miso soup once a day. Your body will get warmer and it will be easier to pass through the cold winter season. Mu tea can also help clean out toxins and drugs such as LSD, marijuana, etc.

In November the weather starts getting colder. If you decide to make daikon pickles (takuan) for winter, select a dry, sunshiny day to dry them. If your region has a rainy season, you should dry the daikon out before it begins. While drying in the sun, the daikon absorbs the sun's energy and therefore gives you much vitality when you eat it. Takuan pickles are made with rice bran and salt, and are a very important food for macrobiotic people.

String up and hang the leaves of the daikon to dry and make them into pickles too. The leaves contain calcium, iron, and other minerals. They should be eaten at the same time as the roots. These pickles help to increase the intestinal bacteria that take part in digesting your food. This is why they are important for good digestion.

George Ohsawa said simple food like brown rice, gomashio, miso soup, and three-year-old takuan pickles supply complete nutrition. I hope each house makes their own pickles so you can enjoy pickles that have your own individual character and taste in them.

In Japan there are two celebrations of the full moon in September and October. A small table is taken outside onto the veranda and fifteen different kinds of vegetables and fruits are paired on a large tray which is round like the full moon. Fifteen pieces of mochi formed into round shapes are served on another tray. Wild pampas grass is cut and displayed on the right side of the table in a flower vase, and the whole display is illuminated by candlelight.

In September the full moon is called 'bean full moon' because soybeans harvested at this time taste especially good. The freshly-picked beans are boiled in their pods in salted water like string beans. The October full moon is called the 'potato full moon' because albi (satoimo) is harvested at this time. We serve them fresh at this festival. The whole family goes to the veranda before dinner and prays to the moon, giving thanks for the new crop. The autumn sky is very clear and the moon shines brilliantly. Parents and children give thanks together, bathed in this tranquil light. You can imagine the beautiful memory this makes. The moon cannot talk but the Japanese think it is a god who affects the growth of vegetables, so we give thanks to it for giving a bountiful harvest. This time is perhaps the most beautiful because all the summer's activity has come to rest. We pause and look back with thanks over the last summer. The moon is large, and the light seems to spill over its edges, cascading down in the pure twilight air like a waterfall on the living of the earth below.

The next morning we take all the vegetables left over from the previous night's celebration, mix them with mochi, and cook this in a clear soup. This mochi soup is usually eaten at only one other time – on

New Year's day. So this soup is really special. We thank the full moon again for the chance to have this special soup.

When autumn is at its height and the rice has been cut and bundled, and the countryside is covered with the colors of the changing leaves, then we go to the mountains and have picnics. We make imoni, which is cooked albi potato. Each group brings an iron pot, albi, age (deep fried tofu), mushrooms, and miso, and carries these in a hand wagon into the mountains, traveling one or two miles. We select a place where there is a beautiful mountain stream for water to wash the albi and cook with. Then everyone gathers big stones and makes a fireplace. After that they all gather wood, pine needles, and leaves for the fire. When the fire is made and lit, water is brought from the stream and the big iron pot is set to rest on the stones. The albi, age, and mushrooms are cooked together whole for a few hours. The sunny skies and pure mountain air whet your appetite, and the fire gives the simmering soup a smoky flavor that is delicious. The whole group cooks together, eats together, and plays together – enjoying the autumn gold.

Imoni is a good custom. Our lives are so busy every day, but if we forget to enjoy nature, life can become very lonesome. So please make plans to enjoy a picnic on some sunshiny autumn day, and enjoy the changing colors of the leaves. When we see the colors changing, our minds and bodies instinctively prepare for winter. We think about making pickles, storing vegetables, and cleaning house.

It is also nice to be able to see the town where you live from a distance. We can see how nature is so great and beautiful and our lives are so small and insignificant. Sometimes we need to see how our lives fit in with the natural world. Then we can return to our daily routines with a deeper spirit that makes daily life smoother and more peaceful.

Hunting chestnuts and mushrooms is good recreation for autumn. Chestnut trees grow very quickly. After three years, they bear fruit. So someday many friends can enjoy hunting chestnuts.

Every month nature changes, so your menu should change also. Full moon, Thanksgiving, Christmas, New Year's – many beautiful celebrations come with the cold season. If you really enjoy these celebrations it means you have a special quality of spirit that keeps you from ever growing old. It means your mind has space for enjoying. With some people, though their bodies get old, their feelings stay young. To keep your feelings always young, you must have good cooking. So please study how to cook well.

Grains

239. Chestnut Rice

5 cups brown rice
7 cups water
1 lb. fresh chestnuts
1 tsp. salt
5″ strip dashi kombu cut as shown

Soak unhulled chestnuts overnight and take off the dark outer skin and inside papery skin. If they are large, cut them in half.

In a pressure cooker bring 7 cups of water and kombu to a boil. Remove kombu, add washed rice, chestnuts, and salt and gently stir well. Then put the cover on and cook for 20 minutes on a low flame. Then turn the flame up high until pressure comes up. After pressure is up, turn the flame down low and cook for 45 minutes. Shut off flame and when pressure comes down, remove the cover and serve.

240. Tendon

Cooked brown rice (#1, #2)
Tempura

Sauce
½ cup soup stock (#39)
3 Tbsp. soy sauce
1 tsp. ginger juice

Mix sauce ingredients, bring to a boil and keep hot. For making tempura see #66. Dip hot tempura in sauce and decorate each bowl of hot brown rice with three pieces and pour 1 tablespoon sauce over each bowl. Cover each bowl with a rice bowl cover and serve immediately. If you use cold tempura, bring the sauce to a boil, add cold tempura and bring to a boil without cover. Remove tempura, place on hot rice, pour 1 tablespoon of sauce over each bowl, cover each bowl and serve.

241. Walnut Rice

5 cups brown rice
7 cups water
1½ cups walnuts, roasted
⅓ cup soy sauce

Grind lightly roasted walnuts in a suribachi until half ground, add soy sauce and grind again for about 10 minutes until they are just a little lumpy.

Pressure-cook rice as in #1. After rice is cooked, take off cover and spread walnut sauce on top. Replace cover and let sit for 5 minutes. Then mix rice and walnut sauce and serve. The combination is good with green vegetable ohitashi, clear soup, any kind of pickles, or toasted nori.

242. Bancha Rice, Pressure Cooked

5 cups brown rice
7 cups strong bancha tea
½ tsp. salt

After washing rice, mix with bancha tea and cook the same way as for chestnut rice (#239). If you are not using a pressure cooker, add 1 or 2 more cups of water. (See boiled rice recipe #2.)

243. Rice Balls *(Musubi)*

Cooked brown rice
Shio kombu or piece of umeboshi
Nori for covering

Rice balls are good for traveling. Cold rice usually doesn't taste good, but it becomes tasty when made into rice balls.

Sometimes it is difficult for pregnant women to eat rice, but they can usually eat it in the form of rice balls because a rice ball compresses the rice and makes it more yang. They become filled with the *ki,* or life energy, of the person making them.

George Ohsawa used to cure sick people by serving them plain rice balls (without nori). One rice ball was cut into 10 pieces and each piece was chewed 100 to 200 times. This helped sick people recover quickly. When you try to cure sick people, however, you must feel a deep, sincere desire that the sick person get better because this feeling is transmitted to the rice.

Before making rice balls your hands should be clean. If you wash with soap, make sure you completely rinse your hands to avoid soapy-tasting rice balls. Put bancha tea in a bowl, wet your hands in the tea and hold the rice in your left hand. In the center put two to three pieces of shio kombu (#143) or a piece of salt plum for flavor. This keeps the rice from spoiling. Shape rice balls as shown.

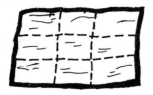

Cover rice balls with nori, gomashio, or sesame shiso (#209), pickled shiso leaves, or shiso leaves pickled in miso. Cut each sheet of nori into nine pieces as shown.

Use two pieces for each rice ball. A whole sheet is too much for one rice ball. Nori is very yin, so too much should not be eaten at one time. If you wet your hands too much with tea, or the rice will get soggy and spoil easily.

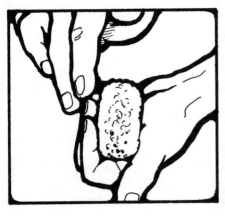

244. Shiso Musubi

Sesame seeds
Shiso leaves
Cooked rice
Water or bancha tea

Chop up the shiso leaves from salted plums, then roast the same amount of sesame seeds and half grind them. Mix together, then stir into cooked rice and make rice balls. (See #243.) To keep rice balls fresh longer, use bancha tea instead of water when you make them. Dip your hands in tea and shape the balls firmly, and lay decoratively on a big plate.

245. Whole Oat Groats

1 cup whole oats
5-6 cups water
½ tsp. salt

After washing the groats, dry roast in a heavy skillet until golden in color, stirring constantly to prevent burning. Pour water over the oats, add salt and bring to a boil. Cover and let simmer over a low heat for several hours or overnight.

For pressure cooking, roast the groats as above, add water and salt, and pressure cook for 1½ hours over a low flame after the pressure comes up. If made the night before, the groats can be left in cooker and reheated in the morning.

246. Buckwheat Groats

1 cup whole buckwheat groats
2 cups boiling water
¼ tsp. salt

If using unroasted buckwheat groats, wash thoroughly and dry roast in a heavy skillet for 10 minutes, or until nut-brown. Or, spread groats on a cookie sheet and roast in a 350° oven for about 15 minutes. Already roasted groats need only to be reroasted for 5 minutes.

Add boiling water and salt to pan and simmer over a low flame for 20 minutes. Serve with nitsuke onions or onion sauce.

247. Thick Buckwheat Cream

1 cup buckwheat flour
2 cups boiling water
¼ tsp. salt

Roast buckwheat flour and salt for a few minutes in a dry pan over a medium-low flame, turning the flour as it needs to be turned. Add boiling water and mix vigorously. Turn off heat and serve immediately. Serve with chopped scallions and soy sauce.

248. Millet

2 cups millet
4 cups boiling water
½ tsp. salt

If pressure cooking millet, roasting beforehand is not necessary. Cook just 20 minutes after pressure comes up. For boiling, add boiling water to roasted millet and cook 30-40 minutes with a tight cover. Serve with nitsuke vegetables or onion-tahini sauce.

249. Millet Kayu

1½ cups millet, washed and
    strained
6 cups water
1 tsp. salt

Put all the ingredients in a pressure cooker, bring to pressure and cook for 5 minutes. Remove from the stove, let it sit for 10 minutes. After 10 minutes use cold water to bring down the remaining pressure, and serve immediately.

Noodles

250. Buckwheat Noodles with Goma Sauce

8oz. buckwheat noodles (see #9)
3 cups soup stock (#39 or #40)
2 heaping Tbsp. sesame butter
5 Tbsp. soy sauce
1 bunch scallions, sarashinegi (#205)
2 sheets nori, roasted and crushed

Mix the sesame butter with 1 cup of soup stock, add 2 Tbsp. soy sauce. If the noodles are cold, put them into hot water to warm them and place in serving bowls. Bring the soup stock to a boil, add 3 Tbsp. soy sauce. Over the noodles pour some sesame butter sauce, then the soup stock, then nori and scallions sarashinegi; or, the sesame sauce, nori, and scallions sarashinegi can be put on the table and the individual can serve himself according to his taste.

251. Homemade Buckwheat Noodles

3 cups buckwheat flour
²/₃ cups boiling water
1 tsp. salt

Mix all ingredients and knead over and over until smooth and shiny. Roll out to about one-tenth of an inch in thickness. Roll up and slice as thinly as possible. Drop into boiling water until done. Drain and separate by pouring cold water over them and draining in a colander. To serve later, place cold buckwheat noodles in a strainer and dip in boiling water for a few minutes.

    Serve with the following condiments: ½ cup sliced scallions; ½ cup grated daikon; 2 sheets nori, roasted and crumbled; and a sprinkle of soy sauce to taste.

252. Chow Mein Noodles

8oz. whole wheat spaghetti,
  broken into small pieces
10 cups water
2 tsp. salt
Oil for deep frying

Bring water and salt to a boil, add noodles, cover, bring to a boil, drain, and wash in cold water. Dry in strainer for 3-4 hours.

Heat deep frying oil and sprinkle one handful of noodles into the hot oil, and deep fry until crispy. When you deep fry noodles, the watery noodles make the oil splatter so use a pan with tall sides and 1½″ oil. Serve prawns with cauliflower and onions (#314) over the fried noodles or with Chinese vegetables supreme (#125).

253. Vegetable Hoto

10 pieces of winter squash,
  1″ square
1 onion, minced
⅓ cup seitan
3 tsp. oil
2 Tbsp. arrowroot flour
1 tsp. salt
2-3 Tbsp. soy sauce
3½ cups soup stock (#39 or #40)
  mixed with 3½ cups water
1 bunch chopped scallions

Noodles
3 cups whole wheat flour
¾ cup boiling water
½ tsp. salt

For noodles: Add enough water to make the dough a little stiffer than earlobe consistency. Roll out to ⅛″ thickness and cut into ⅓″ strips. Boil as in #251. You can also use whole wheat spaghetti.

Saute onion in 1 tsp. oil and add squash. Saute a few minutes. Add salt and soup stock and cook until half done. Add noodles and mix. Cook on medium flame for 10 minutes.

Dust seitan with arrowroot and let sit 5 minutes. Heat a fry pan with 2 tsp. oil and quick-fry seitan until arrowroot becomes transparent. Clean fry pan with ½ cup boiling water and add this to the cooking pot. Place seitan on top of noodles, cover and cook until noodles are tender. Add scallions and season with soy sauce. Cook a few more minutes. Add a little boiling water if necessary. Serve hot.

If there are leftovers, they are good for noodle burgers or croquettes.

254. Udon with Azuki

1 lb. udon noodles
½ cup azuki
1½ cups water
1¾ tsp. salt
1 bunch scallions, chopped
1 tsp. oil
2½ tsp. soy sauce

Cook the azuki beans the same as in #390 (without kombu). Open pot and add ½ tsp. salt. Reserve. Saute scallions in oil over high flame, stirring constantly. Lower flame and add ¼ tsp. salt and soy sauce. Cook for 5 minutes. Reserve. Cook udon with 1 tsp. salt. Drain and mix all ingredients together in a pot. Serve warm in winter, or in the summer put in a square pan and refrigerate. Cut into squares to serve.

255. Broccoli Shrimp Sauce with Noodles

1 onion, sliced thinly
½ cup mushrooms, sliced
3 stalks broccoli, ¼″ sliced,
   top flowerettes
1 carrot, matchsticks
½ lb. shrimp
1 cup bean sprouts
½ cup arrowroot
4oz. whole wheat noodles
Soy sauce

Cook and drain noodles. They should not be overcooked.
   Saute onion until transparent, then add sliced mushrooms. Add broccoli to onions and saute, then add water to cover, bring to a boil, cover and simmer for ½ hour or until vegetables are done. Add shrimp and bean sprouts and more water to the vegetables if necessary. Dilute arrowroot in 1 cup of cold water and add to vegetables. Bring to a boil and simmer until mixture thickens. Add more arrowroot if necessary. The mixture should be quite thick. Add soy sauce to taste. The noodles and sauce can be served separately or the sauce can be poured over a bed of noodles.
   Variations: Brussels sprouts or cauliflower can be substituted for broccoli.

256. Mock Meat Sauce for Noodles

2 onions, finely chopped
1 Tbsp. oil
¼ cup bonita flakes or 1½ tsp.
   ground dried fish
½ cup water
3 Tbsp. miso

Saute onions until transparent, add water and cook for 20 minutes. Add miso and boil until the miso has a fragrant smell. Stir constantly. Add fish and cook for 2 or 3 minutes. Mix the sauce with cooked white udon noodles (or whatever kind you wish to use) thoroughly and cook over a low flame for about ten minutes.

257. Tahini Soy Sauce

2 Tbsp. tahini
2 Tbsp. soy sauce
2 Tbsp. water

Place all ingredients together in a pan and cook, stirring constantly until they have blended and have the consistency of cream. Use over rice, other grains, or vegetables.

258. Thick Soy Sauce

1 tsp. oil
¼ cup soy sauce
½ Tbsp. arrowroot or kuzu
¼ cup water

Warm the oil in a saucepan, add soy sauce and bring to a boil. Add water and continue to boil several minutes. Dissolve arrowroot in small amount of water, add to the sauce and cook until thick, stirring constantly. Serve on grain dishes, etc.

Casseroles

259. Oat Groats with Brussels Sprouts

2 cups oat groats
3 cups water
1 tsp. salt
1 lb. Brussels sprouts, quartered
    through root
Bread crumbs
1 Tbsp. oil
Soy sauce to taste

Wash oat groats. Add them to water and salt and pressure cook for 1 hour. Reduce pressure, saute Brussels sprouts in a skillet and add them to the oat groats. Place in a casserole, season with salt and/or soy sauce to taste. Sprinkle bread crumbs on top and place in preheated 350° oven and bake for 20 minutes, until the top browns evenly.

260. Barley Cabbage Casserole

2 cups barley
3 cups water
½ tsp. salt
1 cabbage
Soy sauce to taste
Bread crumbs

Wash and drain whole barley. Add water and salt and pressure cook 45 minutes. Reduce pressure, uncover and add to this the cabbage which has been cut and cooked nitsuke style (chopped small and sauteed). Mix together, season with salt and soy sauce. Place in casserole, sprinkle bread crumbs on top and bake in preheated 350° oven until golden brown.

261. Parsnip Rice Cream Casserole

Cooked rice cream
Parsnips, sliced diagonally
Oil for sauteing
Salt and/or soy sauce for seasoning
Bread crumbs

Cook rice cream as usual (see #5). Saute parnips until tender. Season with salt and/or soy sauce. In a casserole place a layer of rice cream, next put a layer of parsnips, add another layer of rice cream, a second layer of parsnips. Sprinkle bread crumbs on top, place in a preheated 350° oven and bake 20-30 minutes until golden brown on top.

262. Ryeberry Casserole with Purple Cabbage Nitsuke

2 cups rye berries
3 cups water
½ tsp. salt

Purple cabbage nitsuke
1 purple cabbage, quartered and
    cut fine
4 med. onions, crescents
1-2 salt plum meats (according to
    taste and salt quantity desired)
1-2 Tbsp. oil

Wash rye berries until they drain clear. Add water and salt and pressure cook 45 minutes. Reduce pressure to normal. Uncover and add to this: nitsuke of purple cabbage, onion, and umeboshi plum meat. Simmer together for 20-30 minutes before serving. A delicious combination that makes a nice change from ordinary combinations of grains and vegetables. For variation, crack the rye berries coarsely in a flour mill, wash, drain, and cook as above.

To make purple cabbage nitsuke, saute onions until clear and add cabbage. Simmer until cabbage is well cooked. Season with salt plum meat.

263. Autumn Casserole

1²/₃ cups or 1 lb. azuki beans
3 small brown potatoes
1 cup whole rye
6 cups water
Salt and soy sauce

Wash azuki beans and put in bottom of pressure cooker. Wash, but do not peel, potatoes and cut into quarters. Place on top of the beans. Wash rye, put in cheesecloth and place on top of potatoes. Add water, salt, and soy sauce. Bring to pressure, then lower heat. Cook overnight using an asbestos pad between the flame and pot. Remove cheesecloth, slowly mix and serve in a covered casserole dish.

264. Polenta Casserole

2 cups cornmeal
4½ cups boiling water
½ tsp. salt
3 onions, large diced
1 handful of small mushrooms
2 cups water
1 Tbsp. oil
¼ tsp. salt
1 Tbsp. soy sauce
1-2 Tbsp. arrowroot flour

Cook cornmeal in boiling water with ½ tsp. salt for ½ hour, stirring constantly. Pour onto two plates, spread out and cool until firm.

Saute onions and simmer in water 20 minutes. Thicken sauce with diluted arrowroot and season with soy sauce and ¼ tsp. salt. Simmer a few minutes longer. Place polenta in two layers in casserole with sauce in between and then on top. Sprinkle with mushrooms and bake in covered casserole at 350° for ½ hour.

265. Vegetable Pie

2 cups whole wheat pastry flour
2 med. onions, crescents
1 carrot, matchsticks
1 small whole cabbage,
    1″ matchsticks
1 egg
2 Tbsp. oil
2 tsp. salt

Mix flour and 1 tsp. salt with enough water for pie dough. Add 1 Tbsp. oil. Roll out dough and place in pie pan. Make fluted edge on crust. Bake crust 20 minutes. Saute onions, carrots, and cabbage and add 1 tsp. salt, then cool. Add beaten egg to vegetables. Fill pie and bake a short time at 350° – approximately 10 minutes, until egg changes color.

This is an open-faced pie – no top crust.

266. Onion Strudel

Pie dough
Onions
Tahini or almond butter
Bread crumbs or matzoh meal

Make onion butter by sauteing onions for 1½ hours or longer. Make your favorite pie dough, adding 1 egg for each 4 cups of flour before adding water and oil. Roll the dough thin. Spread onion butter on two-thirds. On the remaining one-third spread tahini or almond butter. Sprinkle with matzoh meal or bread crumbs. Make sure to leave 1 inch with tahini only (no crumbs) for sealing the strudel, and roll it. Cut to desired size or bake whole. If you cut them, bake 20 to 30 minutes at 350°. If you leave it whole, you may bake it longer. It will come out crispier on the top side. (One might try turning this over and crisping both sides.)

Try leeks, Belgian endive, cabbage, etc.

Vegetables and Seaweeds

267. Celery with Scallions

1 bunch scallions, chopped
2 stalks celery, sliced finely
½ tsp. salt or less
1 tsp. oil

These vegetables cook in their own liquid. Saute the scallions in a little oil, stirring constantly. In a few minutes add the celery, sauteing 5 minutes more. Add the salt and cook until the liquid is evaporated.

268. Carrots and Onions Miso

3 med. onions, minced
1 carrot, minced
1 Tbsp. oil
2 Tbsp. miso
½ tsp. salt

Saute onions in oil until golden, add carrots and saute briefly. Add ½ cup water and salt and cook about 15 minutes covered. Add miso and continue cooking uncovered over a low flame for another 10 minutes or until much of the liquid has boiled off.

269. Vegetables with Miso

2 onions, cut in 6 sections
4 cabbage leaves, sliced
1 carrot, sliced
1 Tbsp. oil
2 Tbsp. miso
½ tsp. salt

Saute onions, then cabbage, then carrot. Add 1½ cups water and salt and cook 10 minutes. Add miso and cook another 10-15 minutes. In this recipe there is more liquid remaining than in the previous recipe (#268); this sauce can be poured over rice.

270. Kinpira

3 fresh young burdock, matchsticks
1 med. carrot, matchsticks
1 Tbsp. sesame oil
2 Tbsp. soy sauce
¼ hot pepper, seeds removed and
  sliced in strips (optional)

Heat oil and saute burdock in a covered pan, stirring occasionally. Ten minutes later add the carrot and saute well. Add the red pepper and pour ½ cup water around the edge of the pan. When the vegetables are about half done, season with soy sauce. Fresh young burdock should be stirred gently in order to keep its shape because it cooks fast. When the vegetables are tender, remove the cover and cook off the excess water. Add soy sauce to taste.

Hot pepper stimulates your appetite. If you have hemorrhoids, omit the hot peppers.

271. Boiled Vegetables

Onion
Carrot
Daikon, turnip, or rutabaga
Broccoli
Cauliflower
Scallions
Tofu
Dried mushrooms
Kombu
Fu or bean threads or soba

Make a soup stock by boiling a few dried mushrooms and a piece of kombu in salted water. Take half of the tofu and cut into pieces and deep fry. Soak fu and cut into diagonal strips. If using bean threads, cook according to directions on package. Reserve liquid. Cook soba also if used, but discard liquid.

Now prepare the vegetables by washing and cutting into bite-size chunks, about 1 inch. There should be equal amounts of all ingredients including tofu, plain and fried, and mushrooms.

In a large heavy pot, saute the onions until transparent. Push to one side, add daikon and saute also. Cover with soup stock and bring to a boil. Add carrots. Add more stock and bring to a boil. Continue in this manner until all ingredients are added. Be careful when adding a vegetable so that each vegetable is not mixed with any other (keep onion together, carrots together, daikon together, etc.). Cut up the mushrooms and add them.

This is the order of adding ingredients: onions, daikon, carrots, cauliflower, broccoli, plain tofu, fried tofu, mushrooms, fu (or noodles), scallions. When everything is in, add other reserved liquid and boil for 3 minutes. Add soy sauce to taste.

Serve with rice and it is a meal in itself.

For extra special occasions a few dried shrimp can be added to the soup stock and included in the dish. Alternatively, a beaten egg can be carefully stirred in at the end and cooked just until it solidifies.

272. Watercress

1 bunch watercress, finely chopped
1 tsp. oil
½ tsp. salt or less

This vegetable cooks in its own juice. Saute the vegetable in a little oil, stirring constantly until done. Add salt in the middle of the cooking. Soy sauce may also be added to taste, at the end of cooking.

273. Oriental Style Vegetables

4″ piece of daikon, flat rectangles
1 carrot, flat rectangles
2″ lotus root, ¼″ thin rounds
1 burdock, flat rectangles
1 konnyaku, flat rectangles (optional)
6 Chinese cabbage leaves,
 ½″ diagonals
2 cups water
1 tsp. salt
2 Tbsp. soy sauce
2 Tbsp. kuzu with 5 Tbsp. water

Saute burdock in 1 Tbsp. oil, adding konnyaku, daikon, Chinese cabbage, carrot, and lotus root. Then add 2 cups water and bring to a boil. When half tender add 1 tsp. salt, 2 Tbsp. soy sauce and add kuzu to vegetables to thicken. Place in a deep bowl or deep individual dishes. Can be served with parsley on top.

274. Dried Daikon *(Sengiri Daikon)*

½ cup dried radish, soaked and
    cut 1″ lengths
2 tsp. oil
½ tsp. salt
2 tsp. soy sauce

Cover radish with water and soak 20 minutes. Squeeze out water, reserving the liquid for use later. Cut and saute radish in 2 tsp. oil over medium heat for 10 minutes. Cover with water from soaking, bring to a boil, add salt, lower flame and cook covered about 30 minutes until tender. Add more water and cook again if necessary until water is almost evaporated. Add soy sauce, uncover after a few minutes, stir and serve as a vegetable.

275. Fu Vegetable Cream

5 onions, quartered vertically
3″ piece of carrot, quarter moons
½ cauliflower, flowerettes
10 small pieces of fu
2 heaping Tbsp. whole wheat
    pastry flour
1 Tbsp. parsley
2 Tbsp. oil
2 tsp. salt
Oil for deep frying

Cook flowerettes in salted boiling water, drain, and reserve water. Deep fry fu pieces (#49). Heat 1 Tbsp. oil, saute onions, carrot, and fried fu and cover with water. Add 1 tsp. salt and boil for 30 minutes. In another pan, heat the remaining tablespoon of oil, toast the flour until it has a nut-like fragrance – do not burn. Cool the flour, add the cauliflower water, bring to a boil and cook until it is thick and has no lumps. Salt to taste, pour the sauce over the sauteed vegetables and cauliflower and mix together, being careful not to break the vegetables or the fu. Taste for salt and soy sauce. Add if necessary.

    Serve this dish in a bowl with minced parsley or minced orange peel as a garnish.

276. Vegetable Rolls

6-8 med. onions, crescents
2 med. zucchini, quartered and
    thinly sliced
4 cups uncooked buckwheat groats
    (toasted)
30 leaves of Swiss chard, cabbage,
    or Chinese cabbage
1 Tbsp. oil
2 tsp. salt
Soy sauce

Steam the leaves until they are soft, but not well cooked. In a pan heat up 1 Tbsp. oil, saute the onions and zucchini and cook until half tender. Add the toasted buckwheat groats and salt. Place this mixture in each leaf. Tie with kampyo or use toothpicks to hold together. Place the rolls on the bottom of a heavy pot. Using water, vegetable stock, or remaining water from the steamed leaves, pour 2-3 inches into the pot. Bring to a boil, simmer slowly for 1-2 hours. Add salt and soy sauce to taste about 30-40 minutes before serving.

277. Jerusalem Artichokes

2 cups Jerusalem artichokes,
    matchsticks
1 tsp. oil
¼ tsp. salt
2 tsp. soy sauce

It belongs to the small sunflower family. Originally it grew in Belgium. The Japanese use it to make alcohol and pickles.

    After washing, slice. Saute in oil. Season with salt and soy sauce. Cook 30 minutes, adding water if necessary. It is very good in rice bran pickles (#203) or miso pickles (see *Calendar Cookbook*, #263).

278. Sliced Kombu Nitsuke

4oz. sliced kombu
5 pieces age, cut in ⅓″ strips
Soy sauce for seasoning

Any Japanese food store has sliced kombu seaweed, but be careful of green kombu, this is dyed. Soak the kombu in water to cover for 20 minutes, then cut in 1½″ pieces. Strain kombu water or set in a bowl and use the top water. Place this water in a pressure cooker, add the sliced kombu, bring to full pressure, reduce flame to low and cook 15 minutes. Remove from stove and allow pressure to return to normal. Remove the cover, add the age, bring to a boil without the cover and cook for a few minutes. Add the soy sauce and cook for 20 minutes more.

279. Mekabu Nitsuke

3.4oz. mekabu, cut into ½″ pieces
1 Tbsp. soy sauce

Mekabu means the part of the wakame seaweed near the root. High in minerals, it is more yang than regular wakame.

Soak the mekabu overnight in 4 cups of water. Filter the soaking water through a cotton cloth, use 1 cup of the soaking water and 2 cups of plain water and pressure cook mekabu for 1 hour. After pressure has come down to normal, add 1 Tbsp. soy sauce and cook until the water has evaporated slightly. Use any leftover mekabu water in nitsuke or noodle sauce or miso soup.

Cooked Salads

280. Broccoli Salad

1 bunch broccoli
1 heaping Tbsp. whole wheat
      pastry flour
3 Tbsp. French dressing (#77)
1 Tbsp. salt

To 5 cups of water, add 1 heaping Tbsp. pastry flour and 1 Tbsp. salt, bring to a boil, add broccoli and boil until tender, but not soft, without cover. Strain, and wash quickly in running water to remove the starch. Set aside to cool, then cut into small pieces, and mix with French dressing.

281. Cauliflower Salad

1 small cauliflower
1 heaping Tbsp. unbleached
  white flour
4 Tbsp. French dressing (see #77)
½ cup mayonnaise (see #75 or #183)
5 cups water

To 5 cups of water add 1 Tbsp. salt and 1 Tbsp. flour and bring the whole cauliflower to a boil. Cook until tender, wash under running water to remove starch, and set aside to cool. Break it up into small flowerettes and mix in French dressing. Serve in a glass salad bowl covered with mayonnaise sauce.

282. Cauliflower Carrot Salad

1 cauliflower
3 carrots
6-8 cups water
½ cup parsley, chopped
Mayonnaise (#75)

Boil water with a pinch of salt and steam cauliflower uncovered by placing whole cauliflower (with leaves) stem down. Bring to a boil again, cover and let bottom cook and top steam until done. Cool, remove leaves, cut the stem from the bottom, and proceed by pulling each flowerette apart, cutting stem when necessary. Boil carrots 20 minutes and cut into rounds. Mix cauliflower, carrot, and parsley gently with mayonnaise.

283. Watercress Sesame Salad

3 bunches watercress
½ cup unhulled sesame seeds
1 Tbsp. soy sauce

Wash watercress, drop into a large pot of boiling salted water and boil 5 minutes with no cover, or until cooked. Squeeze out water and cut into ½″ lengths. Toast sesame seeds and mash well in a suribachi until it becomes like a paste. Add soy sauce to taste. Mix well with watercress and serve.

Variation: Prepare 1 bunch spinach as watercress and boil 2 carrots separately for 20 minutes. Cut carrots into 1½″ rectangles, mix with spinach, and dress as above.

284. Chinese Cabbage Roll

5 large Chinese cabbage leaves
1 bunch spinach
1 sheet nori

Place cabbage leaves in 8 cups boiling salted water with the leafy part up and cook uncovered. When the water returns to a boil, immerse leaves and remove when soft, setting aside in a strainer to cool. Prepare spinach likewise in the same water.

Squeeze cabbage leaves and spinach separately on a sushi mat. Then layer cabbage leaves (alternate end to tip) on sushi mat, topping with spinach. Leave a 1″ border around spinach. Place a sheet of nori on top and roll the mat, squeezing out excess water. Cut the roll into 1″ pieces.

Serve plain with a little soy sauce or add to top of nabemono stews (see #370).

Soups and Stews

285. Onion Squash Stew

2 small onions, quartered
Squash (2 times amount of onions), cut in 1″ squares
5 cups soup stock (see below or use #39 or #40)
3 heaping Tbsp. whole wheat pastry or unbleached white flour
1 cup water
½ tsp. salt
1 tsp. oil

Soup stock
1 bone (leftover organic chicken, or fish)
7 cups water
1 tsp. salt
¼ tsp. pepper

Boil soup stock over a low flame 1½ to 2 hours until reduced to 5 cups. Saute onions and squash with ½ tsp. salt in a little oil. Add stock and salt. Cook until tender. Toast flour in a dry pan, cool and add water. Simmer 15 minutes and add to the vegetables. Simmer awhile longer.

286. Vegetable Stew with Kuzu

3 med. onions, 6 crescents
½ lb. string beans, cut on diagonal
5 age, cut in 3 pieces
1 small carrot, cut into diagonal slices
½ cup fresh mushrooms, whole
1 stalk celery, ½″ rounds
1 lb. tofu, cut in 1″ cubes
3″ piece dashi kombu cut part way through every inch

1 tsp. minced ginger
½ tsp. salt
2-3 Tbsp. soy sauce
2 Tbsp. kuzu or arrowroot
3 cups water
Oil for deep frying

Deep fry onions and carrots. Cook string beans in boiling salted water and reserve.

Place kombu in the bottom of a pan. Add ginger, celery, mushrooms, carrot, onions, tofu, age. Add water and salt and cook 10 minutes. Add soy sauce and cook until tender. Dilute kuzu, add and cook a few minutes. Add soy sauce to taste. Add string beans at the end.

287. White Oyster Stew

½ lb. oysters
2 onions, ⅓″ diced
1 carrot, ¼″ diced
2 Tbsp. sake
4 Tbsp. whole wheat pastry flour
4 cups soup stock (#39)
1 Tbsp. minced parsley
10 mushrooms, thinly sliced
4 Tbsp. sesame oil
2-3 tsp. salt

Wash oysters in salted water and drain. Heat up 1 Tbsp. sesame oil, add oysters and saute until they shrink. Add 1 more Tbsp. oil to the side of the pan. Add onions, mushrooms, carrots and saute. Add 1 tsp. salt, 2 cups of soup stock and bring to a boil over high flame. Heat up frying pan, add 2 Tbsp. oil, add pastry flour, roast until a fragrant smell is given off and set aside to cool. Add 2 cups soup stock and sake, mix well and place in a cooking pan with oysters. Bring to a boil over medium flame. Add 1 or 2 teaspoons more salt and cook for 20-30 minutes more over medium flame. Serve immediately with minced parsley.

288. Vegetable Stew with Sesame Rounds

4 onions, 8 crescents
2 carrots, half moons
½ cauliflower
½ cup fresh mushrooms, cut in half
½ cup whole wheat pastry flour
1 heaping Tbsp. minced parsley
1½ Tbsp. oil
2-3 tsp. salt

Dough
½ cup sesame seeds
½ cup whole wheat flour
½ tsp. salt
Oil for deep frying

Wash and lightly roast sesame seeds. Mix with whole wheat flour, ½ tsp. salt and knead until dough is as soft as your earlobe. Divide into eight equal pieces, make round shapes and deep fry.

Heat 1 Tbsp. oil in a fry pan, saute onions until transparent, add mushrooms and carrots and saute for a few more minutes. Add water, cover vegetables, bring to a boil, add 1 tsp. salt and cook until tender.

Heat up ½ Tbsp. oil in another pan, roast whole wheat pastry flour until a fragrant smell is given off and set aside to cool. Mix with 1½ cups of water. Add this mixture to the cooked vegetables, bring to a boil, add 1 or 2 more teaspoons of salt and add fried rounds. Cook for 20 minutes more with cover. Boil flowerettes in salted water, add to stew, bring to a boil and serve immediately with a garnish of parsley.

If you want more flavor, add two or three pieces of bay leaf to the vegetables when cooking.

289. Buffalo Stew

1 cup whole dry corn
1 cup beans
1½ cups assorted vegetables
    (onions and carrots, etc.)
Sage
2 Tbsp. seitan
2 Tbsp. soy sauce
4″ piece kombu

Soak the corn for 24 hours, then put it in a heavy pot with 3 cups of water and a piece of kombu. Bring to a boil, place an asbestos pad under pot and simmer very low overnight.

Soak the beans (pinto, navy, kidney – whatever kind you choose) overnight and cook by themselves in 2½ cups water until tender but firm.

Vegetables can vary – any root vegetable (carrots, parsnips, onions, burdock), also green pepper, winter squash – anything that will hold up fairly well. Cut these into small chunks. They can be sauteed first or added to the corn raw and simmered.

At this point combine corn, beans, vegetables, seitan and enough water to make a thick stew and simmer until tender and a nice gravy is made – season with soy sauce and sage and simmer a short while more.

About 1 cup dry corn with proportionate amounts of other ingredients will serve 4-6. This is a very hearty stew.

290. Oatmeal Potage

2 cups rolled oats
10 cups water
1 tsp. salt
1 tsp. oil

Saute oats slowly in the oil, stirring constantly. Cool, add water and salt and cook over low flame until desired consistency. Stir occasionally. Sprinkle with minced parsley, watercress or some other green. You can make this potage with wheat, grain milk, or buckwheat flour.

291. French Onion Soup

3 onions, thin crescents
4 cups soup stock (see below)
1 tsp. oil
Salt to taste
Soy sauce to taste

Saute the onions in oil. Add the soup stock and cook until done. Season with soy sauce and salt and simmer 5 minutes longer. Serve over dried bread or with croutons.

Soup stock

3″ piece kombu
1 Tbsp. bonita flakes
6 cups water
½ tsp. salt
1 Tbsp. soy sauce

Bring 3 cups of water and kombu to a boil, strain and reserve kombu. Add 3 more cups of cold water, add kombu, bring to another boil and cook for 30 minutes. Add bonita flakes, bring to a boil and cook for 1 minute. Remove from the flame – allow bonita flakes to settle, strain bonita and kombu, add salt and soy sauce.

292. Egg Drop Soup

1 onion, chopped
1 Tbsp. oil
1½ tsp. salt
3 Tbsp. soy sauce
9 cups water
¼ cup chirimen iriko
    (small dried fish)
½ bunch raw scallions, chopped
1 beaten egg, white only

Saute onion in oil, add the fish, saute it well, add water and cook for 20 minutes. Add salt. Bring to a boil and stir in the egg until it is cooked. It will take a few minutes for the egg to harden. Add soy sauce. Serve with chopped raw scallions.

293. Buckwheat Cream Soup

1 cup buckwheat flour
2 tsp. oil
7 cups water
1 tsp. salt
5 scallions, sarashinegi (#205)
Nori, roasted and crushed

Saute flour in oil a few minutes and let cool. Add water and boil until thickened. Add salt and cook covered for 20 minutes. Pour into soup bowls and serve with sarashinegi (#205) and roasted nori. You may also saute onions and add to the cream while it is cooking.

294. Azuki Bean Soup

1 cup azuki beans, soaked with
    2″ × 2″ piece kombu in 3
    cups water for 4 hours
1 handful string beans, cut ¾″
2 onions, diced
4 cups water
1 tsp. salt

Use equal amounts of azuki beans, string beans, and onions. Saute onions and string beans lightly in pressure cooker. Add azuki beans, kombu, and cooking water. Bring pressure up and cook for about 45 minutes. Let pressure come down, add salt and 4 cups water and cook covered for 20 minutes. If necessary, add soy sauce to taste.

295. Vegetable Soup Au Polenta

2 white turnips, cut large pieces
2 onions, quartered
1 carrot, diagonals
1 tsp. oil
7 cups water
1½ tsp. salt
1 cup cornmeal (prepared as
    bechamel #187)
1 Tbsp. parsley, minced
Soy sauce to taste

Saute onions, turnips, and carrots in 1 tsp. oil. Add water and boil about 30 minutes until tender. Prepare cornmeal as bechamel sauce (see #187), add to vegetables and boil slowly over a low flame. Season with salt. Cook 45 minutes. Add soy sauce and simmer a few minutes longer. Serve with parsley as a garnish.

Variation: Millet flour or corn flour can be used for thickening.

296. Creamed Miso Soup

5 small whole onions
1 small carrot, ½″ diagonals
½ tsp. salt
1 cup whole wheat pastry flour
3 tsp. oil
6 cups water
2 Tbsp. miso

Saute onions in a pressure cooker in 1 tsp. oil until slightly transparent, add carrots, 2 cups of water, ½ tsp. salt, and cover. Cook under pressure for 5 minutes. Or, cook in a saucepan until done, but firm. Saute the flour in 2 tsp. oil until it is slightly darker in color and has a nut-like fragrance, stirring constantly. When done, let it cool. Make a paste of the flour, gradually adding in 4 cups of water altogether. Add this paste to the vegetables, and bring it to a boil. After the soup thickens, cook for 10 minutes. Add miso and cook for an additional 5 minutes. Simmer slowly.

297. Carp Soup (Koi Koku)

1 carp
Burdock root, 3 times as much
    as carp, shaved
3 heaping Tbsp. miso
1 Tbsp. oil
Bancha tea leaves

Roast bancha tea leaves which have been boiled already for tea, then tie into a bag or cheesecloth. Remove bitter part of carp (the gall bladder) carefully so as not to burst it. Do not remove scales. Cut up fish into ½″ slices. Saute burdock until smell is gone. Add slices of carp. Put used tea leaves on top of carp. Add enough water to cover. Simmer 3 hours or until bones are soft. Take out tea leaves. Thin miso with a little water and pour over carp. Simmer for an additional hour. (If you use a pressure cooker, cook for 2 hours and let pressure go down. Test to see if bones are soft. If not, continue cooking with pressure until done. Then add miso and proceed as above.) Eat everything in this dish, including the bones. Add grated ginger to taste when serving.

298. Kenchin Soup

1 burdock root, shaved
7″ piece of daikon, flat rectangles –
   1½″ long, ½″ wide, ⅛″ thick
1 med. carrot, quarter moons
2 med. shiitake mushrooms, or
   5 fresh mushrooms, matchsticks
1 bunch scallions, 1½″ rounds
1 lb. tofu, strained and diced ½″
5 albi or taro, cut bite-size
1 Tbsp. sesame oil
5 cups water or stock (#39 or #40)
3 Tbsp. soy sauce
2 tsp. salt

Sprinkle cut taro with 1 tsp. salt.

   Heat sesame oil and saute in this order: burdock, shiitake, daikon, albi, and carrot. Add tofu, saute, and add soup stock or water. Boil over medium flame, add 1 tsp. salt and soy sauce. Simmer 30 minutes or until vegetables are tender. Add scallion, bring to boil once more, and serve. This soup needs to be sauteed well for taste.

299. Daikon Bechamel Soup or Sauce

1 large daikon (shave ¼″ thick
   and 1½″ long)
¼ cup carrots, minced
½ cup onions, minced
1 tsp. salt
1 tsp. oil

Saute onions in the oil. Add carrots, then add daikon. Add salt and 1 cup of water and cook until tender. Remove vegetables and cover with onion bechamel sauce.

Onion bechamel sauce

¼ cup onions, minced
½ tsp. salt
1 cup whole wheat flour
1 Tbsp. oil
2 Tbsp. white wine or sake

Saute onions in oil and add 1 cup whole wheat flour roasted with 1 tsp. oil. Cool and add 2 cups of water, including the vegetable cooking water. Bring to a boil and slowly add white wine or sake. Cream together well.

   Add ½ tsp. salt, bring to a boil and cook on low flame for 20 minutes.

300. Metropolitan Soup

⅓ cup barley
⅔ cup red beans or pinto beans
2 med. onions, crescents
1 med. carrot, ⅓″ diced
½ stalk celery, ¼″ diced
1 Tbsp. oil
2 tsp. salt
1 tsp. soy sauce

Soak barley in ⅔ cup water overnight. Pressure cook for 15 minutes. Soak beans in two times water overnight and pressure cook for 40 minutes. Saute onions until transparent, add carrot and celery and water just to cover and cook for 20 minutes. Add salt, cooked barley and beans, and cook for another 30 minutes. Season with soy sauce to taste. If you use red beans, this soup turns pink and is really beautiful.

Beans

301. Split Pea Potage

3 cups split peas
7 cups water
3 small onions, minced
2 celery stalks, minced
1 Tbsp. oil
1 Tbsp. salt
2 bay leaves

Soak peas 1 hour. Saute onions until transparent. Add celery. Strain peas and reserve water. Place peas on top of vegetables without stirring. Add soaking water around the edge of the pan. Do not stir. Bring to a boil, add bay leaves, and cook 30 minutes or until soft. After soft, add salt and cook 20 minutes until creamy. Remove bay leaves and slowly mix to serve. Top with crushed corn chips for color and taste.

302. Chili Beans

3 cups pinto beans, soaked overnight
  or at least 5 hours in 8 cups water
3″ × 3″ piece of kombu, wiped with
  a damp kitchen towel
2 small onions, crescents
1 Tbsp. sesame oil
¼ tsp. chili powder
¼ tsp. cayenne
1 Tbsp. salt

Pressure cook beans for 45 minutes with the kombu. Saute onions. When transparent, add all the beans. Bring to a boil, covered, and sprinkle salt on top. Turn down flame and cook 30 minutes. Add spices and cook 10 more minutes. Mix, half mash, and serve.

Good with tortillas (#110) or hot cornmeal pan bread (#332).

303. Soy Burgers

2 cups soybeans
1 cup minced onion
1 cup minced carrot
1 Tbsp. sesame oil
1 tsp. salt
⅓-¼ cup buckwheat flour
Oil for deep-frying (or pan-frying)
½ cup chopped scallions

Boil soybeans in 4 cups water for 2 hours or until tender, adding more water if necessary. Strain, then blend until smooth. Should equal 4 cups.

Saute onion in a covered pot. Add carrot and salt. After the vegetables are soft, evenly mix in the blended soybeans very well. Remove to a bowl, add scallions, and allow to cool. Add flour and mix well.

Shape into burgers. Either deep- or pan-fry. Season with soy sauce or ginger-soy sauce, or grated ginger. Serve on whole wheat hamburger buns with your favorite ingredients.

304. Baked Chick Peas

1 cup chick peas
2 minced onions
1 tsp. salt
2 cups water

Cook chick peas by the desired method. Add onions with salt and cook 20 minutes. Place in a small casserole. Reserve the liquid from cooking chick peas to use in bechamel sauce.

Bechamel sauce

1 cup whole wheat pastry flour
1-2 Tbsp. oil
4-5 cups water
1 tsp. salt

Heat oil in a saucepan. Add flour and roast until nut-like fragrance is obtained. Cool, return to stove and add liquid gradually, stirring continuously. Add salt and season with soy sauce if desired. Pour over chick peas and bake in a 350° oven for 30 minutes.

305. Hummus

2 cups cooked chick peas
1 tsp. sesame oil
3 small cloves of garlic, grated
1 heaping Tbsp. sesame butter
1 tsp. salt
1-2 tsp. lemon juice

Puree or blend the cooked chick peas with some water reserved from their cooking. Heat the oil and saute the garlic until it is brown in color. Add the blended chick peas and the salt. Bring this to a boil and cook on a low flame for 20 minutes.

Dilute the sesame butter with some liquid from the cooking chick peas and add this to the chick peas. Bring this to a boil once more. Let cool, add lemon juice, mix well and serve.

Natto – Natto is a fermented soybean product not well known in America; it has been used by many Japanese families for centuries. It has an unusual taste which is not easy for some modern people to appreciate. But just as enemies can become your best friends, natto can grow on you if you are persistent. It has a faint resemblance to Roquefort cheese, perhaps because both are high in protein and both are the result of fermentation. It serves as an excellent source of protein for non-meat-eating people. It is available in Japanese markets if you cannot find the time to make your own.

Soybeans are difficult to digest. However, by allowing bacteria to digest them for us, which occurs in the fermentation process of making miso, soy sauce, and natto, they become a very nutritious, easily assimilable food. Natto is the simplest soybean preparation. It is more yang than tofu but more yin than miso or soy sauce, because the yang factors of time and salt are not applied.

It will keep in the refrigerator, and can be served at any time with no preparation; thus it is good to have around for unexpected attacks of hunger or hungry guests.

306. Homemade Natto

3 cups soybeans
10 cups water
6 one-pint paper containers

Wash mature dry soybeans, soak overnight in 10 cups water.

Drain and discard water. In a deep pot (not a pressure cooker) add beans and water to cover by 1½″. Bring to a boil on medium flame and half-cover. Turn to low flame and cook about 30 minutes. When the foam reduces, cover and simmer 4-5 hours, until beans are tender. Crush one bean between your thumb and little finger or fourth finger to check for tenderness. Do not stir or the beans will break; broken beans reduce the fermentation.

Strain liquid and reserve for use in clear or miso soup. Place 1 cup of the hot soybeans in each white cardboard container (such as small paper take-out boxes), fold in the covers, and place all the filled containers in a large double paper bag. Close up the bag, tie it with string, and place in the oven. The oven should be around 98°-104° or the heat of the pilot light only; do not turn the oven any higher. Note: Do not use your oven for any other purpose while making natto. Leave the soybeans in the oven for 3 nights. Remove after the third night – they should be ready. (If you cook a larger quantity of beans, it is necessary to stack the containers on top of each other. After the second night, switch the bottom to the top and vice versa. Let them stay another full day.)

Open the container covers and let natto cool. Depending on your oven and the season, natto may over-ferment. If there is an ammonia smell, remove all the natto from the containers and spread out for half a day in a cool place. The smell will evaporate and the good smell will return.

The finished product has a dark tan color, and the beans retain their shape but are covered by a stringy substance. Natto can be kept frozen for one or two months, and refrigerated about a week. To serve, try 'scrambled natto,' recipe #307.

307. Scrambled Natto

1 container of natto (as #306)
⅛ tsp. salt
1 Tbsp. soy sauce
2 heaping Tbsp. sliced scallion or
　　pickled daikon leaves

Mix natto, salt, and soy sauce. Then blend the mixture well. Add chopped scallion or pickled daikon leaves and scramble again. Serve with rice. To eat, put 1 teaspoonful of scrambled natto on brown rice and eat together.

Natto is a good source of protein. You can stop a craving for animal foods by eating scrambled natto.

Special Holiday Dishes

308. Stuffed Turkey

12-15 lb. turkey
½ lemon
3 Tbsp. salt

Marinade sauce
⅓ cup soy sauce
⅔ cup water or ⅓ cup sake
2 Tbsp. grated ginger juice
2 tsp. salt

Stuffing
3 cups roasted brown rice
  (golden color)
6 cups boiling water
½ cup minced onion
½ cup minced celery
½ cup shiitake mushrooms,
  finely chopped
1 Tbsp. sesame oil
6 cups dried, cubed whole wheat
  bread (⅓″ cubes)
3 tsp. salt

Wash turkey well inside and out, remove soft red parts from inside and dry all over with paper towel. Rub outside of turkey with ½ lemon. Rub 3 Tbsp. of salt inside and outside. Let turkey sit about 30 minutes. Mop off liquid inside and outside with paper towel. This removes the bloody smell and the turkey smell.

Mix soy sauce, water, and grated ginger juice with 2 tsp. salt. Brush this sauce on inside and outside of turkey. Let it sit 2-3 hours, brushing turkey with sauce three or four times during this period.

Add boiling water to rice plus 1 tsp. salt and bake in covered casserole in oven for 1 hour at 350°.

Saute onion until transparent in 1 Tbsp. sesame oil, add mushrooms and saute, then add celery and saute. Add 2 tsp. salt, cooked warm rice, and let cool. Then add bread cubes and mix well.

Stuff turkey neck and stomach loosely and sew together. Place turkey, wings spread, on a rack on a cookie sheet (to catch drippings) and bake for 45 minutes at 450° until completely brown. Remove turkey and wrap in double thickness of aluminum foil. Return to rack, breast up, and bake 7 hours at 300° or 10 hours at 250°. When turkey is completely cold, remove foil. Remove stuffing and reheat in oven if desired. Use juices on cookie sheet and in foil for gravy.

If more stuffing is desired, make bouillon with giblets following directions for chicken bouillon (#43), adding salt. Pour bouillon over remainder of bread and rice in a casserole and bake at 450° for 45 minutes with cover. This stuffing is tasty but different than turkey stuffing. It is excellent the day after Thanksgiving.

Note: Using aluminum foil makes the turkey and turkey skin soft and moist.

Turkey stock———Using leftover bones, scraps, skin, giblets, etc., plus any vegetable scraps, cook for several hours as for bouillon. Remove all meat and discard bones and scraps. Use in preparing soups.

309. Whole Wheat Bread for Stuffing

5 cups whole wheat flour
1 cup unbleached white flour
2⅓ cups warm water
½ tsp. yeast
1 Tbsp. oil

Dissolve yeast in warm water for 5 minutes. Add oil and salt. Mix in flour and knead until earlobe consistency. Cover with wet cloth and leave in warm place until doubled. Punch down and let rise once more. Then roll into loaves and place in oiled pans. Score bread – two parallel lines about 1″ deep. Place in cold oven and heat to 350°. Bake about 1 hour until golden brown. Stuffing bread is better one day old.

310. Turkey Dressing

Bread cubes from 3-4 loaves
Giblets, chopped
2 stalks celery, chopped
1 bunch scallions, chopped
Salt and soy sauce
1 bunch Swiss chard, chopped
1 bunch parsley, minced
½ lb. mushrooms, sliced
3 cloves garlic
Sage (optional)

Boil giblets and celery and scallions in a little water. Add whole garlic cloves. Then add mushrooms, Swiss chard and parsley. Add salt and simmer. Remove garlic when done.

Soak bread cubes in giblet water. Add bread cubes to the giblets, and vegetables, more liquid if needed, and salt and soy sauce. Refrigerate overnight for best flavor.

311. Russian Soup

1 cup roasted rice (high flame)
5 small whole onions
2 med. turnips, quartered
2 med. potatoes, quartered
1 large carrot, cut diagonally
    ⅓″ thick
1 Tbsp. sesame oil
10 cups water (or turkey stock, #308)
1 Tbsp. salt
Parsley, minced

Bechamel sauce
½ cup whole wheat pastry flour
2 tsp. oil
1 cup water

Heat oil, saute potato until slightly transparent, add whole onions, then turnips, then carrots, sauteing for a total of about 10 minutes. Add roasted rice, mix and saute for a few minutes. Add 10 cups of boiling water or turkey stock, bring to a boil and simmer 5 to 6 hours, mixing occasionally. This soup is good cooked all day. Add 1 Tbsp. salt after it has cooked 1 hour.

Make bechamel sauce, add to soup, taste for salt, bring to a boil and simmer 30 minutes more before serving. If soup is too thick, add water or stock. If soup is thick, it is good for a snack or for an entire meal.

If you are in a hurry, cook this soup in pressure cooker, using less water (about 2″ above vegetables). Cook 45-60 minutes under pressure. When pressure is down, add more water, bechamel sauce, and salt. Cook without pressure about 30 minutes longer. Serve with minced parsley.

Variations: Russian soup is thick when cold. It is delicious as pie filling. If necessary to thicken soup, use oatmeal, cooked rice, or bread crumbs to absorb liquid. Another way to use leftover Russian soup is to saute a thinly sliced potato, cover with water and cook until tender. Add Russian soup and more water if necessary. Make a bechamel sauce by first roasting a pinch of curry, then flour. Add this to mixture and cook 20-30 minutes. Serve over half a bed of rice with hijiki or kombu and tasty pickles such as cucumber mustard pickles.

312. Gefilte Fish (Japanese Style)

½ lb. raw tuna, finely chopped
1 onion, chopped
1 tsp. ginger, grated
½ cup whole wheat pastry flour or
    whole wheat flour
1 Tbsp. miso
1 Tbsp. arrowroot

Grind chopped tuna in a suribachi. Add ginger, chopped onion, flour, miso, and arrowroot, blending all together and mashing in suribachi. Form into tiny balls, drop into boiling water and cook for 3 minutes. Put toothpicks into each ball and serve.

313. Glazed Mackerel Nitsuke

1 lb. mackerel, bass, or
    other small fish
3 med. onions, ½″ crescents
2 med. carrots, irregular wedges
3 med. shiitake mushrooms,
    soaked and quartered
3 med. potatoes, ½″ irregular wedges
Chinese snow peas, 3 per person, or
    1 bunch scallions, sliced 1½″
2 cups soup stock (#39)
3 Tbsp. soy sauce
1 tsp. salt
3 Tbsp. arrowroot flour
Oil for deep frying

Marinade
2 Tbsp. soy sauce
2 tsp. minced ginger
2 Tbsp. sake

Mix marinade and marinate fish for 20 minutes, mixing from time to time. Strain off marinade, cover fish with arrowroot, let sit for 5 minutes, and then deep fry.

Place mushrooms, potatoes, onions, and carrots in pot and add soup stock. Bring to a boil, simmer until half done, add salt and soy sauce. Before they are completely tender, add mackerel and snow peas or scallions. Taste for seasoning and adjust according to desire. Dissolve arrowroot in cold water and add. Cook until the mixture thickens and then serve.

314. Prawns with Cauliflower and Onion

8 prawns
1 med. onion, crescents
1 cup cauliflower, small flowerettes
½ tsp. salt
1 Tbsp. oil
4 cups water
4 tsp. soy sauce
1 Tbsp. kuzu or arrowroot diluted
    in 3 Tbsp. water

Remove shells and veins from prawns. Salt and let stand for 10 minutes. Saute prawns until pink, in 1 Tbsp. oil. Remove. Saute onion and cauliflower. Add ¼ tsp. salt and 2 tsp. soy sauce. Cover and cook 5 minutes. Add water and boil 15 minutes. Add ¼ tsp. salt and 2 tsp. soy sauce. Add shrimp and bring to a boil. Add kuzu or arrowroot and bring to a boil, stirring constantly. Serve over rice.

315. Shrimp Curry

24 shrimp
½ tsp. curry powder
1 tsp. salt
2 Tbsp. oil
2 cups kombu stock (#39)
3 scallions, minced
1 Tbsp. kuzu or arrowroot (approx.)
    diluted in a little water

Remove shells and veins from shrimp. Heat curry powder in oil, add salt and stir until smooth. Add shrimp and saute until they turn color. Add stock gradually. Dilute kuzu or arrowroot and add, stirring constantly until thickened. Cover. Bring to a boil and cook 5 minutes, then add minced scallions. Serve over rice.

316. Scallops Gratin

6 scallops, ⅛″ pieces
1½ cups white sauce (#187)
5 small potatoes
5 Tbsp. milk or water
1 Tbsp. sesame oil
1 egg yolk
1 tsp. salt

Cut scallops into ⅛″ pieces and sprinkle with salt and pepper. Sprinkle potatoes with 1 tsp. salt and place on vegetable steamer in pressure cooker with 1 cup water. Cook 20 minutes, then peel (if desired) and mash. Heat oil in frying pan, add mashed potato and saute. Add milk or water and continue cooking until it gets thick. When the potato no longer sticks to your fingers, add egg yolk and mix.

Mix scallops with white sauce and spoon into a casserole pan. Put the cooked potato into a cake icing bag. By squeezing the bag, make an attractive 'potato icing' decoration on top. Then put in a hot oven and bake. Serve immediately in small dishes.

If you can find 3″ by 4″ shells from clams, oysters, scallops, etc., put the sauce and shellfish mixture in each one, decorate the edge with mashed potato icing and bake in the oven until potato turns light brown. On each small plate set a folded napkin, place one shell on top, and serve.

317. Azuki Chestnut Kanten

1 cup azuki beans
1 cup dry chestnuts
⅛ lb. tofu, mashed
2 bars kanten
1 tsp. salt
1 Tbsp. yinnie syrup
Pinch of lemon rind

Soak azuki and chestnuts in 3 cups of water about 6 hours. Bring to boil and add ½ cup of cold water. Repeat this 2 more times until beans and chestnuts are cooking in 4½ cups of water. Cook until tender, add 1 tsp. salt, remove cover and cook 20 minutes more, stirring gently from bottom to top until little liquid remains.

Rinse kanten, break into pieces and soak in 4 cups of cold water about 20 minutes. Bring to boil and cook 20 minutes. Reserve ½ cup kanten juice. Add chestnuts and beans to kanten and cook 20 minutes more without cover. Rinse serving dish with cold water. Pour in hot mixture.

Mash tofu in a suribachi and slowly mix in reserved warm kanten juice. Add yinnie syrup and pinch of lemon rind, bring to slight boil, cook a little, and pour over kanten after it has started to become firm. Cool thoroughly.

Variation: One egg white can be substituted for the tofu.

Fried Foods

318. Buckwheat Croquettes

½ cup buckwheat groats
1 cup boiling water
¼ tsp. salt
1 tsp. oil
1 large onion, minced
Whole wheat flour
Oil for deep or pan frying

Saute groats in oil for 5 minutes, stirring constantly. Add salt and boiling water, cover, lower flame and cook 10 minutes. Then let steam in its own absorbed water for another 10 minutes before taking off the cover. Saute onions in oil and mix with groats. Add enough whole wheat flour and water to make dough a consistency which will make small balls that hold together. Roll each ball in whole wheat flour and deep fry until outside is crisp. Check by cutting one in half to see if the center is cooked. These may also be pan fried by making the batter thinner and dropping by spoon into the oiled pan.

319. Yam Croquettes

6 small yams, cooked
½ tsp. salt
Whole wheat flour
Oil for deep frying

Puree cooked yams, add salt and simmer over low heat until firm enough to form balls. Wet hands and shape into walnut-sized balls. Roll in whole wheat flour and deep fry until golden brown (about 60 seconds). Drain and serve.

Variations: Pureed squash, sweet potatoes, carrots, or parsnips can be used instead of yams. Nuts and/or raisins can be added.

320. Lotus Root Balls

1½ cups lotus root, grated
1 cup onions, minced
1 tsp. salt
1½ cups whole wheat flour
Oil for deep frying

Mix ingredients well. Form into little balls and deep fry. This can also be made with carrots.

321. Seasoned Tempura

3″ carrot, 1½″ matchsticks
½″ lotus root, ⅛″ rounds
3″ burdock, 1½″ matchsticks
Oil for deep frying

Tempura batter
1 cup whole wheat pastry flour
½ tsp. salt
1 Tbsp. soy sauce
1 heaping Tbsp. arrowroot
1 cup cold water

Mix batter the same as in #66. Lightly boil vegetables until half soft, drain and cool. Heat oil as in #66, then lower temperature to about 300°. Dip vegetables into batter and deep fry. Serve with grated daikon seasoned with soy sauce.

322. Collard Green Tempura with Tofu

1 lb. tofu
10 large collard greens
¼ cup arrowroot powder
¼ cup pastry flour
½ cup tempura batter (#66)
Oil for deep frying

Cut tofu in half. Slice each half into five pieces and place on a cotton dish towel which is over a board tipped toward the sink. Cover tofu with a towel and place another board and a thick telephone book on top for about 30 minutes to remove liquid. Wash collard greens and dry with paper towels. Combine dry arrowroot powder with pastry flour. Roll tofu in this mixture. Make tempura batter. Dip one side of tofu only in batter and place batter side down on top side of collard green leaf. Holding edges of leaf with both hands, dip underside of leaf in batter and fry. When leaf looks crispy on edges, turn it over and cook a few minutes longer until tofu looks yellowish. Remove to strainer placed in pan to drain.

Serve with fresh grated daikon and/or soy sauce.

323. Burdock Roll

2 med. burdock, 5"-7" lengths
1 cup whole wheat flour
2 tsp. oil
⅓ cup water
¼ tsp. salt
1 tsp. grated ginger
2 tsp. soy sauce
Deep frying oil 3" deep

Scrub and cut burdock and saute in 1 tsp. oil. Add a small amount of water and cook until half done. Add soy sauce and ginger and cook until tender. Cool. Add salt and 1 tsp. oil to flour and rub in thoroughly with hands. Add water and knead lightly until slightly softer than ear lobe. Roll dough to ⅛" thickness. Roll burdock in dough overlapping about ½ inch and seal, pinching ends of dough closed, rounded to the shape of the burdock. Heat oil as in #66. Deep fry burdock until color of the dough deepens. Turn burdock over and fry until both sides are brown. Remove to strainer set in pan, then to paper towels.

Slice into pieces 1½" long. Stand pieces on end when serving, accompanied by grated daikon.

Variation: Two medium carrots about 7" long can be substituted for the burdock. Carrots are sliced diagonally.

Note: If you are in a hurry, saute burdock in pressure cooker. Add ½ cup water and 2 tsp. soy sauce and cook for 20 minutes from time pressure is up.

324. Deep Fried Kombu

Kombu
Corn oil, 2″ deep

Clean kombu by going over it with a damp cloth. Cut half the kombu with scissors into 1″ × 4″ pieces and tie into a loose knot. Cut the rest into 1½″ × 3″ pieces, make a slit in the center and pull one end through the slit. Deep fry in 2 inches of corn oil. Good for a snack.

325. Tofu Raft

½ lb. tofu
⅓ cup burdock, grated
⅓ cup albi or taro, grated, plus
   ¼ cup whole wheat pastry flour
1 sheet nori, cut into 8-10 pieces
Oil for deep frying

Crumble tofu same as in ganmodoki (see #67) and mix it with vegetables. If you have no albi or taro, use flour only to hold pieces together. Put batter on nori ⅓″ thick, cut into rectangles (about 8 per sheet of nori), and deep fry.

    Serve with grated daikon and soy sauce, or grated minced parsley on a mound of grated daikon with soy sauce to taste.

326. Split Burdock Logs

2 burdock, cut into 2″ pieces
3″ × 3″ piece dashi kombu
3-5 shiitake mushrooms
Salt
Soy sauce
Tempura batter
Oil for deep frying

Pressure cook the 2″ pieces of burdock until tender. Cut in half lengthwise but not all the way through. Flatten out by pressing with your fingers. Make a tempura batter, drop the pieces of burdock in the batter and then deep fry in hot oil. Use a tempura batter similar to the one in the Mock Chicken recipe (see #68).

    Then place some dashi kombu and shiitake mushroom on the bottom of a pan, cover with 2 cups water, bring to a boil, add salt and soy sauce to your taste. Add burdock, and simmer covered for 15 minutes. Reserve kombu and mushrooms for other dishes and serve burdock logs with a little of the liquid.

Pickles

327. Cabbage Salt Pickles

2 cabbages (6″ diameter, about
    2 lbs.), cut 1″ squares
2 Tbsp. salt, approx.
1 piece dashi kombu, 4″ square,
    matchsticks
3 Tbsp. orange or tangerine skin,
    matchsticks

Take cabbages apart, wash and dry. Set aside two or three outer green leaves. Sprinkle 1 tsp. salt in bottom of container (glass, porcelain, or wood). Place half of the outer cabbage leaves in container followed by ¼″ deep layer of cabbage and one quarter of the kombu and orange skin, sprinkling ½ tsp. of salt over the top. Repeat this layering of ingredients 3 more times. Finish off with a layer of remaining outer leaves and 2 tsp. salt.

Cover with wooden lid and press down with a 7 pound stone. When water comes up a day or so later, lighten the pressure to 2-3 pounds.

In the summer you can eat these pickles in three or four days. In the winter they are really good after ten days. Before eating, partially drain off liquid, leaving a little moisture on the bottom of container. Refrigerate.

328. Chinese Cabbage Salt Pickles

6 heads medium-sized Chinese
    cabbage (about 4″ diameter)
1 cup crude salt
3″ × 12″ piece kombu, matchsticks
3 dry red chili peppers (approx.
    1½″ long), thin rounds
1 orange or tangerine skin,
    matchsticks

Wash cabbages, setting aside three outer green leaves. Cut 3″ deep into stalk crosswise +. Pull cabbage apart into quarters. Make two 1″ deep cuts into stalk end of each quarter. Sprinkle 1½ Tbsp. salt in bottom of dry container. Place half of the outer cabbage leaves in container. Place chunks of cabbage snugly in a layer on bottom of keg, topping with one-quarter of the orange skin, kombu, chili peppers, and 2-3 Tbsp. salt. Repeat this layering three times. Finish off with a layer of salt – about 2 Tbsp.

Place wooden lid on cabbage using 20 pounds of pressure. When liquid comes up a couple of days later, lighten pressure to about 5 pounds.

If you wish to keep these pickles over a month, first dry washed cabbages outside in shady place for a day and use ¼ cup additional salt.

329. Fresh Daikon Nuka Pickles

25-30 fresh daikon
12 cups rice bran (nuka)
3-4 cups salt

Remove daikon leaves. Wash leaves and radishes and dry in sun one day. Roast rice bran lightly over medium flame in cast iron or stainless steel skillet until color changes slightly. Cool. Mix salt and rice bran thoroughly. Sprinkle bottom of keg with two handfuls of rice bran. Place a layer of daikon in keg all going in the same direction. Sprinkle three handfuls of rice bran over daikon. Place second layer of daikon on top of first layer in opposite direction, i.e., heads over tails. Again sprinkle three handfuls of rice bran over daikon. Third layer of daikon is placed crosswise or at right angles to previous row. Fourth row of daikon is placed the same as layer three except with tails over heads of layer three. Continue layering daikon in this manner until keg is filled, sprinkling three handfuls of rice bran between each layer. Then place daikon leaves on top of daikon, filling in all spaces. Sprinkle remaining rice bran over daikon leaves. Put wooden cover on keg using a 20-30 pound stone for pressure. After five days, water will be up to top. Lighten pressure to about 5-10 pounds.

Pickles will be ready to eat about two weeks later. They will keep in a cool place for about two months in winter.

To improve flavor, cut a piece of kombu 4″ × 12″ into about 24 pieces ½″ square, placing a few pieces on top of each layer on top of rice bran.

Sometimes 2 cups of orange or apple skins can be used on top of daikon leaves. When water comes up to the top, discard fruit skins.

If these pickles are too salty, use 2-3 cups salt.

330. Eggplant Mustard Pickles

2 lbs. young, small eggplant
4 Tbsp. salt
1 cup rice koji
1 cup mustard powder
½ cup dashi kombu stock (#39)

Sauce
⅔ cup soy sauce
5 Tbsp. yinnie syrup
1 Tbsp. salt

Wash eggplant and halve them lengthwise. Salt eggplant and put in vegetable press, putting about ½ cup of water around the edges. Press down hard two or three days. Remove eggplant and cut into strips ½″ wide. Squeeze strips hard to remove excess water.

To make the sauce, mix soy sauce, yinnie syrup, and salt and bring to a boil. Cool and pour into a bowl. Saturate eggplant with sauce.

Add boiling water to mustard powder until it is thick and creamy. Pat thin layer of mustard mixture on bottom and sides of small bowl. Cover mustard with rice paper. Fill bowl with boiling water. Place two or three red (burning) coals (wooden coals) into bowl for about 10 minutes, after which throw out coals and water. Slowly remove rice paper and turn bowl upside down for about 20 minutes. Then thoroughly mix mustard in the bowl. Add rice koji to mustard and mix well. Add soup stock and mix well. Spread a thin layer of this mixture on the bottom of a clean, dry earthenware container. Add eggplant strips in a layer 1½″ thick and snugly placed. Continue making layers of eggplant with mustard sauce between, finishing off with mustard sauce on top.

Cover with rice paper, then clay cover, and seal with sticky tape. Keep in a cool place and eat these pickles in a week.

Variation: See #83.

Breads and Desserts

331. Pressure Cooked Bread

4 cups cooked grains
4 cups whole wheat flour or
    combination of flours
2½ cups warm water
1 tsp. salt

Mix equal parts flour and leftover cooked grains. Vary flours and grains according to season, etc. Combine flour, salt, and cooked grains. Mix together well before adding any extra liquid as the liquid from the grains (and vegetables when they are used) is often enough to make a good batter needing only a small quantity of added liquid. Cover with a damp cloth and raise in a warm place for 4-6 hours. Place 1″ of water in bottom of pressure cooker. Put rack on bottom of cooker. Pour batter into a lightly oiled pan that fits inside the pressure cooker. Batter usually rises during cooking and can clog air vents and even cause top to blow off cooker. Place pan in pressure cooker, cover, bring water to a boil, and steam for 1-2 hours before placing pressure cooker weight on top of cooker. Uncover and check to see if there is enough water in pressure cooker. Recover, place weight on top of cooker and bring to full pressure. Lower heat and pressure cook for 2 hours. Reduce pressure, remove bread pan from pressure cooker and place on a cake rack to cool. Looks 'globby' on top, but as it cools, moisture on top is reabsorbed into bread, giving it a pudding-like taste and texture. This is a rich bread that is very filling when eaten in small amounts. It is also very satisfying and easy to digest. Good for lunches, on hikes, when traveling, etc.

Optional items to add: Leftover cooked vegetables, soba water, cooked raisins, cinnamon, etc.

332. Cornmeal Pan Bread

2 cups fine ground cornmeal
6 cups boiling water
1 tsp. salt
Oil for pan frying

Place cornmeal in a heavy cooking pot. Slowly add 4 cups boiling water, and mix. Then add 2 more cups water but do not mix – try to keep it under the cornmeal for steaming. Cover, bring to boil, then turn to low for about an hour.

Allow to cool to room temperature. Remove warm corn mush to wet bread pans and allow to cool. Turn pans upside down and remove corn mush. Slice with a wet knife into ½″ thick slices. Heat and oil a heavy fry pan. Fry slices of corn mush uncovered, 7 minutes or until slightly browned on one side, then 5 minutes on the other side.

Serve hot corn bread with chili beans (#302) and fresh green salad.

333. Corn Popovers

1½ cups corn flour
½ tsp. salt
1½ cups boiling water
2 Tbsp. oil
2 eggs

Mix flour and salt. Add boiling water all at one time to blanch the flour. Add oil and beat well. Add unbeaten eggs one at a time. Beat hard by hand or with an egg beater or electric beater. Drop on greased cookie sheet. Place in a cold oven, turn heat to 400° for 20 minutes, reduce to 350° and cook 10-20 minutes longer until golden color. The secret of getting them to pop well is placing them in a cold oven and turning to a high temperature – the sudden high temperature causes them to pop. Can also cook in a muffin tin instead of a cookie sheet. Fill each cup of the muffin tin only half full after you have preheated and oiled the tin. Good served with hot applesauce.

334. Toren's Cake

1½ cups flour
3 Tbsp. carob powder
1 tsp. baking soda
½ tsp. salt
½ cup corn oil
¼ tsp. vanilla extract or bean
1 cup apple juice or cider, or
   ½ cup soba water plus
   ½ cup cider
1 cup apple butter and raisin
   puree mixture
Nuts, optional

Mix all dry ingredients together thoroughly in a large mixing bowl. In a separate mixing bowl combine all liquid ingredients. When using soba water, if there is time, let this ferment a day or two before making the cake. The fermented soba water is very leavening and makes a much lighter cake. If you use vanilla bean instead of liquid vanilla extract, use about ½″ or ¾″ of vanilla bean. Split the piece of vanilla bean full length so that the flavor will come out and add it to the juice. Bring it to a boil and simmer for about 20 minutes. Remove the bean and cool this extract completely before adding to the liquid mixture. Then, add the liquid ingredients to the dry ingredients and mix well together. An egg beater or electric beater makes a lighter cake batter, but is not absolutely necessary. You can beat by hand with a wooden spoon. Bake in a preheated oven at 350° for 30-45 minutes, or until it tests dry. Add roasted, chopped walnuts or filberts to the batter for special occasions. Dust the nuts in flour before adding them to the batter. This keeps them from absorbing moisture from the cake batter and makes a nuttier taste when baked. Fits an 8-inch square or round cake pan.

335. Loaf Cake

1 small yam, chopped very fine
1 apple, chopped
¼ cup raisins
¼ cup roasted nuts
½ cup corn oil
3 egg yolks
2 cups flour
Water to make thick cake batter
¼ tsp. salt
3 egg whites, beaten stiffly

Mix well. Fold in stiffly beaten egg whites. Can add ¼ tsp. orange rind. Bake at 350° in preheated oven for 1 hour.

336. Cake Icing

1 box yeasted rye crackers
1½ cups apple or white grape juice
1 Tbsp. tahini
½ tsp. cinnamon
1 cup currants

Soak crackers in apple or grape juice. Add tahini, cinnamon, and currants. Blend. No cooking is required.

337. Muffin or Cookie Icing

1 cup raisins
1 Tbsp. carob powder
½ bar kanten
2¼ cups water

Boil raisins in 1½ cups water. Mix in carob powder to taste. Break kanten into small pieces and soak in ¾ cup of water for 20 minutes. Bring to a boil and then simmer 20 minutes. Add to raisin-carob mixture and simmer for 10 minutes. Cool and blend, or beat with an egg beater to obtain desired icing texture.

338. Tahini Custard

1 bar kanten, diluted in 2½ cups
    apple juice with a pinch of salt
4 Tbsp. sweet rice flour
2 Tbsp. tahini
Lemon peel

Heat diluted kanten, adding bit of lemon peel. Blend sweet rice and tahini in 2½ cups of water and add to hot kanten. Cook over medium flame; wisk from time to time. Allow to cool and pour into sundae glasses and refrigerate.

Serve with toasted chopped almonds on top, or apricot cream made with cooked and blended dried apricots.

339. Raised Donuts

1 cup grain milk or oat milk
¾ cup apple butter or raisin puree
3 eggs (optional), beaten well
1 Tbsp. salt
1 Tbsp. yeast
5 cups unbleached white flour or
    3 cups white, 1 cup rice and
    1 cup whole wheat pastry flour
1 tsp. grated orange rind
Oil for deep frying

Combine dry ingredients (except yeast) in a bowl. Mix yeast with ½ cup warm water and let sit for 15 minutes. Stir well to make sure yeast is completely dissolved. Mix beaten eggs, apple butter or raisin puree, and grain milk in a bowl. Add this gradually to dry ingredients with dissolved yeast, stirring well. Add grated orange rind. Raise in a warm place 2 hours, covered with a warm, damp cloth. Punch down and roll out to ½" thickness, and cut with a donut cutter. Raise again for 2 hours, covered with a warm, damp cloth in a warm place. Heat corn oil about 3-4 inches deep in a pot and deep fry donuts and centers until golden brown.

340. Carrot Macaroons

1 cup whole oats
⅓ cup shredded carrot
3 Tbsp. peanut butter

Pressure-cook whole oats in 3 cups of water overnight. Mix shredded carrot into the cooked oats. Add peanut butter. If the mixture is too wet, add whole wheat flour. Spoon onto a cookie sheet. Bake at 375° for 50 to 60 minutes. Keep refrigerated.

341. Ladyfingers

7 cups grated carrots
1 cup raisins or currants
Tahini
Pinch of salt

Mix grated carrots and raisins. Add tahini to hold the mixture together (or for taste) and a pinch of salt. Put in baking dish no more than ½″ thick. Bake at 375° for 10 minutes. Take out and cut into rectangles 3″ long by 1″ wide. Bake another 10 minutes. This recipe also makes a good pie filling.

342. Persimmon Pudding

8 persimmons, approx.
3 eggs
1½ cups whole wheat pastry flour
1 tsp. baking powder
½ tsp. salt
¼ cup oil
2 cups grain milk
1 tsp. cinnamon
½ cup chopped nuts
½ cup chopped raisins
1 tsp. grated fresh ginger

Remove pits from persimmons, blend in blender – should make almost a quart of puree. Beat in eggs, flour, baking powder, salt, oil, grain milk, cinnamon, and ginger. Add nuts and raisins. Bake pudding in an oiled 9″ by 9″ baking dish at 325° until firm – about 1 hour.

343. Plum Pudding

1 cup rye flour
½ tsp. salt
1½ cups grated carrot
1 cup grated yam or sweet potato
½ cup raisins
1 cup chopped prunes
4-6 Tbsp. sesame oil

Mix ingredients well and pour into greased baking dish. Place baking dish in water in covered pan and bake, steaming for approximately 1½ hours at 325°.

Optional but better: Add 1 beaten egg or 1 tsp. baking soda and 8-10 yinnies (melted in ¼ cup water in double boiler) to pudding.

344. Vanilla Sauce

½ cup whole wheat pastry flour
½ cup tahini
1½ cups apple juice mixed with
    1½ cups water
Vanilla and salt to taste

Roast the flour in the tahini. The oily part from the top of the jar is ideal for this. Cool. Slowly add apple juice which has been diluted with an equal amount of water. Avoid lumps. Slowly bring to a boil, adding more liquid until the consistency is like heavy cream. Add salt and vanilla to taste. Cook on low flame with flame tamer for 45 minutes.

Winter

a. Umeboshi Ginger Pickles (*Macrobiotic Kitchen* or *Chico-San Cookbook* – #126), and Sake-Kasu Pickles (*Calendar Cookbook*, #158). #88 – Gyoza and sauce. #86 – French Bread. #371 – Yose Nabe. b. Yose Nabe items, raw.

Grains

345. Oyster Rice
346. Shrimp Sake Rice
347. Fish Rice
348. Chicken Ojiya
349. Egg Ojiya
350. Mochi
351. Baked Mochi
352. Deep Fried Mochi
353. Boiled Mochi
354. Orange Miso Mochi
355. Yaki Mochi Nabe
356. Wrapped Mochi
357. Bonita Mochi
358. Oroshi Mochi
359. Rice Patties
360. Lentil and Rice Loaf
361. Buckwheat Potato Casserole

Vegetables

362. Stuffed Cabbage
363. Stuffed Acorn Squash
364. Carrots with Sesame Seeds
365. Carrots with Walnuts
366. Winter Vegetable Miso
367. Fresh Daikon Nitsuke
368. Salmon Vegetable Pie
369. Farofa (Brazilian Dish)

Stews

370. Tofu Vegetable Nabe
371. Yose Nabe
372. Radish Turnip Nabe
373. Vegetable Nabe with Mochi
374. Oyster Nabe
375. Oyster Nabe with Miso
376. Chiri Nabe
377. Boiled Tofu (Yudofu)
378. Furofuki
379. Udon Sukiyaki
380. Vegetable Oden (Nikomi Oden)
381. Country Style Chicken Stew

Soups

382. Miso Soup
383. Squash Potage
384. Daikon Miso Soup with Salmon
385. Clear Chicken Soup (Mizutake)
386. Country Chicken Soup
387. Country Soup with Salmon
388. Winter Kenchin Soup
389. Sake-No-Kasu Soup with Salmon

Beans

390. Azuki Winter Squash Nitsuke
391. Soybean Nishime
392. Chick Pea Sauce for Millet
393. Lentil Soup
394. Lentil Stuffed Pancakes
395. Lentil Roll
396. Bean Combinations for Winter

New Year's Recipes

397. Clear Soup Zoni
398. Rolled Egg
399. Black Bean Nishime
400. Vegetable Nishime
401. Albi Nishime
402. Crispy Dried Fish (Tazukuri)
403. Glazed Dried Fish
404. Celery Sesame Salad
405. Chrysanthemum Turnip Salad
406. Kinton (Pudding)
407. Apple Kanten

Special Dishes

408. Chawan Mushi (Japanese Egg Custard)
409. Chicken with Sweet Rice Stuffing
410. Vegetables and Chicken Nitsuke
411. Chinese Cabbage Stuffed with Chicken
412. Farm Style Goat Cheese

Fried Foods

413. Jinenjo Roll with Nori (Nagaimo Norimaki)
414. Lotus Root Rolls
415. Stuffed Lotus Root
416. Lotus Root Fritter
417. Squash Croquettes
418. Mock Burdock Loach

Sauces and Dressings

419. Brown Sauce
420. Ginger Sauce
421. Mustard Sauce
422. Bonita Sauce
423. Sweet Kuzu Sauce
424. Vinegar Sauce
425. Marinade
426. Umeboshi Onion Dressing
427. Sesame Dressing

Pickles

428. Dried Daikon Pickles
429. Daikon Koji Pickles
430. Turnip Koji Pickles

Breads and Snacks

431. Sesame Bread
432. Buckwheat Bread
433. Party Bread
434. Raisin Bread
435. Carrot Bread
436. Rye Bread
437. Oatmeal Sunflower Gluten Bread
438. Party Rolls
439. Rye Rolls
440. Whole Wheat Buns
441. White Buns
442. Karinto
443. Spiral Karinto
444. Squash Muffins
445. Buckwheat Azuki Pancakes

Desserts

446. Amasake
447. Amasake (Flour)
448. Amasake Manju (Steam Cake)
449. Steamed Amasake Roll
450. Baked Amasake Roll
451. Amasake Karinto
452. Amasake Cookies
453. Amasake Cake
454. Amasake Wedding Cake with Frosting
455. Unyeasted Amasake Donuts
456. Yeasted Amasake Donuts
457. Amasake Crescents
458. Pumpkin Pie
459. Simple Pumpkin Pie
460. Half Moon Chestnut Turnovers
461. Mincemeat Filling
462. Oatmeal Cookies
463. Cranberry Relish
464. Soft Gingerbread Cake
465. Carob Christmas Cake
466. English Christmas Pudding

Winter Cooking

The cold season needs a warm atmosphere, so one of the best dishes to serve is nabemono, the Japanese stew. At the table a steamy fragrance arises from the pot as it is served and it creates a warm atmosphere. It may be served any number of ways: nabe – noodles with vegetables, seitan, tofu; uosuki – 3 or 4 kinds of fish with tofu and scallions; oyster nabe – oysters with vegetables seasoned with miso; yosenabe – mountain vegetables and garden vegetables mixed with shellfish in one pot; tofunabe – boiled tofu with scallions, bonita, soy sauce and minced orange peel. It should be served in a beautiful casserole. Traditionally, the container was kept warm on a small charcoal brazier at the table. Today you can use an electric warmer. This is best for the winter dishes.

Nabemono contains a variety of combinations of noodles, vegetables, wheat gluten, tofu, and fish. It is served steaming hot and is very nutritious. It makes any gathering a warm, happy family group. There are many kinds of nabemono in this cookbook, so please enjoy these with your family and friends during the cold season.

Winter provides a very good opportunity to yangize yourself because cold weather strengthens and contracts. So you can appreciate cold weather.

During the cold season (a yin time), we need more yang cooking methods – for example, using less water and cooking for a longer time. If your body is in a yin condition, try using some buckwheat flour in place of whole wheat flour. Root vegetables are more yang than the leafy types, so use more root vegetables during the cold season. This is natural because these vegetables stay fresh through the winter if properly stored. When you cook leafy vegetables like cabbage, use less water. After sauteing them, cover and let them steam in their own juices.

Ojiya is a vegetable soup made into a thick gruel by adding rice and flavoring it with miso. This makes the body much warmer than miso soup alone. See #348-#349.

You can evaluate whether you are taking the right amount of liquid by watching how much you urinate. Adults should urinate 3-4 times a day.

It is a good idea to serve 2 or 3 slices per person of pickled vegetables at each meal. Any kind of pickle is okay but in winter the takuan pickle (dried daikon in rice bran and salt) is best. Or rice bran pickle (#79).

Old people and children should take less salt. Miso soup should be made less salty. Adolescents and adults, however, can use yaki miso (baked miso, #147). If you crave more miso, you can add this to your own bowl.

Most of the recipes in this section are nice dishes to serve when you expect guests for dinner. Many different fish recipes are included. In the temperate latitudes these are appropriate recipes for winter. For most daily meals, however, a simple menu of grains and vegetables is adequately nourishing, delicious, and beautiful. But if you expect company and want to welcome them with variety, your whole family can enjoy gourmet food also.

In the following menus, you can omit chicken or fish if you prefer and still make very good meals. Dashi kombu used in place of chicken or fish gives nearly the same taste. The natural fermentation of soy sauce has a flavor which enhances every food. Mock chicken, goose, or duck recipes can be substituted for chicken or fish to create meals which should satisfy any animal-food-eating guest.

Any vegetables in these recipes can be substituted according to season. You need only watch yin yang balance. From that point you should try to make your own creations.

In winter we cook nabemono (stews) using vegetables, noodles, fish, shellfish, and sometimes chicken. This is better balanced than chicken or fish only, and the taste is more harmonious. I use more than three times vegetable foods to animal foods. In this section I don't explain cooking fish or chicken by themselves – but if you do, you must make balance by marinating them. Commonly in Japan they serve broiled fish with just grated daikon; this is enough for balance since they are eating white rice. But we are using brown rice in our diet, a much stronger food, and so we need to marinate animal foods. Use either fresh ginger juice and salt, or ginger juice with sake and soy sauce. Marinate for 20 minutes (see my *Calendar Cookbook,* #10 and #95).

A long time ago when my children were small we lived in Chico, California. Often we were invited to parties, children's birthdays, etc., sometimes with fried chicken dinners. The next morning, not only I but my husband also had terrible nightmares, usually with knives and blood. Later, when we moved from Chico to Carmichael, my son asked me to please cook a traditional American Thanksgiving turkey dinner. So I asked my husband, then got an organic turkey. This was the first time I roasted a turkey; I didn't know how to cook turkey, so I opened my copy of *Zen Cookery* and also asked a Japanese friend with an American husband how to cook a regular American-style turkey. I learned both styles, then decided how to balance with marinating. At my children's birthdays I tried fried chicken, American-style. One American boy living with us said, "I never tasted such good fried chicken in my life!" We ate both turkey and fried chicken prepared this way and never had nightmares. Maybe using the marinating style helped make balance (see *Calendar Cookbook,* #78, for fried chicken).

Every month I talk to my cooking students at our Vega Study House: If your husband wants fish, please cook with balance. Even if he wants steak, you must cook it. He may have been raised on meat and still wants it sometimes. If you don't, he will go to a restaurant anyway – and home cooking is better than restaurant cooking. Home cooking creates better communication in family relationships.

I have never cooked steak yet. But if I did I would have to think how to balance it – maybe I would use garlic, wine, horseradish, etc. If you study yin yang philosophy you can think how to cook. To learn a new style, study other cookbooks and practice your cooking. You can even learn from Italian, French, or American cookbooks, adapting them to macrobiotic style.

In a special case where someone gets sick and has no appetite for more than ten days, this is a really dangerous time. Ask what kind of food they want to eat. If a sick person asks for a steak, don't worry – give it to him. This is a kind of shock treatment. He may have an appetite after that and become strong. Then, return to normal macrobiotic cooking.

A long time ago in New York when my first baby was born I took a bath in water that became cold – we didn't have enough hot water. I caught a cold. My heart condition is abnormal by birth, and maybe the pregnancy and delivery were too much for me. I may have had a fever for three weeks, and no appetite. I just drank water. I was breastfeeding but not eating. I lost thirty pounds. Finally, I had difficulty breathing and was hospitalized. I craved salty pickled fish eggs, but I didn't know if Japanese stores in New York had that kind of food; so my mother sent me salty pickled salmon and codfish eggs. My husband brought me white rice balls with both kinds of fish eggs. He laughed, "Why do you like that kind of fishy taste?" But I ate a couple of them and then my appetite came back. I had enjoyed both these foods in my childhood; maybe somewhere, some body cells had memory for these foods – even after five years of the brown rice and vegetable diet. Or maybe after three weeks of fasting, some old foods were eliminated and needed to be replaced.

A macrobiotic member in Japan had diarrhea a year after starting the diet – for a year she could not stop it. Then she ate a piece of steak and it stopped the diarrhea. So even salty fish eggs or steak can be a medicine. Foods can be stronger than drugs.

In the order of the universe, man relies on the vegetable world. George Ohsawa said if you enjoy life you can enjoy fish, not necessarily every day, but it is a food for occasional enjoyment. Grains, vegetables, seaweeds, and beans – these are very simple foods, but please change your cooking all the time. People will be tired of the same style. My students say cooking is really fun because there is a lot of variety. Please create your own cooking style.

Grains

345. Oyster Rice

5 cups brown rice
7 cups water
½ lb. small fresh oysters
1 tsp. salt
2 Tbsp. soy sauce
2 Tbsp. sake
1 cup fresh mushrooms, sliced thin
½ cup watercress, chopped

Place the oysters in a strainer, sprinkle with salt, mix well and wash under running water. Set aside. Wash rice and add with water and salt to pressure cooker. Cover with a regular pan cover and bring to a boil over a hot flame. Then add the oysters, mushrooms, soy sauce, and sake and mix slowly from top to bottom. Now lock the pressure cover on the pot and bring up to a full pressure over a high flame. When at full pressure, turn heat to low flame and cook 45 minutes. After pressure returns to normal, mix in watercress and serve immediately.

346. Shrimp Sake Rice

4 cups brown rice
5 cups water
½ lb. shrimp
1½ tsp. salt
2 Tbsp. sake
1 cup fresh mushrooms, sliced thin
1 heaping Tbsp. parsley

De-vein the shrimp (remove black strip from along backbone with bamboo skewer) and wash in cold water. Bring to boil 5 cups water, add shrimp and bring to boil again over high flame. Cook until shrimp turn a red color, remove from heat and set aside to cool. After completely cold, take the shrimp out of the water and remove shells. Place shrimp on a dish. Filter cooking water through cotton cloth.

After washing the rice, put it in a pressure cooker, add the shrimp water and plain water to make 5 cups altogether. Add sake, mushrooms, and salt and bring to a boil over a low flame for 20 minutes, then turn up high. Cook the same as oyster rice (see #345). After pressure returns to normal, mix shrimp with hot rice and serve garnished with parsley.

347. Fish Rice

2 pieces white-meat fish
  (2″ × 3″ squares)
4 cups brown rice
5 cups soup stock (#39)
1 tsp. salt
2 Tbsp. soy sauce
1 tsp. ginger juice
2 Tbsp. sake
2 bunches watercress

Sprinkle fish with ½ tsp. salt. Mix ginger, 1 Tbsp. soy sauce, and 1 Tbsp. sake. Marinate fish in sauce for 20 minutes. Cook this fish on both sides on a Japanese metal toaster or pan fry in a slightly oiled pan with cover. Then break up the fish into small pieces.

After washing the rice, add 5 cups soup stock, 1 Tbsp. soy sauce, and 1 Tbsp. sake. Also add the leftover marinade sauce. Bring to pressure on high flame, then turn flame low and cook for 45 minutes. Shut off flame and let sit until pressure goes down.

Pass watercress through boiling salted water (½ tsp. salt) and set aside to cool. Cut into ¼″ pieces. Mix watercress and fish with rice and serve.

Ojiya – Bring to a boil twice as much soup stock as cooked rice, add the rice and slowly mix. Put the cover on and bring to a boil over high flame. After boiling, cook for 45-60 minutes over a low flame without stirring. When done, serve immediately. If you wait until the ojiya cools, it will be sticky like glue – so you should serve it while it is still hot.

If you use chicken or fish in ojiya, this goes best with plain kombu stock. Vegetables and tofu go well with kombu and chuba iriko or bonita stock. Stock for ojiya should taste a little saltier than ordinary clear broth.

If you use shellfish, remove them to a bowl after ojiya comes to a boil. Shellfish become hard when cooked for a long time. When ojiya has cooked completely, return the shellfish to the pot.

If you use fish and the ojiya has too fishy a taste, add chopped parsley, watercress, or scallions, mixing into pot just before turning off the flame. This gives more flavor and removes the fishy smell.

If you like vegetable ojiya, see soup section #382-#389 for recipes. Any kind of soup is okay – choose whichever you like. Also, you can season with miso instead of soy sauce. All kinds of ojiya make you feel warm, so they are good for winter or cold days.

With ojiya, any of the following condiments may be used: grated fresh ginger, sarashinegi, roasted and crushed nori, or minced orange rind.

348. Chicken Ojiya

1 chicken drumstick, minced
3 cups cooked rice
½ lb. tofu, 1/3″ cubes
1 bunch scallions, diagonals
7 cups water
1 Tbsp. sake
1 tsp. salt
1 Tbsp. soy sauce
1 heaping Tbsp. minced parsley

Bring water to boil, add sake, scallions, chicken and salt, soy sauce, and cold cooked rice. Bring to boil again over high flame, then turn low and cook for 50 minutes. Add cut tofu, bring to boil and cook 5 minutes. Shut off the flame. Sprinkle with the parsley and serve immediately.

349. Egg Ojiya

2 eggs, fertile, organic
3 cups cooked rice
6″ piece carrot, quarter moons
4″ piece daikon, flat rectangles
1 bunch scallions, ½″ rounds
7 cups soup stock (#39)
1 Tbsp. oil
2 tsp. salt

Heat up oil, then add daikon and carrot and saute. Add the soup stock and bring to boil. Then add the salt and cooked rice; bring to boil over high flame. Turn low and cook for 1 hour. Then add scallions. Beat eggs, then pour over the ojiya. Shut off flame. Mix and serve immediately.

Mochi

Mochi is a special Japanese food dating from ancient times. Sweet brown rice is more yin than regular rice, and more glutinous. If you serve regular brown rice everyday, your stomach never grows tired. But if you eat sweet brown rice every day, your stomach would quickly grow tired and you would lose your appetite, because it is richer, more yin food. So the Japanese serve these only occasionally: ohagi (sweet brown rice balls covered with sesame seeds, azuki beans, or roasted soybean powder); mochi (pounded sweet rice); amasake (sweet rice drink); yinnies (ame, or sweet rice candy); or mirin (sweet rice wine for cooking).

Here I would like to explain about mochi. Sweet brown rice is steamed and pounded – a yangizing process. A very condensed food, charged with energy, is produced.

All Japanese celebrate the New Year by offering pairs of round mochi, one small and one large, one on top of the other. These are displayed on the family altar to the ancestors and on the kami-sama (altar to God), in the study areas, working areas, and kitchen. The round shape is smooth with no rough edges. So we hope the year ahead will go this way too, with no rough edges, but with family harmony and everything going smoothly. One mochi is bigger than the other; the big one symbolizes the parents, the small one the offspring. This also represents yin and yang, which are never exactly identical or equal. Always one is greater than the other.

We decorate the top of the mochi with kombu, which stands for long life, because kombu seems to live forever, never growing old in the ocean. The Japanese say 'yoro kobu' which means 'celebration of a long wonderful life.' We hope the New Year will be splendid in the same way. Then a tangerine and tangerine leaves are put on top. The old word for tangerine in Japanese was 'dai-dai' which means 'forever.' In a special prayer in which we say 'dai-dai' we are expressing our hope that our children and grandchildren will continue forever and our family will never die out.

On New Year's Day, a family meal is served. Each family celebrates in their own home.

Mochi contains a very high quality starch and is very easy to digest because it is pounded and broken down. When you eat it, you get very warm and feel great vitality because the pounding compacts and compresses it. When you eat it much energy is released. If you think this is nonsense, try it youself.

After you eat mochi, the stomach and intestinal enzymes digest it and change it into glucose. It digests more quickly than regular rice because being more yin, the starch decomposes more easily (like fruit, which is yin and decomposes very easily).

When you eat mochi, serve it with daikon (large white radish) or natto (steamed fermented soybeans). Most people usually overeat mochi because it is so condensed and so delicious. So, daikon and natto are served with it to help digestion. When you eat much starch, more vitamin B_1 is needed; this is also found in natto and daikon.

Mochi helps people who have weak stomachs and are skinny. Sumo wrestlers eat mochi often for energy and for building up their solid muscles. Japanese farmers who are very active eat mochi often to build up their bodies. In winter, Japanese country folk would save broken brown rice which is left when rice is milled. This was made into flour and added to mochi.

If a pregnant mother eats mochi often, the baby will have great durability as it grows up because the mochi gives it such a strong foundation. This foundation becomes the source of great durability later in life. Just as mochi is flexible and strong, so the child becomes like this. Mochi also helps the nursing mother produce more milk.

Mochi makes a good snack. It is especially ideal for growing children. It satisfies their desire for treats between meals and gives them a nutritious, body-building food at the same time.

350. Mochi

5 cups sweet brown rice
7 cups sweet brown rice flour
5 cups water

Rinse sweet rice in pan of water until water becomes clear. Soak 24 hours (fig. 1). Put soaked rice and water in a pressure cooker, cover and cook using a flame a little higher than medium. Bring to full pressure, turn down and cook for 20 minutes (fig. 2). Turn off the heat and let it stand for 45 minutes (fig. 3). Pound with a suricogi (wooden pestle, fig. 4). Mix flour with very hot rice and pound again (fig. 5). Wet both hands in cold water and knead rice (fig. 6). Dip hands in cold water each time before handling hot rice. When most of the rice grains are broken down, the kneading process is completed.

Bring water to a boil in rice steamer. Put a wet cloth inside the pan after water begins to steam. Place mochi-flour mixture on top of the wet cloth and cover with the same cloth. Steam-cook at high heat for 20 minutes (fig. 7). Pierce mochi with a dry chopstick – if nothing sticks to it when it is withdrawn, the mochi is done (fig. 8). Spoon out a lump of mochi, form it into a ball, and coat it with the covering you prefer (fig. 9). Also shape the mochi into 3″ flat rounds, put a dab of cooked azuki in the center (fig. 10). This is called daifuku.

If you have some extra mochi, make 2″ diameter flat rounds, or large loaf shapes, and cover with flour. Leave this until cool. If using loaf shapes, slice mochi ½″ thick the day after making it. You will need a cutting board, knife, and wet dish towel. When cutting mochi, put all your weight on the knife and press down. After a while the knife will get sticky, so keep the knife wet and clean. Store mochi in the freezer – can keep for 6 months. Bake or fry before serving.

If you want to store mochi dry for later use as snack, first form the mochi into bread dough shapes and cut it into ⅛″ thin slices or ⅓″ square pieces for snacks and keep in a clean dry place for 10 days. After drying, you can keep it in a covered jar for a long time. When you serve this dry mochi, toast it first in a dry fry pan, or deep fry and sprinkle with salt, amasake, or yinnie syrup. Deep fried, it makes good croutons for potage, miso, or clear soup. After cutting mochi, keep it fresh in a plastic bag, tie and freeze. It will keep a long time this way.

If not frozen, mold will easily grow on mochi. However, this is not harmful. Just scrape it off with a knife. If it becomes very moldy and dry, scrape off the mold and soak the mochi in water. Wash off the flour and keep it covered with cold water in a cool place. Change the water after three days. After 5 days the mochi will get soft. Then let it drain for ½ day before using it. Cut the mochi into 1″ square pieces, heat up a fry pan and toast both sides for 5 minutes with cover until mochi is soft. Then you can serve it with any kind of sauce or dish.

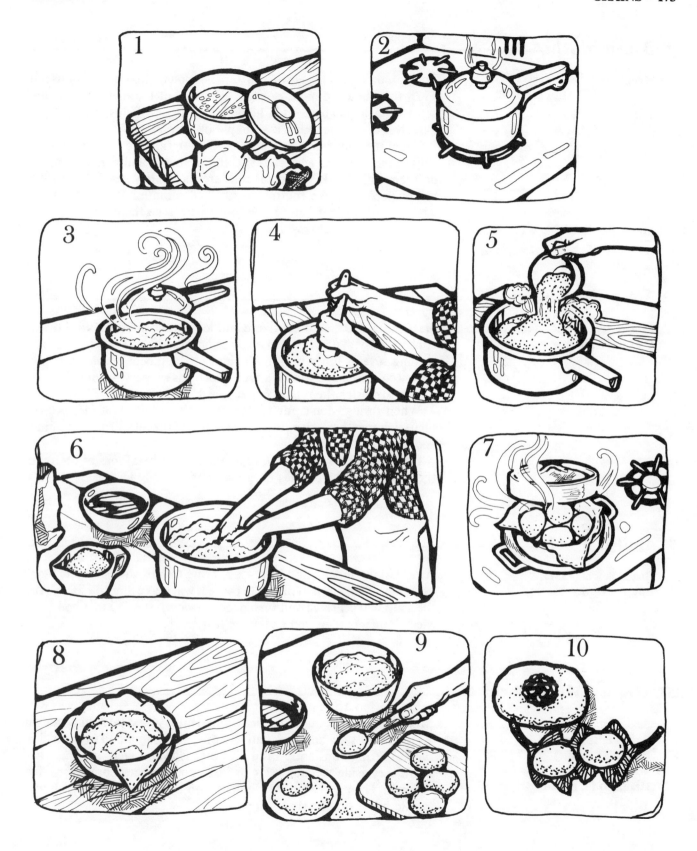

351. Baked Mochi

Mochi

To cook on top of a gas stove, a Japanese metal toaster is very useful. Turn the flame up high, put mochi on top of the metal toaster and cover with a pie pan. This holds steam in and helps it bake more quickly. As it cooks turn it a couple of times.

If you use the oven, preheat it to 450°, until the oven racks are hot (this prevents the mochi from sticking to them), and place the mochi on them to bake. If the metal rods are too widely spaced, put silver foil on top and bake the mochi for 7-10 minutes. When the mochi have puffed up, but before they pop open, take them out.

A toaster oven also works well.

352. Deep Fried Mochi

Mochi
Oil for deep frying

Heat oil to 350°, shut off flame and let sit for 5 minutes until the oil cools slightly. Turn the flame to medium high, add mochi and fry – turning several times until both sides of the mochi become a golden yellow color. Then drain on a rack which has a reservoir for saving the oil, and transfer them to a paper towel.

When frying, don't put too many in the oil at one time, because they stick together. Also, the temperature of the oil will drop too much and they won't cook well.

If the mochi taste too oily, toast them on a metal toaster on top of the stove. This evaporates excess oil and the oily taste.

353. Boiled Mochi

Baked mochi (#351)
Soup of choice

After baking mochi, add it to soup, bring to boil, and simmer. Don't use a high flame to boil mochi because it will make them dissolve. Also the soup will get thick and turbid. So, always just bring to a boil once, then simmer – then you can serve it immediately.

354. Orange Miso Mochi

Baked mochi (#351)
Barley miso (mugi)
Rice miso (kome)
Water and sake
Orange rind, grated

Mix barley (mugi) miso and rice (kome) miso ½ and ½. Add water and a little bit of sake and mix until creamy. Bring to a boil over medium flame stirring constantly until all water is evaporated and miso gets shiny. Set aside to cool. Mix in just enough grated orange rind to flavor it. Then spread baked mochi with this sauce and garnish with a little bit of orange rind.

355. Yaki Mochi Nabe

12 pieces of mochi, 2″ × 3″
½ lb. white meat fish
½ cup flour
1 bunch watercress
1 cup grated daikon radish
2 eggs, fertile, organic (optional)
8 cups soup stock
1 tsp. salt
3 Tbsp. soy sauce
Oil for deep frying

Tempura batter (see #66)
⅔ cup whole wheat pastry flour
⅓ cup water
1 egg
2 Tbsp. sesame seeds

Deep-fry mochi and drain off excess oil. Cut fish into bite size pieces, cover with flour, dip in tempura batter and deep-fry. Wash watercress and cut into 2″ pieces.

Decorate a big plate with fried mochi, fish tempura, and watercress. Put grated daikon in a bowl in the center. Beat 2 eggs and reserve them in a small bowl.

Bring soup stock to a boil, add 1 tsp. salt and 3 Tbsp. soy sauce. Add ½ of the bowl of grated daikon to the soup stock. Add two beaten eggs and stir. Then add mochi, fish tempura, and watercress. Bring to a boil and serve immediately at the table on a small warming unit if you have one.

Keep adding more daikon, mochi, tempura, and watercress as it is used up by your guests and family.

356. Wrapped Mochi

1 piece baked or boiled salmon
2 Tbsp. mayonnaise (see #75)
⅓ cup boiled crab
2 Tbsp. French dressing (mix 1 Tbsp. rice vinegar, 2 Tbsp. olive or corn oil, and ½ tsp. salt)
3 Chinese cabbage leaves, 1″ matchsticks
1 apple, 1″ matchsticks
2 Tbsp. peanut butter
1 tsp. mustard paste (see #83)
2 sheets nori

Break salmon into small pieces and mix with 1 Tbsp. mayonnaise. Break crab into small pieces and mix with 1 Tbsp. French dressing. Squeeze water from cabbage and mix with 1 Tbsp. French dressing and apple. Toast nori and cut each sheet the long way into 8 pieces and put this into serving dish. Mix the peanut butter with the mustard paste. Now take all the dressings to the table and let each person make his own choice of sauces. Finally, each one can wrap his mochi with a strip of nori and enjoy them.

357. Bonita Mochi

Mochi
Water for boiling
Soy sauce
Bonita, fresh-shaved

Bake mochi in the oven or on top of a gas stove. Then boil it in plain water. When mochi gets soft, remove it to the serving plate. Put a drop of soy sauce on each square and top with fresh-shaved bonita. Serve immediately.

358. Oroshi Mochi

Baked mochi (#351)
Daikon, grated
Soy sauce to taste
Nori

Grate daikon, squeeze out a little of the water, add a small amount of soy sauce and mix. Roast nori, cut with scissors into long threadlike strips. Pass the baked mochi through boiling water. Set on serving dishes and cover each piece with grated radish. Then garnish the center with a pinch of nori strips.

Another good topping for mochi is azuki squash (see #390).

359. Rice Patties

2 cups cooked rice
1 cup chopped, roasted walnuts
1 cup bread crumbs
4 Tbsp. chopped onion
1 tsp. savory
Salt to taste
1 Tbsp. oil
¼ cup chopped green pepper
  (optional)
Liquid and flour as needed
Oil for frying

Form into patties, adding flour and liquid (grain milk or water) as needed. Fry and drain.

360. Lentil and Rice Loaf

2 cups cooked rice
1 Tbsp. chopped onion
1 Tbsp. browned whole wheat flour
⅓ cup chopped, toasted nuts
1 cup cooked lentils, pureed
1 Tbsp. oil
3 Tbsp. grain milk or water
Sprinkle of savory

Mix all ingredients until earlobe consistency, adding flour as needed. Form into loaf in baking dish or casserole and bake in 350° oven until browned.

361. Buckwheat Potato Casserole

1 cup cooked buckwheat groats
4-5 Idaho potatoes
1 chopped onion
Chopped parsley
½ cup feta or goat milk cheese
  (optional)

Liquid mix
2 cups cooked rice cream (#5)
  or kokkoh
2 beaten eggs
Dash of salt
Soy sauce to taste

Slice the potatoes thin. Place into a greased baking dish, in alternate layers: potatoes, buckwheat, onions, parsley, and the liquid until all ingredients are used. Top with cheese if desired and bake approximately 1 hour at 350° or until done.

Vegetables

362. Stuffed Cabbage

8-10 large cabbage leaves
⅓ cup seitan
3-4 scallions, chopped
3-4 Tbsp. leftover rice
3″ × 4″ piece kombu
Oil for sauteing
Soy sauce
Arrowroot or flour

Parboil cabbage leaves in salted water or stock for 2 minutes. Drain and save the water. Saute the scallions, then the seitan. Mix with the rice and season with soy sauce. Fill each cabbage leaf, roll it up and secure with a toothpick. Place the kombu in the pan with water from cooking the cabbage. Add the cabbage rolls and simmer for 20 minutes. Remove rolls and keep warm. Thicken juices with arrowroot or flour and serve with the rolls.

363. Stuffed Acorn Squash

3-4 acorn squash
2 small carrots, quarter moons
3 med. onions, minced
1 small head cabbage, thinly sliced
5 shrimp or ⅓ cup seitan, sliced ¼″
1 tsp. oil
1 egg (optional)

Bechamel sauce
1 cup whole wheat pastry flour
1 Tbsp. oil
1½ cups water

Cut acorns in half and remove seeds. Cut small piece off bottom of each so they will sit balanced, and place them on a cookie sheet.

Heat the oil, add the onions and saute until transparent. Add cabbage and saute until color changes. Then add carrots and when the color changes, add the salt to taste and the shrimp or seitan. Cook 10 minutes with the cover off. If ⅓ cup seitan is substituted for the shrimp, chop the seitan and mix with the cooked vegetables before mixing in the bechamel sauce. Do not cook.

Make the bechamel sauce with salt to taste. Mix into the cooked vegetables. Add 1 beaten egg (optional) to the mixture now. Stuff the mixture into the squash pieces and put oil on the edges of the squash. Bake at 350° for 1 hour.

364. Carrots with Sesame Seeds

2 carrots, matchsticks
1 Tbsp. corn or sesame oil
3 Tbsp. sesame seeds
½ tsp. salt
2 tsp. soy sauce

Saute the sesame seeds in a small amount of corn or sesame oil for a few minutes. Add the carrots. Add a little water to cover the bottom of the pan, salt and cover; cook on a low flame. When the vegetables are cooked and all the moisture is evaporated, add soy sauce to taste. Cook an additional 5 minutes.

365. Carrots with Walnuts

2 carrots, matchsticks
3 Tbsp. walnuts
½ Tbsp. oil
1 tsp. salt
½ cup water

Roast walnuts in a dry pan, grind, and reserve. Heat oil and saute carrots with salt, add water and cook on low flame until liquid is almost evaporated. Combine with walnuts, cook a little longer and serve.

366. Winter Vegetable Miso

½ cup burdock, shaved
1 cup onion, crescents
½ cup squash (any winter squash),
    ½″ diced
¼ cup carrot, diagonals
¼-⅓ cup mugi miso
2 Tbsp. sesame oil

Heat pan. Saute burdock in oil until smell is gone, add onion, and saute until color is transparent. Add squash, carrot, and shiso leaves. Add ¼ cup water, bring to a boil until tender. Add 3 Tbsp. of water to the miso and mix well. Add to cooking vegetables. Slowly and carefully mix in the miso. Then bring to a boil until miso smell is gone. Shut off flame. These miso vegetables can be served either cold or hot. If you use more onion, it will taste sweeter. Some children don't like miso soup, though they need miso. So this is an appetizing way of serving it.

Garnish with minced parsley or celery tops.

367. Fresh Daikon Nitsuke

1 med. daikon (1½″ diameter),
    matchsticks
2 tsp. oil
½ tsp. salt
2 Tbsp. soy sauce

Saute daikon in oil with cover for 5 minutes. Add salt and 1 Tbsp. soy sauce and slowly mix. Lower heat for a few minutes so that vegetable releases its own juice. Then raise to medium flame, cook about 20 minutes or until tender, stirring occasionally. Shut off flame. Sprinkle 1 Tbsp. soy sauce on top. Mix and serve.

368. Salmon Vegetable Pie

Fresh salmon (or tuna)
2-3 onions, minced
3-4 stalks celery, thin rounds
4 green olives (optional)
Pie dough (see #92)
Bechamel sauce (see #187)
Soy sauce
Oil
Salt

Prepare pie dough, roll out shape to pie tin. Bake pie shell until light golden color and then cool it. Make bechamel sauce.

Saute onion and celery in the oil until transparent and tender. Add to the bechamel sauce and cook until flavors blend. Flake the cooked fish and add to the bechamel sauce mixture just before ready to bake. Add sliced olives for special occasions. Season with soy sauce and salt to taste. Pour into the pie shell and place in preheated 350° oven to heat through – 10-15 minutes. Delicious.

For variety from time to time, change the flour and/or vegetables used.

369. Farofa (Brazilian Dish)

Vegetables of your choice
Cornmeal, well roasted
Oil
Salt and soy sauce to taste

Take your favorite vegetables (broccoli, cauliflower, carrots, burdock, kale, or collards) and cut fine. Saute with some onion in a little more oil than usual. When nearly done, add some well-roasted cornmeal (there should be more vegetables than cornmeal). Sprinkle in a few drops of water if it seems dry. Season with salt and soy sauce. Place a tight cover on pan and let it steam for awhile. It should come out fluffy. Serve hot.

Stews

370. Tofu Vegetable Nabe

½ lb. tofu, cut 1″ cubes
½ head Chinese cabbage, 1″ squares
½ bunch spinach, 2″ lengths
1 carrot, flower shape or diagonals
1 burdock, long diagonals
4″ piece dashi kombu
4 cups water, approx.
1 bunch scallions, 1½″ diagonals
Soy sauce and salt to taste

Place kombu on the bottom of a pot. Add burdock, then add Chinese cabbage and carrot in separate sections on either side of pot. Cover with water ½″ over vegetables. Add soy sauce and salt to taste, cook uncovered until tender. Add spinach, tofu, and scallions and slightly boil. Combine 1 Tbsp. fresh lemon juice with 2-3 Tbsp. soy sauce and serve individual portions as a dipping sauce for vegetables and tofu.

The traditional Japanese way to serve nabe is with the serving pot in the middle of the table. Individual bowls are served, and extra broth can be added as desired.

371. Yose Nabe

½ lb. chicken (or shrimp, shelled and deveined)
10 oysters, washed in salted water
5 med. shiitake mushrooms, soaked and cut ¼-½″ pieces, or ½ cup fresh mushrooms
2 carrots, flower shape
1 bunch watercress, top leaves only
1 bunch scallions, ¼″ diagonals
½ head Chinese cabbage, use inner leaves only, 2″ rounds
4 cups soup stock (#39)
2 Tbsp. soy sauce
2 tsp. salt
½ lb. whole wheat noodles or saifun

Place the cabbage in the center of the pan. Place the chicken, shiitake, carrots, oysters, and watercress around the cabbage. Bring soup stock to a boil in another pot and add salt and soy sauce. After it has boiled, pour it over the vegetables, bring to a boil again and cook until the vegetables are tender. Add noodles or saifun (if using saifun, cover with boiling water and let sit one hour) and simmer until warm. Top with chopped scallions. As you serve, add more items to the nabe pan.

372. Radish Turnip Nabe

4" × 1½" piece daikon, cut in half
   lengthwise, then ⅓" half rounds
5 turnips, ⅓" crescents
5 Chinese cabbage leaves
3 pieces of age (store-bought or
   homemade), bite-size pieces
1 bunch scallions, diagonals
2 heaping Tbsp. mugi miso
⅛" piece dashi kombu cut part way
   through every 1"

Boil daikon in salted water until tender, do the same with turnip. Boil cabbage leaves a few minutes in salted water, stack leaves on a sushi mat, roll up, then cut into ½" rolls.

Around the edge of an 8" shallow pan, make a bank of miso against the sides. Pour 3 cups of water into the pan gently so as not to disturb the miso, turn the flame to high, add kombu and bring to a boil. Then gently place each vegetable in a separate section: Daikon, cabbage, age, turnip, and scallion. Bring to a boil and cook for 10 minutes. The miso slowly dissolves into the vegetables as they stew and gives them a wonderful flavor. If possible, bring the pan to the table and cook with a heating unit. Serve with toasted mochi, boiled noodles, or soba. These are nice to add, especially if you have extra juice. This dish is good for the cold season because it makes your body warm very quickly.

373. Vegetable Nabe with Mochi

10 pieces baked mochi (see #351)
1 bunch scallions, diagonals
1 piece fu (dried wheat gluten),
   ½" strips
3 pieces mock goose (ganmodoki,
   #67), cut in ¼" pieces
8" piece dashi kombu, slice in
   1" pieces
2 Tbsp. soy sauce
2 tsp. salt
Oil for deep frying

Cut fu with scissors and deep fry.

Bring 5 cups water to a boil and cook the kombu for 1 hour. Add 2 tsp. salt, remove kombu pieces, add 2 tsp. soy sauce and half of the other ingredients (mochi, scallions, fu, ganmodoki) and bring to a boil. Bring the pan to the table and serve from a hotplate or warming unit. Add the other half of the ingredients after the first serving has been made.

374. Oyster Nabe

1 lb. fresh oysters
2 bunches scallions, diagonals
2 bunches watercress,
   top leaves only
1 block tofu, 10 1" cubes
½ pkg. harusame
2 cups soup stock (#39)
½ tsp. salt
2 Tbsp. soy sauce

Wash oysters in salted water and drain. Bring a little water to a boil, add harusame and cook 5 minutes. Drain.

Decorate a big plate with all ingredients. Bring soup stock to a boil, add salt and soy sauce and ½ the remaining ingredients. Bring to a boil and serve steaming hot at the table. Keep it hot at the table on a hot plate or heating unit. After serving the first time, add the rest of the ingredients.

A sprinkle of orange rind on each dish is nice when you serve.

375. Oyster Nabe with Miso

1-2 lbs. oysters (Washington)
3 bunches watercress,
  top leaves only
3 pieces (¾ lb.) tofu, 1″ squares
1 lb. Chinese cabbage, 1″ diagonals
½ cup miso (½ barley and ½ white)
2 bunches scallions, long diagonals
1 Tbsp. orange peel, grated
½ cup soup stock (#39)

Cook miso in heated pan until fragrant, without burning. Cool. Mix in orange peel. Using a shallow iron or Corningware pan, spread miso across the entire pan. Add the soup stock. Arrange the vegetables in the pan with the oysters. Cook over medium heat; do not overcook. Add more stock as necessary. Add more water if too salty. Mix in miso around the pan with chopsticks or ladle.

376. Chiri Nabe

1 lb. white meat fish such as cod,
  red snapper, or bass
3 small turnips, thin crescents
1 small Chinese cabbage, 1″ squares
2 bunches scallions, ¼″ long
  diagonals
2 bunches watercress or spinach,
  1″ lengths
1 lb. tofu, 1″ cubes
6″ piece kombu
5 cups water
3 Tbsp. sake

If you use whole fish, cut the head into 1½″ square pieces, rub with 1 Tbsp. salt to remove the strong smell, wash off completely before using.

Soak kombu in water for 2 hours with sake. Bring water to a boil and remove kombu. Add fish and turnips, cook until half done and add Chinese cabbage. Cook until turnips are tender. Then add scallions and watercress. Cook only for a few minutes. Add tofu. Serve with lemon sauce in a side dish. This dish is not oily, rich, or heavy; it has a very delicate enjoyable taste. If you have leftover soup stock or sauce, it can be served over noodles.

Lemon sauce

1 Tbsp. lemon juice
1 Tbsp. soy sauce
¼ tsp. grated ginger (optional)
1 scallion, minced and washed
  (optional)

Mix ingredients together and serve on the side.

377. Boiled Tofu (Yudofu)

1 lb. tofu, 1″ cubes
3″ square kombu
Orange peel, grated
1 heaping Tbsp. chopped scallion
1 Tbsp. bonita flakes
3-4 Tbsp. soy sauce

Cut kombu comb-shape and place in pot with 5 cups of water and soak 30 minutes. In a smaller porcelain bowl or tall teacup, place 3-4 Tbsp. soy sauce with bits of orange peel, scallion, and 1 Tbsp. bonita flakes. Place this sauce cup in the center of the pot. Bring the kombu stock to a boil uncovered, and add tofu to the stock. Cook until tofu rises to the surface. Remove tofu and serve with the warm dipping sauce.

Variation: Add fresh lemon juice to the dipping sauce.

378. Furofuki

1 daikon, 1″ rounds
3 turnips, quartered
6″ piece kombu
⅓ cup sweet rice

Orange miso
3 Tbsp. mugi miso
1 Tbsp. sesame oil
3 Tbsp. boiling water
¼ tsp. orange peel

Place kombu on bottom of pan, add daikon and turnip and cover with water. Also add ⅓ cup of sweet rice tied up in a small cotton bag. Add salt according to taste, bring to a boil and cook on a medium flame for about 2 hours until the vegetables are tender. Longer cooking makes the vegetables taste sweeter. This dish can be served at the table in an earthenware or Corningware pan. In serving, add miso to the stock and drink it. You can use kome miso, sesame miso, scallion miso, oily miso, or orange peel miso.

Saute miso in hot oil about 5-7 minutes, until a good miso fragrance is produced, but be careful not to burn it. Add the water and bring to a boil. Add the orange peel and remove from flame.

This dish makes you warm in cold weather. It is necessary to have a clean pan and cooking dishes with daikon and turnip or the taste of the foods previously cooked in the pan will conflict with the taste of the daikon and turnip.

379. Udon Sukiyaki

1½ lbs. udon, spaghetti, or homemade noodles
1 lb. tofu
10 pieces wheat cutlet (#49), cut in bite-size pieces
3 bunches scallions, diagonals
5 med. shiitake mushrooms, soaked 20 minutes, cut in half or ½ lb. fresh mushrooms
10 pieces baked mochi (#351)
½ head Chinese cabbage, cut in 1″ pieces
1 bunch watercress
5 cups soup stock (#39 or #40)
1 tsp. salt
2 Tbsp. soy sauce

Homemade noodles
5 cups unbleached flour
1 tsp. salt
1⅓ cups cold water

Mix flour and salt, gradually adding the water. Knead until earlobe consistency. Roll out to ⅛″ thickness. Flour the top of the dough and fold it over in half. Flour again and fold again – repeating the process until folded dough is about 2″-3″ in width. This makes it easier to cut the noodles. Be careful not to press too hard on the dough, so that it doesn't stick together. Bring 8 cups water to a boil with 1 tsp. salt. Add noodles. Cook until tender, rinse in cold water, and strain off the water. Pick up a handful of noodles and twist them so that they resemble a circle. Place them in a serving bowl.

To make the sukiyaki, arrange all the vegetables on a platter. Place soup stock, salt, and soy sauce in a pot and bring to a boil. Add Chinese cabbage and cook for a short time. Add the other ingredients and the noodles. Cook for 5 minutes and serve immediately.

Sukiyaki can be cooked and served at the table for nice variation. Other vegetables, white fish, chicken, etc., can be used for special occasions.

380. Vegetable Oden *(Nikomi Oden)*

10″ piece daikon, 1″ rounds
2 carrots, ½″ rounds
10 taro, washed well
4″ lotus root, ⅓″ rounds
1 piece konnyaku, cut in 12 pieces
10 Brussels sprouts, quartered
    through roots
24″ piece nishime (thin) kombu
5½ cups water
3 Tbsp. soy sauce
Mock chicken (#68) or
    mock goose (#67) or
    tofu rafts (#325)

Mustard sauce
1 Tbsp. dry mustard
½ Tbsp. hot tea

Soak kombu in water for 10 minutes until a little soft – to remove sand. Strain kombu and reserve water. Tie kombu in knots, then slice into 3″ pieces. Place tied kombu in the bottom of a big pot. Add daikon, taro, konnyaku, carrot, and lotus root in layers, then add the kombu water and enough plain water to cover. Add 2 Tbsp. soy sauce. Bring to boil. Continue to cook oden until tender (about 1 hour). Add more soy sauce to taste (similar in taste to clear soup).

Boil Brussels sprouts in salted water for 7 minutes without cover, strain, and let cool. Then add oden for a few minutes to warm up. Serve with mustard as a condiment if you like. (Not recommended for people with hemorrhoids.)

To make mustard sauce, mix dry mustard and hot green or bancha tea well in an ovenproof bowl. Invert the bowl over a burner on low heat for about 5-10 minutes until it gives off a potent mustard smell and is slightly browned. Serve on the table, to be mixed with soy sauce or oden sauce. This is a very good condiment for Chinese cabbage pickles or pressed salad.

Note: Oden can be served in any season by substituting the vegetables of that season.

381. Country Style Chicken Stew

1-2 pieces chicken meat
1 onion, ¼″ crescents
1 med. daikon, large shaved
1 med. carrot, cut as daikon
1 med. burdock, shaved
3 med. shiitake (soak and remove
    stems)
1 konnyaku, cut bite-size
1 lb. albi, ½″ irregular wedges
5 cups soup stock (#39)
1 Tbsp. oil
1½ tsp. salt
1½ Tbsp. soy sauce
2 Tbsp. kuzu

Heat oil, saute the onion, burdock, shiitake, daikon, carrot, and konnyaku. When color changes, add the chicken and albi. Saute a short time and add a pinch of salt. Add the soup stock or water and bring to a boil. Add salt and soy sauce and cook on medium heat. (Note: Taste the vegetables, not just the soup stock, before salting.) Dissolve kuzu and add to soup. Serve hot.

In hunting season, there may be quail, pheasant, or other hunter's luck available.

Note: I use the edge of a sake cup or a teacup to cut konnyaku.

Soups

382. Miso Soup

1″ piece of daikon, 1½″ in
    diameter, matchsticks
5 scallions, ¼″ lengths
2-3 strips of wakame, cut
    in small pieces
5 cups water
1 tsp. sesame oil
2 Tbsp. miso

Heat oil, saute daikon until slightly softened. Add 5 cups water, bring to a boil, add wakame and cook until the wakame is soft. Add scallions, bring to a boil, then turn off. Put the miso into a metal strainer and mash it through into the soup; whatever won't go through the strainer, turn it over into the soup. Serve immediately.

Use this as a basic miso soup recipe, substituting other vegetable combinations for daikon and scallions.

The following are good winter combinations for soups. Onion and wakame should accompany all these.

onion – turnip	turnip – wakame	Chinese cabbage – wakame
burdock – scallion	Chinese cabbage – turnip	radish – age
albi – daikon	wakame – any soup greens	Chinese cabbage – daikon
squash – scallion	carrot – turnip	albi – scallion
scallion – daikon	scallion – sweet potato	dried daikon
cabbage – daikon	albi – carrot	burdock – daikon
radish – carrot	onion – cabbage	beet – onion
	Chinese cabbage – wakame	

Please take one of these combinations in miso soup once a day. Mugi miso is best for general use. Adults should use 1 heaping teaspoon of miso each day. Children and old people should take 1 level teaspoon or ½ teaspoon per day. If you take miso in some form every day, as soup or vegetable nitsuke, etc., your body will not crave meat, chicken, fish, or especially dairy products.

---

383. Squash Potage

1 med. squash (acorn, butternut,
    banana, cut in squares or other)
4 large onions, quartered
1 tsp. salt
1 Tbsp. oil
3 Tbsp. whole wheat pastry flour
Soy sauce to taste

Saute onions and squash in oil for about 5 minutes. Add ½ cup water and salt and pressure-cook for 20 minutes. Remove cover when pressure is down. Place ingredients in a blender or a food mill and make a puree. To 8 cups of puree, add 3 cups of water.

Roast the flour in the oil. Cool. Make a paste with 1 cup water and add this gradually to the squash puree, stirring constantly to prevent lumping. Add soy sauce to taste. Simmer 5 minutes (or until thickened) and serve. Garnish with parsley and croutons.

Variation: Cook whole cauliflower in salted water for 7 minutes, bottom side up, cut into flowerettes, and add to potage with croutons.

384. Daikon Miso Soup with Salmon

½ salmon head (fresh, not salted)
2 daikon, thick shaved
2 onions, minced
1 Tbsp. oil
Miso to taste

Saute minced onions in 1 Tbsp. oil. When the color changes, add chopped salmon and saute 5 to 7 minutes. Add daikon and saute a few minutes more. Then add water to cover vegetables. Cook on medium flame until tender. Add miso. It is good to cool this completely. Then reheat on stove just before serving for best flavor.

385. Clear Chicken Soup *(Mizutake)*

½ young chicken, cut in 6 pieces
7 cups water
Salt and soy sauce to taste

Lemon sauce
½ cup soup stock (#39)
2 Tbsp. soy sauce
2 tsp. lemon juice

Bring water to a boil and add chicken; do not cover. Cook on a low flame until bubbles appear, skim the top of the water. Cook for 1 hour or until the meat separates from the bone. A low flame keeps your stock from getting dark. Bring it to the table, place it on a hibachi or some small heating unit. Reheat and serve with salt and soy sauce.

Lemon sauce may be served as a side dish. To prepare, bring ½ cup soup stock and 2 Tbsp. soy sauce to a boil, let cool, and add 2 tsp. lemon juice.

For condiments, try grated ginger or sarashinegi (#205). For a good balance you may want to serve this with Chinese cabbage, carrot, watercress, etc., but it tastes best when eaten alone. It is better than fried chicken.

386. Country Chicken Soup

1 lb. chicken with bone
1 lb. small albi or taro, whole
1 carrot, irregular wedges
6″ daikon, thick shaved
1 small bunch scallions, ⅓″ rounds
5 med. shiitake, soaked in water, or
   1 cup fresh mushrooms, quartered
⅓ cup barley miso (or ½ barley
   miso and ½ rice miso)
8 cups water

Bring water to a boil and add the chicken. When marrow and potassium come out of the bone, skim off the bubbles and discard but leave the chicken in the pot. Continue cooking at low boil for 50 minutes. Add the vegetables and cook until tender. Dilute the miso and add to the soup. Cook 10 minutes longer until vegetables absorb the miso taste. Add the scallions and bring to a boil. Remove from stove and serve. Adding more of a variety of vegetables, selected with a balance of yin and yang, increases the flavor and richness of this soup.

The secret of this recipe is the long cooking time which makes the chicken tender and tasty, as well as the blending of the miso with the vegetables.

387. Country Soup with Salmon

½ salted salmon head, cut into
   small pieces
10″ piece daikon, 1½″ shaved
1 carrot, ⅓″ half moons
3 small onions, ½″ crescents
3 med. potatoes, irregular wedges
5 cups water
1 tsp. ginger juice
1 Tbsp. oil
Soy sauce and salt to taste

Saute the salmon head, then add potatoes, onions, daikon, and carrot. Saute well, then add the 5 cups water. Cook until tender. Taste first before adding salt and soy sauce as needed. Add 1 tsp. ginger juice before turning off the flame. Remove from heat and serve immediately.

Any salted fish or other vegetables may be used. (Use albi instead of potatoes for those who are sick.)

388. Winter Kenchin Soup

4″ piece daikon, ¼″ quarter moons
1 carrot, half moons
1 lb. albi, remove skin,
   irregular wedges
1 lb. tofu, strain water and squeeze
   by hand
3 Tbsp. sake-no-kasu
2 Tbsp. miso
½ tsp. salt
1 Tbsp. oil
6 cups water
5 scallions, ¼″ rounds

Dissolve sake-no-kasu in hot water or cut into small pieces. Saute the daikon, albi, carrot, and broken (mashed) tofu in that order, add 6 cups water and salt and bring to a boil. When the vegetables are half done add the sake-no-kasu and cook for 10 minutes. Add the miso and cook an additional 5 minutes. Add scallions. Sprinkle with orange rind and serve.

389. Sake-No-Kasu Soup with Salmon

½ daikon or turnip,
   ¼″ quarter moons
1 carrot, ¼″ quarter moons
1 med. burdock, shaved
1 filet of salmon
3 Tbsp. sake-no-kasu
⅓ cup mugi miso

Saute burdock, daikon, and carrot then add salmon in one piece. Saute well, then add boiling water to 1″ above the vegetables. Bring to a boil and cook until tender. Add boiling water to sake-no-kasu and cream together. Add boiling water to miso and blend. Add both to the soup and cook 5 minutes more.

Sake-no-kasu is a residue left over from sake-making and makes the body warm. It is available in Japanese food stores in many large cities.

Beans

390. Azuki Winter Squash Nitsuke

1 cup azuki beans
3 cups water
4 cups sliced winter squash
    (butternut or Hubbard)
1 tsp. salt
2″ × 2″ piece kombu

Soak the washed azuki beans with kombu in 1½ cups cold water at least 5 hours, or overnight. Bring them to a boil on a high flame, add ½ cup cold water and bring to a boil again. Repeat this procedure twice more and cook on low flame.

When the beans are tender (about 1 hour) add the sliced squash and salt and continue cooking until the squash is tender. Stir the nitsuke so that some of the squash gets mashed, similar to a puree.

This dish is beneficial to those who have diabetes or kidney diseases. It can also be used as a covering for mochi, or as a filling for muffins.

391. Soybean Nishime

1 cup dry soybeans
3 med. burdock, irregular wedges
3 carrots, irregular wedges
2 cups kombu, cut 1″ square (soak
    in water to cover, 10-20 minutes)
1 Tbsp. sesame oil
1 tsp. salt
1 Tbsp. soy sauce

Roast soybeans in a dry pan until beans have 2-3 spots of brown color. Saute burdock in open pressure cooker until smell is gone, add beans and saute for 5 minutes. Filter kombu water through a cotton cloth and add to burdock, beans and kombu. Bring pressure up over a high flame and cook 20 minutes over medium flame. Shut off. After pressure returns to normal, take off cover, add carrot, bring to a boil until pressure is up, then shut off flame and remove from heat. Take off cover, add salt and soy sauce, and cook for 20 more minutes. Toss vegetables and mix bottom and top. Without cover, evaporate the juice. Soybeans are quite yin, so cook them with something yang, like burdock and seaweed, hijiki, onion, carrot, or lotus root. If you have fresh lotus root, add 1½ cups of lotus root to make a very delicious dish.

392. Chick Pea Sauce for Millet

2 cups millet
2 cups chickpeas
2 med. onions, ⅓″ crescents
1 carrot, diced in ⅓″ cubes
5 cabbage leaves, cut in ½″ squares
1 square dry tofu or ¼ lb. fresh tofu
1 Tbsp. oil
1 tsp. salt
2 Tbsp. minced parsley

Soak 2 cups chickpeas 4-5 hours in 4 cups water, pressure-cook 45 minutes and let pressure return to normal naturally.

Soak, squeeze, and repeat soaking dry tofu until water is clear, changing water several times. Cut into ⅓″ squares. If you can get hard style fresh tofu, use ¼ lb.

Heat the oil, saute the onion until it is transparent, add the tofu, cabbage, and carrots. Add the cooked chick peas, cover with water and bring to a boil. When the vegetables begin to soften, add the salt and cook until the vegetables are tender.

Wash the millet, add to 4 cups of boiling water with ¼ tsp. salt. Pressure-cook for 20 minutes. To serve, cover the millet with the sauce and garnish with parsley. Millet cooked this way is similar to cous-cous in taste.

393. Lentil Soup

1 cup lentils
3 med. onions, thin crescents
1 carrot, ¼″ quarter moons
½ stalk celery, ¼″ diced
1 Tbsp. oil
2 tsp. salt
4-5 cups boiling water
1 tsp. soy sauce

Soak lentils in 2 cups water and pressure-cook 20 minutes.

Heat oil, saute onion until brown, add carrot, saute a few minutes, add celery, saute a few minutes, add boiling water and cook for 10 minutes over low flame. Add cooked lentils and salt and cook for 40 minutes.

Season well with soy sauce and serve hot. Sprinkle with minced parsley.

394. Lentil Stuffed Pancakes

1 cup cooked or leftover lentils
1 cup buckwheat flour
1 Tbsp. arrowroot flour
2½ cups water
½ tsp. salt

Mix buckwheat flour, arrowroot flour, salt, and water; heat oil, and make two or three 4″ diameter thin crepes (pancakes), and fry. When half done, add 1 heaping Tbsp. of lentils and fold up pancake on both sides. Turn over and fry both sides in covered pan. This is a country dish from Belgium; simple, but the combination of buckwheat and lentils is very tasty. Especially good for winter.

395. Lentil Roll

Leftover lentils
Pie dough (see #92)

Roll out dough into rectangular shape. Spread cooked, leftover lentils (or other vegetables and/or beans, etc.) on top of dough and roll as if making a jelly roll. Join ends of roll together, making a 'brioche' shape to the lentil roll. Place on an oiled, pre-heated cookie sheet and bake 30-45 minutes at 400°. Cut into ½″-¾″ pieces. A delightful way to use up leftovers. Good for snacks.

396. Bean Combinations for Winter

— Cook pinto beans and azuki beans together. Add onions that have been cooked until transparent, season with salt. Tastes like chili.

— Lima beans with kombu: Pressure-cook kombu a long time. Boil lima beans, add to kombu and pressure-cook together. Add to this a mixture of sauteed onions and bonita flakes and simmer 30 minutes. Season with diluted miso to taste.

— Soak soybeans 12-24 hours. Pressure-cook, then add sauteed lotus root (cut into thick slices) and sauteed chopped onions. Cook down for a few hours, adding soy sauce when beans are soft. Tastes like pork and beans.

— Soak soybeans, then dry. Deep fry, sprinkle with salt, and drain on a paper towel. Makes a delicious snack.

— Red kidney beans and rice: Cook beans and add sauteed onions. Mix with cooked rice. Wrap in partially boiled cabbage leaves and bake as is or place in a casserole and pour bechamel sauce over and bake.

New Year's Recipes

397. Clear Soup Zoni

10 pieces baked mochi, 2″ × 3″ (#351)
7 leaves Chinese cabbage, 1″ squares
½ bunch watercress or
** ½ bunch spinach**
1 sheet nori, roasted and crushed
2 cups boiling water
5 cups soup stock (#39 or #40)
½ tsp. salt
3 Tbsp. soy sauce

Cook greens in salted water, cool, then cut in 1½″pieces. Place cabbage inside pot, adding 2 cups boiling water and salt. Cook until half done. Add soup stock, bring to a boil and add soy sauce and mochi. When mochi becomes slightly soft, serve immediately with cooked greens and nori sprinkled over soup as garnish.

398. Rolled Egg

4 eggs, beaten
1 med. onion, minced fine
2″ carrot, minced fine
3 Tbsp. soup stock or water
1 Tbsp. sake
½ tsp. soy sauce
½ tsp. salt
Oil

Saute onions and carrot with salt, covered, until tender. Let cool completely. Add beaten eggs and remaining ingredients. Brush fry pan with oil and pour in egg mixture. Cook with cover over low to medium flame for 3-5 minutes. Scoop out egg onto plate, then turn over into re-oiled fry pan and cook uncovered until slightly brown (1-2 minutes). Put bamboo sushi mat on top of fry pan and turn over. Then roll as in picture. Let cool about an hour and slice ½″ thick – diagonal or round.

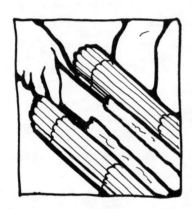 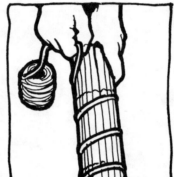 

399. Black Bean Nishime

2 cups black beans
4 cups water
1½ tsp. salt

Soak washed black beans in 4 cups cold water for an hour. Bring beans to a boil in same water and cook covered 1½ hours over low flame. Add salt and cook covered ½ hour more over low flame.

Cook 5 more minutes without cover.

400. Vegetable Nishime

1 med. burdock, irregular wedges
1 konnyaku, 1″ × 2″ squares
2″ lotus root, eighths lengthwise,
    then irregular wedges
1 small carrot, quartered lengthwise,
    then irregular wedges
3 tsp. oil
3 tsp. soy sauce
¼ tsp. salt

Heat 1 tsp. oil and saute burdock until its smell is gone. Add a little water, bring to boil and cook 20 minutes. Add 1 tsp. soy sauce and continue to cook until tender. Cook lotus root the same as burdock.

Heat 1 tsp. oil and saute konnyaku well until bubbles are gone. Add 2 tsp. soy sauce. Cover and cook 20 minutes, mixing a few times. Add ¼ cup water to carrot and bring to a boil. Lower to medium flame, cover and cook 10 more minutes. Add ¼ tsp. salt and cook until tender.

Serve on 5″ long bamboo skewers – 2 per person – burdock, lotus root, konnyaku, and carrot.

401. Albi Nishime

10 med. albi
1 tsp. oil
½ tsp. salt
2 tsp. soy sauce

Scrub albi and scrape off hairy outer skin. Heat oil and saute whole albi. Add ½ cup cold water, ¼ tsp. salt, and bring to a boil. Cook 20 minutes. Add ¼ tsp. salt and soy sauce. Cook until tender.

It will be less salty when cold on the following day. Serve 2 albi per person.

402. Crispy Dried Fish *(Tazukuri)*

1 cup tazukuri
3 Tbsp. soy sauce
1 Tbsp. oil

Heat oil. Saute small fish until crispy. Add soy sauce and keep shaking pan to distribute sauce evenly. Cook until dry. Do not use chopsticks to stir fish as they will break off the heads and tails.

403. Glazed Dried Fish

2 cups tazukuri
2 Tbsp. soy sauce
2 Tbsp. sake
1 Tbsp. yinnie syrup

Roast tazukuri in dry skillet until well dried and brownish in color. In another pan cook together, uncovered over low flame, soy sauce, yinnie syrup, and sake for 5 minutes until mixture becomes thick. Add roasted fish and shake pan until sauce covers fish. Remove to a dish to cool.

404. Celery Sesame Salad

3 stalks celery, thin diagonals
5 Tbsp. sesame seeds
1-2 Tbsp. soy sauce

Place celery in strainer and dip in and out of pan of boiling water. Shake strainer to cool celery. Roast sesame seeds until easily crushed between thumb and 4th finger. Grind seeds in suribachi into butter. Add soy sauce and mix until creamy.

Add cooled celery to creamy sauce after squeezing out excess water in celery between the palms. Mix thoroughly in sauce and serve, or place celery in small individual plates and top with sesame sauce.

405. Chrysanthemum Turnip Salad

2 lbs. large turnips
10 chrysanthemum leaves or
   lettuce leaves
1 Tbsp. salt

Dressing
5 Tbsp. rice vinegar
1 orange rind, grated
2 Tbsp. salt

Wash and cut turnips into 1″ cubes. Then, never lifting the tip of the knife from the cutting board, and cutting into the cube ⅔″, cut cross-hatch into turnip cubes, about ⅛″ across. Sprinkle with salt and let sit 30 minutes until soft. Squeeze out water. Combine dressing ingredients and mix with turnips. Leave in deep bowl so dressing covers turnips for one or two days.

Serve the turnip on a chrysanthemum leaf; press down on cut surface of turnip cubes and spread, to simulate a bloom. In center of 'chrysanthemum' place a pinch of orange rind.

Variation: If turnips are not available, use daikon.

406. Kinton (Pudding)

2 cups sweet meat squash or yams
2 cups dry chestnuts
1½ tsp. salt
1 tsp. minced orange skin

Steam whole squash or yams. Remove skins while hot, add 1 tsp. salt, and mash.

Wash chestnuts and cover with ½″ of warm water, soaking for 2 hours. Use cold water if soaking overnight. Cook chestnuts until half done (about 30 minutes). Add ½ tsp. salt and finish cooking. Drain off liquid and set aside. When cool, mix whole chestnuts with mashed squash and bring to a boil uncovered. Cook about 10 more minutes until thick like mashed potatoes. Mix in orange skin and remove from heat. Serve cold.

407. Apple Kanten

3-5 apples
1 cup sliced apples, peeled
2 bars kanten
3 cups water
3 Tbsp. yinnie syrup or honey
1 tsp. salt

Wash apples, cut each in 8 pieces. If not organic, peel. Remove seeds, then slice thin. Cover with water and cook 20-30 minutes until tender. Puree by food mill or using colander with suricogi. If too watery, cook again to evaporate excess liquid.

Wash kanten in cold water and squeeze out. Soak 5 minutes in 3 cups water. Bring to a boil, add salt and sliced apples and simmer uncovered about 15 minutes. When white foam comes to the surface, skim it off. Add apple sauce and sweetener and cook 5 more minutes, stirring frequently. Rinse a mold with cold water, place kanten in mold, and chill. When completely cold, cut as you wish and serve.

Special Dishes

408. Chawan Mushi (Japanese Egg Custard)

2 eggs, beaten
1 onion, sliced thin
1 small carrot, matchsticks
2 cups soup stock (#40)
1 Tbsp. bonita flakes
1 Tbsp. soy sauce
Optional: lotus root balls (#320) or
    pieces of white meat chicken or
    pieces of fish (red snapper, sea
    bass, etc.). Chicken or fish to be
    marinated with 1 Tbsp. soy sauce
    for 10-20 minutes.

Prepare the soup stock by soaking a 2″ piece of dashi kombu in 2 cups water for 4 hours. After soaking, cook with ¾ tsp. salt for 20 minutes. Add 1 Tbsp. bonita flakes and 1 Tbsp. soy sauce, bring to a boil, then strain and cool. Beat egg and add to this stock when cool. Saute vegetables in oil until tender. Put the vegetables (and lotus balls and fish or chicken) in the bottom of the custard cups (covered ones if possible) and pour the egg-stock mixture over them to the ¾ mark. Set the cups on a rack in a pressure cooker with 1 cup water. Cook 5 minutes under pressure or 15-20 minutes in a steamer or in the oven in a pan filled with a little water.

Serve as a soup course.

409. Chicken with Sweet Rice Stuffing

1½ lb. whole chicken
2 cups water or soup stock (#39)
1 tsp. minced fresh ginger
5 Tbsp. mirin (optional)
2 Tbsp. sake
3 scallions, chopped

Stuffing
½ cup sweet brown rice
3 shiitake mushrooms, soaked in
    ½ cup warm water, then cut
    ¼″ squares
1 stalk celery, ¼″ squares
⅓ cup almonds, slivered
1 Tbsp. sake

Wash sweet rice, place it and ½ cup water in a small bowl, place in top of steamer, and steam for 40 minutes; or place 2 cups water in a pressure cooker and in a small bowl place ½ cup water and ½ cup sweet rice, then bring pressure up using high flame until pressure gauge jiggles, and continue over high flame for 20 minutes. Then shut off. After pressure comes down, remove cover. Mix almonds, celery, mushrooms with cooked rice. Stuff the washed chicken. To wash chicken, remove blood and wipe with a paper towel. Stuff chicken a little over half full, allowing room for expansion as it cooks. Heat 2 Tbsp. of sesame oil in a wok or deep saucepan. Fry both sides of the chicken until it is a beautiful brown color, then add 2 cups water or soup stock, mirin, soy sauce, sake, chopped scallion and 1 tsp. minced ginger. Bring to a boil, then reduce to low flame and cook until tender, about 1½ hours. Turn frequently and cook evenly on all sides. Set decoratively on a large plate.

410. Vegetables and Chicken Nitsuke

½ lb. chicken, sliced thin
1 lb. albi, bite-sized irregular wedges
2 pieces konnyaku, bite-sized
    irregular wedges
1 med. burdock, bite-sized
    irregular wedges
½ lb. fresh mushrooms
1 med. carrot, bite-sized
    irregular wedges
1 bunch watercress, 1″ pieces
1½ cups soup stock (#39)
1 Tbsp. sake
½ tsp. salt
2 Tbsp. soy sauce

Marinate the chicken for 20 minutes in 1 Tbsp. sake and 1 Tbsp. soy sauce. Cook the albi and konnyaku separately in salted water until they are half done.

Boil the soup stock, add ½ tsp. salt and 1 Tbsp. soy sauce. Add burdock, mushroom, and carrot and cook 20 minutes. Add chicken, albi, and konnyaku and cook on medium flame until done. Add water as necessary. Cook covered until all juices evaporate. Add watercress last, mix in gently and cook a few minutes longer.

Optional vegetables include: Lotus root, pine mushrooms, and fresh chestnuts.

411. Chinese Cabbage Stuffed with Chicken

1 small Chinese cabbage

Stuffing
½ lb. chicken, minced
4 med. shiitake mushrooms, soaked
    and minced or ½ lb. fresh
    mushrooms, sliced thin
2½ tsp. salt
5 scallions, sliced
1 egg
1 Tbsp. sake
2 Tbsp. soy sauce

Soup stock
  5 cups soup stock (#39)
  1 tsp. salt
  1½ Tbsp. arrowroot or kuzu

Remove the outside leaves of the Chinese cabbage and save for another dish. Boil whole cabbage in salted water until slightly soft, then cut full length in half. Mix remaining ingredients and stuff between the leaves. Tie each half in two places with kampyo. Steam for 20 minutes or pressure-cook by bringing cabbage up to full pressure, turning it off and allowing it to come down to normal. This dish can also be cooked by placing it in soup stock as follows:

Bring soup stock and salt to boil, place cabbage lengthwise in stock, cook until tastes blend together well. Cook 20 minutes on a medium flame, then take out cabbage and place it on a platter. Add dissolved arrowroot or kuzu to stock. Cook until stock thickens slightly, cut cabbage at table, and serve with stock over it.

412. Farm Style Goat Cheese

½ gallon raw goat's milk
Lemon juice
Salt

Bring ½ gallon raw goat's milk to a boil in a heavy pot, stirring constantly. When it reaches a rolling boil, turn it off and add lemon juice, stirring slowly until milk separates into curds and whey. Add salt. Strain whey from curds through chessecloth. Hang cheesecloth suspended until fairly dry, or place cheesecloth in a cheese form (a small square box with screen or holes in the bottom).

This cheese must be refrigerated. It is delicious eaten as is or sliced and fried in a little oil.

Fried Foods

413. Jinenjo Roll with Nori *(Nagaimo Norimaki)*

½ lb. nagaimo, grated
¼ lb. minced onion
2 sheets nori cut in 6″ pieces
1 heaping Tbsp. whole wheat
    pastry flour
1 tsp. minced orange rind
½ tsp. salt
Oil for deep frying

Mix grated nagaimo, onion, flour, and ½ tsp. salt and add 1 tsp. orange rind. Then make a roll a little less than the length of the nori and roll up in the nori; or make a gyoza shape, folding up in the nori, and deep fry. Serve with lemon sauce.

Lemon sauce
2 Tbsp. soy sauce
2 tsp. lemon juice
2 Tbsp. water

Mix ingredients well.

414. Lotus Root Rolls

1½ minced onions
½ cup grated carrot
1½ cups grated lotus root
1 tsp. salt
1 cup whole wheat flour
4 Tbsp. sesame oil

Mix all ingredients. Make ½″ by 1½″ long rectangular croquette shapes (or any shape you like). Oil cookie sheet with 4 Tbsp. sesame oil, place rolls on sheet, and bake in 450° oven for 15 minutes. Turn over and bake at 350° until slightly golden brown. Serve hot.

415. Stuffed Lotus Root

7″ long whole lotus root
1 cup water
½ tsp. salt
⅓ cup scallion miso
½ cup tempura batter (#66)
Oil for deep frying

Wash lotus root and cook with water and salt for 30 minutes. Set aside to cool. Cut off one end of the lotus root and stuff all the holes all the way to the other end with scallion miso, using a chopstick. Then dip the whole root in tempura batter and deep-fry until golden. Slice ⅓″ thick and serve.

Scallion Miso
1 bunch scallions, cut ⅓″ pieces,
    using roots (separate roots,
    greens, and whites)
1-2 Tbsp. oil
1-1½ Tbsp. miso

Saute first the roots (chopped fine) then the greens until the color changes; finally add the whites. Stir gently so as not to mash the pieces. Add miso without mixing. Cover pan and cook for 5 minutes – steam will make miso soft. Then mix and cook without cover a few minutes more.

416. Lotus Root Fritter

2 pieces of lotus root 7″ long,
    ½″ diagonals
½ cup buckwheat flour or
    whole wheat pastry flour
1 tsp. salt
Oil for deep frying

Set buckwheat flour on a flat plate and coat lotus root pieces. Then shake off excess flour and deep fry. Drain oil completely and set aside to cool. Bring 2 cups of water to a boil, add fried lotus root pieces, 1 tsp. salt, and cook over medium flame until all water evaporates. After 20 minutes, add more salt if you like.

Then take each slice, cut it in half the long way and display each piece back to back as shown. This is called ya bane style (ya means archery and bane means feather); that is, it looks like arrow feathers.

417. Squash Croquettes

1 acorn or butternut squash
1 onion, minced
1 tsp. oil
1 tsp. salt
1 cup bread crumbs
½ cup whole wheat pastry flour
½ cup tempura batter (see #66)
Oil for deep frying

Pressure-cook squash for 10 minutes or steam for 20 minutes and mash.

Saute onion in 1 tsp. oil and mix with mashed squash and 1 tsp. salt. Let cool before adding flour and mix well. Make croquette shapes, dip in tempura batter, cover with bread crumbs or cracker meal, and deep fry until crispy. This goes well with vegetable ohitashi or pressed salad.

418. Mock Burdock Loach

1½ burdock, grated
1½ carrots, grated
1 minced onion
1 sheet nori, cut in 8 pieces
1 tsp. salt
⅓ cup whole wheat pastry flour
Oil for deep frying

Mix all ingredients – vegetables, flour, and salt – and put on the cutting board ⅓″ thick and 4″ long. Cut into loach size pieces (approximately ⅓″ diameter by 3½″ long) with spatula and deep-fry until golden. After draining, wrap with a piece of nori and serve with grated daikon. You can also make kuzu sauce (see #55) to cover instead of nori.

Sauces and Dressings

419. Brown Sauce

1 small onion, minced large
1″ piece carrot, minced large
2 med. mushrooms, minced large
1 Tbsp. oil
1-1½ Tbsp. whole wheat pastry flour
1½ cups kombu stock or bouillon
1 Tbsp. apple butter
1 tsp. salt

This sauce is good served on eggs, turkey, or cooked vegetables.

Saute onions, carrots, and mushrooms over medium flame for a long time until they are brown. Add pastry flour and cook until sauce is brown, then add 1½ cups stock. Add apple butter and cook 20 more minutes.

Puree or blend vegetables, taste for salt, and cook longer if thicker sauce is desired. Garnish with chopped parsley.

Variation: Madera sauce – add 2 Tbsp. sake to hot brown sauce.

420. Ginger Sauce

1 tsp. fresh grated ginger
5 Tbsp. soy sauce

Mix well. Good for boiled tofu, cold tofu, and baked, boiled, or fried fish.

421. Mustard Sauce

1 tsp. mustard paste (see #83)
5 Tbsp. soy sauce

Mix well. Good for chicken, fish, shellfish, sashimi (raw fish), oden (vegetable stew), and Chinese cabbage pickles.

422. Bonita Sauce

½ cup shaved bonita
1 cup water
3 Tbsp. soy sauce

Bring the water and soy sauce to a boil, add bonita. Bring to a boil again, remove from heat, set aside to cool. Strain. Good for cooked tofu, vegetables, or noodles.

423. Sweet Kuzu Sauce

Marinating sauce (#425)
Kuzu or arrowroot

Mix the marinating sauce (#425) with kuzu or arrowroot. Good for baked or boiled fish, because it gives a shiny attractive glaze to the food.

424. Vinegar Sauce

5 Tbsp. rice vinegar
2 Tbsp. soy sauce

Bring to boil then set aside to cool. This is a good sauce for salad, chicken mizutake (#385), or chiri nabe (#376).

425. Marinade

7 Tbsp. mirin (sweet rice wine)
3 Tbsp. soy sauce

Bring good quality mirin to a boil without a cover and boil for 10 minutes until it thickens slightly. Add soy sauce, bring to boil and set aside to cool. Good for marinating chicken, fish, or shellfish, or as a sauce for sushi (raw fish on vinegared rice).

426. Umeboshi Onion Dressing

3 onions
3 umeboshi plums, pitted
Sesame oil, generous amount
1 Tbsp. lemon juice (optional)
1 Tbsp. tahini

Saute onions in oil. Place in blender with plums, tahini, and enough water or salt plum juice to make the dressing the consistency of mayonnaise. Blend in the lemon juice if desired.

427. Sesame Dressing

4 Tbsp. roasted ground sesame seeds
1 Tbsp. soy sauce
3-5 Tbsp. boiling water

Grind sesame seeds well and mix with soy sauce and boiled water in a suribachi. Mix well. If you want a thicker sauce, bring to a boil and evaporate. Good for cooked vegetable salad or vegetable dishes. A flavorful, highly nutritious sauce.

Pickles

428. Dried Daikon Pickles

1 pkg. dried daikon (approx. 8oz.)
3" × 3" piece dashi kombu,
⅛" matchsticks

Sauce
⅔ cup soy sauce
⅔ cup soup stock
¼ cup natural rice vinegar

Wash dried radish quickly in a strainer. Squeeze out water. Mix sauce ingredients together and add kombu and radish. Leave for 24 hours in porcelain or glass container in a cool place, mixing two or three times. Serve with rice.

Note: If you are in a very yin condition (not in good health) do not use rice vinegar. Substitute umeboshi juice.

429. Daikon Koji Pickles

Step I:
20 daikon, 12" × 1½"
1 cup salt
½ cup cold water

Step II:
Daikon from step I
1-1½ cups salt
2 dry red chili peppers (optional)
7 cups rice koji
5" × 12" piece kombu, 1" squares

Step I: After washing daikon, sun-dry one day. Remove small slice at each end of daikon and set aside. Sprinkle a handful of salt in bottom of container. Place a layer of daikon snugly in keg, then a handful of salt. Repeat this layering three times, setting the daikon at right angles to the previous layer. Pour ½ cup of cold water around the circumference of the container. Cover with wood lid and use 30 lb. pressure. In 3-5 days the water will be on top. Rinse daikon in own liquid and drain off the liquid.

Step II: Mix 7 cups koji with salt. De-seed peppers and slice in thin rings. Sprinkle 2 handfuls of koji-salt mixture into bottom of container. Place a layer of daikon in container topped with about ⅓ of the kombu and peppers. Repeat this layering about two more times. Cover with wood lid and apply 15 lbs. of pressure. After liquid comes to the top, lighten pressure to about 5 lbs.

Serve 10-20 days later. These pickles should be eaten in a month, before they become sour tasting.

430. Turnip Koji Pickles

Step I:
2 lbs. small turnips with leaves
3 Tbsp. salt

Step II:
Turnips from step I
1 Tbsp. salt
¾ cup rice koji
4" × 4" piece dashi kombu, 1" squares
1 dry red chili pepper

Step I: Separate leaves from turnips and wash both thoroughly. Cut turnips into quarters. Sprinkle 1 Tbsp. salt over bottom of container. Mix turnips and leaves with 2 Tbsp. salt. Place in container snugly. Cover with wood lid and apply 5 lbs. pressure. After 3-4 days, squeeze out water and place in dry container.

Step II: Mix koji and salt. Layer salted turnips in dry container alternating with salt-koji mixture, kombu, and chile pepper rings evenly divided between layers of turnips. Press down with your hands. Cover with wood lid and use 5 lbs. pressure.

Ten to twelve days later, pickles are well-flavored and ready to serve.

Breads and Snacks

431. Sesame Bread

1½ cups sesame seeds and 1 cup
    raw wheat germ, toasted together
2 cups whole wheat flour
2 cups whole wheat pastry flour
2 cups brown rice flour
1½ tsp. sea salt
2-3 cups liquid

Combine dry ingredients. Warm the liquid (the amount varies according to the texture of the flours used). Mix well together. Warm and oil bread pans, fill to ¾ full and bake at 325° until it tests dry, about 45-60 minutes. Oil is not necessary in this bread because the roasted sesame seeds add oil to the bread batter, sufficient for daily eating.

432. Buckwheat Bread

1½ cups freshly ground
    buckwheat flour
3 cups whole wheat flour
1 cup brown rice flour
1 cup cornmeal
2 tsp. salt
1 Tbsp. soy sauce
⅓ cup safflower oil (optional)
2-3 cups liquid

Combine all dry ingredients. Add warmed liquid portion and soy sauce. Knead into a batter, earlobe consistency. Warm and oil bread pans and add dough. Place in a cold oven, turn temperature to 350° and bake 2 hours, or until it tests dry and has a golden crust.

433. Party Bread

4 cups whole wheat flour
1 cup cornmeal
2 cups sweet rice flour
1 cup brown rice flour
1 cup rye flour
1-1½ cups cooked raisins
1 cup chestnut puree
3 cups raisin syrup
¼ cup fresh apple butter
½-1 cup roasted sesame or sunflower
    seeds, walnuts, or pecans

Cook raisins and reserve liquid as in #233. Combine all dry ingredients. Add 2 cups warm liquid to the flour, then the apple butter and chestnut puree. Mix together well, then add raisins, toasted seeds, or roasted nuts which have been dusted in flour before adding to dough. Knead well and add additional liquid until earlobe consistency is obtained. The liquid should be warm before adding to the flour – this makes a lighter dough. Let rise for 24 hours in a warm place, covered with a cloth rinsed in warm water. Moisten the cloth and re-cover frequently during the rising period. Shape into loaves. Pre-heat bread pans, oil them, add the loaves and bake for 1 hour at 350°.

434. Raisin Bread

4 cups whole wheat flour
1 cup rye flour
1 cup brown rice flour
1 cup oat flour
1 Tbsp. sesame oil (light)
2-3 tsp. salt
½-1 tsp. cinnamon
½ tsp. dry yeast dissolved in
    ¼ cup warm raisin water
    (see #233)
1¼ cups raisin syrup
1½ cups cooked raisins
1 egg, beaten

Mix the flours, salt, and cinnamon together. Add the oil and blend with your fingers so the oil saturates all the flour. Add 1 cup liquid and the beaten egg. Dissolve yeast in ¼ cup warm raisin water and let sit for 15 minutes before adding to the dough. Mix together well. Add raisins which have been dusted with flour. Add remaining ¼ cup liquid if the dough is not desired consistency. Should be earlobe consistency. Cover with a warm moist cloth and let rise until double in size. Knead down, shape into loaves; warm and oil the bread pans, put in the loaves and cover with warm moist cloth until dough rises again. Preheat oven to 350° and bake for 1 hour or until tests dry.

435. Carrot Bread

4 carrots, shaved
2 cups whole wheat pastry flour
1 cup other flour
1 cup toasted sunflower seeds
1½ tsp. cinnamon
1-2 cups raisin water (see #233)
4 Tbsp. oil
2 tsp. salt
1 tsp. nutmeg (optional)

Saute carrots in 3 Tbsp. oil (similar to kinpira, #270) and cook for 2 hours until golden brown and very sweet. Mix together flour, salt, and spices. Add 1 Tbsp. oil and blend in with your fingers. Add 1 cup warm liquid, then the carrots which have been cooled completely. Dust the seeds in flour and add to dough. Mix well together, adding more liquid if earlobe consistency has not been obtained. Add liquid gradually as the juices from the cooked carrots absorb into the dough and change the texture of the dough shortly after the carrots have been added. Bake in a preheated 350° oven for 45-60 minutes or until tests dry. This is a delicious cake-like bread.

For variation: Let the dough rise in a warm place, covered with a warm moist cloth, for several hours. This makes a lighter bread and changes the flavor.

436. Rye Bread

4 cups pumpernickel rye meal
2 Tbsp. oil
3½ cups boiling water
1 cup wheat grits
1½ tsp. salt
¼ cup bran

Mix all ingredients except bran, add boiling water until dough is of earlobe consistency. Let sit overnight in a warm place. Add bran and bake in covered pan 4 hours at 200°. Place another pan of hot water in oven to keep oven moist.

437. Oatmeal Sunflower Gluten Bread

2 cups rolled oats
1 Tbsp. oil
¾ cup toasted sunflower seeds
5 cups whole wheat or
    unbleached flour
½ tsp. salt
1 cup raisins
½ cup gluten flour
Water as needed

Mix ingredients, adding water until dough is of earlobe consistency. Bake in 350° oven for 1½ hours or until done.

438. Party Rolls

4-4½ cups whole wheat pastry flour
    or blend of flours
1 tsp. yeast dissolved in ½ cup
    warm water
1 cup warm soba water
2 tsp. salt
⅓ cup oil

Mix flour and salt in a large mixing bowl. Add oil and blend into flour by hand so that oil evenly saturates the flour. Dissolve yeast in ½ cup warm water and let sit for 15 minutes. Mix well before using. Add liquid yeast mixture to flour. Add warm soba water and mix together well. Mixture will be sticky. Cover bowl with a cloth or Saran wrap and refrigerate overnight. Two hours before ready to serve, remove from refrigerator. Stand at room temperature for ½ hour before working. Knead well on a board. Roll out and cut in shape of Parker House rolls or shape into cloverleaf or bun shape as follows:

Parker House rolls: Roll dough ½″ thick and cut with biscuit cutter. Brush top with warm oil. Holding left forefinger across center of round, bring far side of dough over and press edges of round together. Place about ½″ apart on warmed, oiled cookie sheet or pan. Raise 1 hour and bake in preheated 350° oven for 30 minutes or until browned.

Cloverleaf rolls: Form dough into balls about 1″ in diameter. Place 3 balls in each greased muffin cup and brush with warmed oil. Raise 1 hour. Proceed as above.

Buns: Use a piece of dough about the size of an egg. Shape by hand into bun shape, or into English muffin shape. Raise and bake as above. Allow space for rising in pan. Bake 30-45 minutes, until slightly browned, at 375°-400° in a preheated oven. This recipe will make 32 small rolls or 24 medium sized buns.

For a change: Make raisin or nut bread from this recipe. Double all ingredients except yeast. For liquid portion use 1 cup soba water and 1 cup raisin syrup (see #233). Add 1 cup cooked raisins and 1 cup chopped, toasted nuts when ready to knead. Shape into 3 loaves. Let rise 1 hour at room temperature and bake 1 hour at 325°-350° or until tests dry.

439. Rye Rolls

2 cups rye flour
4 cups whole wheat flour
1 tsp. yeast dissolved in ½ cup
    warm water
1½ cups grain milk, scalded
¼ cup raisin puree
1½ Tbsp. corn oil
2 tsp. salt

Dissolve the yeast in the water. Add remaining ingredients, flours last. Knead well. Set in a warm place. When dough is double in size, beat it down and knead slightly. Form into rolls and place them on a greased pan so they touch each other and rise upward instead of outward. Let rise again until double in size. Bake at 350° for 20 minutes.

440. Whole Wheat Buns

12 cups whole wheat flour
2 cups rice flour
3 cups unbleached white flour
¾ tsp. yeast dissolved in ½ cup
    warm water
2 heaping Tbsp. unbleached
    white flour
6 cups warm water
2½ Tbsp. oil
2 Tbsp. salt

Dissolve yeast in ½ cup warm water and let sit for 5 minutes. Then add 2 heaping Tbsp. unbleached white flour, stir well, and set aside for 5-10 minutes.

Combine the flours with salt and oil, with your hands. This decreases kneading time. Add the yeast mixture and the 6 cups warm water. Knead well. Cover with a wet cloth and set aside in a warm spot for 4 hours to rise to double in bulk. Punch down and let rise again to double size. Punch down and then with wet hands, shape the dough into 1½″-diameter buns and place on a cookie sheet close together – so they will rise upward. Use a 2″ high cookie sheet – the bottom sprinkled with roasted sweet rice flour, cornmeal, roasted brown rice flour, or bulghur.

Place into cold oven and bake at 350° for 45-60 minutes. Remove when done and separate the buns to cool. Makes 64 buns.

You can make good variations by sprinkling top of wet buns with sesame seeds or poppy seeds before baking.

441. White Buns

14 cups unbleached white flour
2 heaping Tbsp. unbleached
    white flour
½-1 tsp. yeast dissolved in ½ cup
    warm water
5½ cups warm water
2 Tbsp. salt
2 Tbsp. oil

Mix and prepare as in #440 – whole wheat buns.

This makes a batter dough so use a wooden spoon for mixing. Shape buns with wet hands. Place cookie sheet into cold oven and bake at 450° hot oven for 60 minutes.

442. Karinto

Leftover pastry dough
Oil for deep frying

Use any leftover pastry dough for karinto. Roll out ¼″ thick. Cut into slabs 1½″ by 4″. Cut a slit lengthwise in center about 2″ long. Pull end of dough through the slit and deep fry.

443. Spiral Karinto

2 tsp. grain coffee
2 cups rice flour
1 tsp. salt
2 cups whole wheat flour
1 cup plus 2 Tbsp. warm water
Oil for deep frying

Mix all ingredients except grain coffee and oil and knead until hard dough is formed. Divide dough in half and mix grain coffee thoroughly into one half. Roll each dough into 8″ by 6″, the light dough to ½″ thickness and the dark to ⅓″. Lay dark slab on light and roll up. Slice to ⅛″ thickness, and deep fry until both sides are lightly browned and crispy.

444. Squash Muffins

4 cups sweetmeat or winter squash
3 cups whole wheat pastry flour
2¼ cups water
1 tsp. salt

Steam squash in ½ cup water on rack in pressure cooker for 10 minutes. Peel and mash, adding ½ tsp. salt. Mix flour with ½ tsp. salt and add 1¾ cups water. This batter is a little heavier than tempura batter.

Heat and oil muffin tins. Fill half full with batter, add 1 heaping Tbsp. of squash. Fill remaining space in muffin tin with batter. Makes 12 muffins. Bake in a 450° hot oven for 30-45 minutes.

Leftover muffins can be reheated on top of the stove. Turn upside down to heat thoroughly, or deep fry them.

Variation: Substitute sauteed vegetables or fried rice for squash.

445. Buckwheat Azuki Pancakes

1 cup buckwheat flour
1-1½ cups water
½ tsp. salt
¼ cup azuki beans
¼ tsp. salt

Cook azuki beans as in #390. Mix flour, water, and salt to form a thin batter. Add cooked beans and stir well. Spoon batter onto a hot greased frying pan as you would for regular pancakes. You will probably have to experiment to get just the right consistency of batter. If batter is too thick, the pancakes will have a raw taste.

Desserts

446. Amasake

2 cups sweet brown rice
¼ cup koji
4 cups water

Amasake can be made from sweet brown rice, barley, wheat, or millet (most any grain).

Rinse rice gently in a pan of cold water. Keep changing the water until it is clear. Soak overnight in 4 cups water. Cook the rice on a flame a little higher than medium. When the pressure comes up, turn down the flame and cook for 20 minutes. Turn off the heat and let stand 45 minutes; cool until the rice can be handled with your hands (approximately 140°-160°). Mix koji with the warm rice and place in a glass or porcelain bowl. *Do not use a metal bowl.* Keep the rice mixture covered in a warm place 3-4 hours and allow to ferment. During the fermentation period, mix from top to bottom several times until the koji is melted. (If you use the oven, cover with a wet towel and leave 8-12 hours – pilot only.) Then put mixture in a pan and bring it to a boil. Turn off the heat as soon as one or two bubbles appear. Allow to cool again and put mixture in a glass jar and keep it in the refrigerator. Amasake can be eaten 5-7 days after this. To eat sooner, keep in a cool place 2-3 days, then serve. To store, bring to a boil (5 minutes) to stop fermentation, then keep in refrigerator (10 days or so).

To obtain a smoother texture, the amasake can be blended in a blender. Amasake can be kept for a long time in a cold place if it is cooked uncovered over a low flame until it changes to a brown color. This is like sugar and can be used as a sweetening in cakes, karinto, donuts, cookies, and pies. To serve amasake as a drink, add boiling water and a little salt, bring to a boil and serve with lemon rind.

447. Amasake (Flour)

7 cups sweet brown rice flour
1 cup koji
8 cups boiling water

Spread the sweet brown rice flour on the bottom of a pressure cooker and add boiling water. Mix together well. Bring this mixture to full pressure with a flame slightly higher than medium. When the pressure comes up, turn down and cook for 20 minutes. Turn off the heat and allow pressure to come down to normal. Cool, mix together with the koji in a glass or porcelain bowl, keep covered and let stand in a warm place for 3-4 hours. During the fermentation period, mix from top to bottom several times until all the koji is melted. Change the mixture to a casserole dish, put in the oven (350°) with a cover and bring to a slight boil. As soon as one bubble appears, remove from the oven and cool. Put in a glass jar and keep the amasake in the refrigerator. This can be eaten 5-7 days later. (To eat sooner, cool as in #446.) Cook the amasake uncovered over a low flame until it has the thickness of apple butter. Use this as a sweetener with a little bit of lemon rind in your baking. Amasake may be used as a filling in crescent rolls. This is very delicious, especially with lemon rind.

448. Amasake Manju (Steam Cake)

2 cups amasake (#446),
    room temperature
2 cups cooked azuki (see #390)
6 cups whole wheat pastry flour
1 tsp. salt

Mix flour, amasake, salt, and ½ cup warm water and knead until it has reached earlobe consistency. Cover with a warm wet towel and let sit overnight. Then knead once again the next day and roll out into a 1"-diameter roll. Cut into 1" thick pieces. Then make flat round shapes 4" in diameter. Make a small round ball with cooked azuki beans and place it in the center and join the edges in, forming a round ball with the beans in the center.

Heat up the steam pan and put a wet towel in the steamer. Put the cakes in around the bottom in one layer only. They expand and stick together if too close to each other. Steam for twenty minutes over a high flame and replace with more. Steamed dough is easier to digest than baked flour products (softer, more water).

449. Steamed Amasake Roll

2 cups amasake (#446),
    room temperature
2 cups cooked azuki (see #390)
6 cups whole wheat pastry flour
1 tsp. salt

Make dough in the same way as in #448 (rectangle shape 10" long and 7" wide). Add the cooked azuki to the center and roll up lengthwise like a jelly roll. Then steam, slice, and serve.

450. Baked Amasake Roll

2 cups amasake (#446),
    room temperature
2 cups cooked azuki (see #390)
6 cups whole wheat pastry flour
6 Tbsp. oil
2 tsp. salt
Egg yolk for brushing

Mix flour and salt, add oil and blend into flour by hand to distribute evenly. Add amasake and prepare in the same way as in #449. Brush the top with egg yolk and bake in a 450° oven for 30 minutes.

451. Amasake Karinto

Amasake (#446), room temperature
Whole wheat flour
Salt
Oil for deep frying

Add whole wheat flour to amasake. Knead until earlobe consistency and add a little bit of salt and roll out to ¼" thin. Then slice in any style you like and deep fry. All amasake recipes have a natural sweetness which children enjoy for desserts and snacks.

452. Amasake Cookies

4 cups amasake (#446),
    room temperature
3 cups whole wheat pastry flour
1½ cups uncooked rolled oats
1 tsp. cinnamon
1 tsp. grated orange or lemon peel
    (optional)
½ cup chopped, roasted nuts or
    roasted sunflower seeds
1 tsp. salt
4 Tbsp. oil
½ cup cooked currants (optional)

Combine dry ingredients. Add oil and mix evenly, add amasake, and currants if they are used. Oil cookie sheet and preheat oven to 350°. Bake 30-40 minutes. When top is brown turn over so that both sides brown evenly. This makes for a more evenly baked cookie.

453. Amasake Cake

3 cups whole wheat pastry flour
2 cups blended amasake
½ tsp. yeast dissolved in 1 cup
    warm water
5 heaping Tbsp. whole wheat
    pastry flour
1 tsp. cinnamon
½ tsp. salt
2 Tbsp. corn oil

White frosting
1 cup blended amasake
1½ cups water
2 level tsp. kanten powder
½ tsp. lemon peel, grated

Dark frosting
1½ cups blended amasake
1 heaping Tbsp. yannoh
    (grain coffee)
2 tsp. kuzu or arrowroot mixed
    with 2 Tbsp. water

The amasake for this recipe should be sweeter. Use recipe #446, substituting 2 cups of koji.

Dissolve yeast in one cup warm water (about 5 minutes). Add 5 heaping Tbsp. of whole wheat pastry flour and mix to a tempura batter consistency. Wait until it rises (about 10 minutes).

After amasake is blended, heat it to body temperature (about 105°). Put 3 cups whole wheat pastry flour in a bowl, add oil and salt and mix by hand until blended. Then add yeast mixture and amasake and sprinkle in cinnamon. Mix with a wooden spoon to a stiff batter. Cover the bowl with a damp cloth and allow dough to rise one hour in a warm place. Then mix batter, cover bowl again with damp cloth, and allow dough to rise one more time.

Heat up cake pans (one large or two medium-sized ones). Oil the pans. Mix batter again and place in cake pans. Place pans in cold oven and heat to 350°. Bake for 30-40 minutes.

For white frosting, add water to kanten and bring to boil without cover. Cook for 10 minutes. Skim off top bubbles, add amasake and stir. Cook for 10 minutes without cover. Add lemon peel and put aside to cool until kanten partially thickens (about 20 minutes). For a dark frosting, you may use yannoh, with kuzu instead of kanten. Mix blended amasake with yannoh, bring to a boil, add dissolved kuzu, again bring to a boil and set aside to cool.

Cut cake in two layers and spread a little apple butter between the layers. Frost all over with amasake frosting. Decorate with crosshatch designs, using a fork.

If you want a white cake, you can use unbleached white flour instead of whole wheat flour or use half brown and half white sweet rice for a nice ivory color.

454. Amasake Wedding Cake with Frosting

2 cups whole wheat pastry flour
1 cup amasake (warm before using, blend in blender)
½ cup corn oil
½ tsp. salt
½ tsp. yeast dissolved in ½ cup warm water
3 heaping Tbsp. flour
1½ tsp. liquid vanilla or ½″ vanilla bean

Sift the flour 3 times and add salt and oil. Use your hands to mix the oil thoroughly with the flour. In a separate bowl add warm water to the yeast. Add to this 3 heaping Tbsp. of flour, mix well and set it aside for 15 minutes until the yeast is completely dissolved. (The flour helps to activate the yeast.) Stir this and add the warm amasake. Mix thoroughly, then add it to the flour, oil, and salt mixture. Using an eggbeater or an electric beater, mix the ingredients until they form a smooth batter. Then add the vanilla. Cover the batter with a damp cloth and let it rise in a warm spot until it has doubled in size (about 1 hour). Punch it down, place in a cake pan and cover it again. Let it rise until it doubles in size again (about 30 minutes).

Cut a brown grocery bag down the seam, open it and place the cake pan on it. Draw an outline of the bottom of the pan on the paper. Cut and place this in the bottom of the pan, which has been oiled. Pour the cake batter on top of this paper. This helps the cake bake evenly and makes it easier to remove from the pan. Bake it at 350° about 45-60 minutes until it tests dry with a bamboo skewer. Remove the cake from the pan and place it on a rack to cool. Do not remove the paper until the cake has cooled. It will then peel off easily and leave an even surface.

This makes an 8″ round layer cake. If you are using tiered pans, adjust the proportions according to the size of each tier. For a tiered cake, purchase heavy cardboard layer dividers from a party shop that has decorations for making home cakes for parties. To elevate between the tiers, use brandy glasses turned upside-down to support each layer, or purchase 'pillars' to use between the layers. Use bamboo skewers placed in the cake and extended into the pillars or brandy glasses to keep the cake from sliding when carrying it to the serving area.

Amasake frosting

2 cups blended amasake
1 tsp. kanten powder
1 tsp. grated lemon peel
½ cup water
1 tsp. vanilla
½ tsp. salt

Add the kanten powder to the water, bring it to a boil, then simmer it for 20 minutes in an uncovered pan with ½ tsp. salt. Skim off any foam from the top and discard it. Add the amasake and cook a few more minutes. Add the lemon peel and vanilla, mix it well, remove from heat and chill it until it sets. This does not mean that it will become firm like kanten jello; instead, it will be soft like frosting. Before covering the cake, mix the frosting with a fork (or an eggbeater or electric mixer). Then spread it on the cake.

For special decorations, cut fruit into small pieces and use as a border design around the cake, or on top of it. If small flowers are available, use them to decorate the wedding cake.

455. Unyeasted Amasake Donuts

6 cups whole wheat pastry flour
2 cups blended amasake
½ cup warm water
1 tsp. salt
½ cup chestnut flour mixed with
    1 tsp. cinnamon
Oil for deep frying

Heat amasake to room temperature. Mix amasake, flour, salt, and water well with a wooden spoon to earlobe consistency. Cover with a wet cloth (or put it into a large covered pot) to set aside overnight at room temperature. Next morning, roll the dough ½″ thickness and shape donuts. The dough becomes much softer, so use water on your hands to handle it and make the donuts. Place the shaped donuts on top of a clean wet dish towel.

Heat fresh oil, 2″-3″ in deep fry pot, over high flame. Preheated oil eliminates excessive oil smell. Remove from flame to cool for 10 minutes. Heat oil again over medium flame. Drop the donuts into the oil without crowding. They will drop to the bottom, but in a few minutes they will expand and rise. Now increase the center hole in each donut by twirling a chopstick inside the hole, moving around in the oil. When color becomes golden, turn and fry other side until it is the same color. Drain in strainer placed inside a larger pan to catch excess oil.

Dust the hot donuts with a mixture of ½ cup chestnut flour and 1 tsp. cinnamon. Set aside on paper towel-covered cookie sheet to cool.

456. Yeasted Amasake Donuts

6 cups whole wheat pastry flour
2 cups blended amasake
2 heaping Tbsp. whole wheat
    pastry flour
½ cup warm water
½-1 tsp. yeast, dissolved in small
    amount of warm water
1 tsp. salt
3 Tbsp. corn oil
½ cup chestnut flour mixed with
    1 tsp. cinnamon
Oil for deep frying

Dissolve yeast and let sit for 5-10 minutes in a warm place. Then mix in the 2 Tbsp. whole wheat pastry flour. Let sit in warm place another 5-10 minutes.

Warm the amasake to room temperature, then stir in the yeast mixture. In another bowl, mix the 6 cups flour, salt, and the 3 Tbsp. oil. By hand, gently blend thoroughly. Mix together the contents of both bowls, add ½ cup warm water and knead like bread dough to blend completely. Cover the bowl with a wet towel and set aside until double in size (about 4 hours). Punch down dough and let rise again for 1 hour. Punch down dough again to remove yeast gases.

Now roll out the dough on a floured board to ½″ thickness and make the donuts with a donut cutter. Put them on a wet cloth. Deep fry and dust as in #455.

457. Amasake Crescents

4 cups whole wheat pastry flour
1 cup amasake butter mixed with
   ½ tsp. grated lemon peel
1 tsp. salt
4 Tbsp. corn oil
1 cup plus 2 Tbsp. cold water

To make amasake butter: After the amasake (#446) has been blended, simmer the mixture, without a cover, for 3-4 hours until apple butter thickness and color. Cool before using.

Mix the flour and oil by hand, blending thoroughly for 5 minutes. Add the salt and water, stir with a fork without kneading. Shape the dough into a ball by hand and roll out on a floured board to ⅛″ thickness. Cut into triangles – base 4″ and sides 5½″. At the base of each triangle place a generous ¼ tsp. of the amasake butter and cover it with a fold of the dough, secured with a bit of water on the edge, before rolling it into a crescent shape. At the end, add a bit more water to hold the tip of the dough in place. Bake in a preheated 450° oven for 30 minutes until slightly golden in color.

If unbleached white flour is desired, add 2 Tbsp. more water to dough mix. Also add ½ tsp. more grated lemon peel to the amasake butter. Very good.

458. Pumpkin Pie

3½ lbs. Hokkaido pumpkin or
   any sweet winter squash
2 eggs, beaten
2 tsp. cinnamon
1 tsp. nutmeg
½ tsp. vanilla
2 tsp. salt
A little oil

Pie crust
  1½ cups whole wheat pastry flour
  1½ cups wheat bran
  3 cups unbleached white flour
  ½ tsp. salt
  1¼ cups corn oil
  ¾ cup water

Cut the skin from the pumpkin or squash and scrape out all the seeds and lining. Cut it into ½″ pieces and saute them in a little oil for about 15 minutes. Add 1 cup of water and pressure-cook for 30 minutes with 2 tsp. salt. Reduce the pressure and remove the pumpkin from the pot. Cool it 30 minutes. Then put it through a food mill. During this blending process, add the beaten eggs, cinnamon, nutmeg, and vanilla.

Combine the flours in a mixing bowl and add the salt. Add the oil, rubbing it by hand until it is completely mixed with the flour. Mix in the water with a fork – do not knead. Roll the dough thinly and place it into pie pans. Bake in a 350° oven for 10 minutes – until pie shells are slightly brown. Remove from the oven and let cool before adding the filling. (This makes 4 pie shells, so you may have an extra shell to use for your favorite recipe.)

Fill the pie shells generously with the cooled pumpkin mixture. Bake the pies in a 350°-375° oven for about 30 minutes, until each is golden brown. Cool them before serving.

This tastes like old-fashioned pumpkin pie. It is delicious.

459. Simple Pumpkin Pie

1 med. pumpkin, peeled and sliced
1-2 handfuls of raisins
Pinch of cinnamon
1 Tbsp. sesame butter
Pie shell (see #458)

Mix pumpkin, raisins, and cinnamon, place in pressure cooker and cook for 20 minutes. Let the pressure come down. Add 1 Tbsp. of sesame butter and blend in blender.

Pour into a 9″ pie shell and bake for 45 minutes until crust is golden.

460. Half Moon Chestnut Turnovers

3 cups whole wheat pastry flour
2 cups dried chestnuts
2 eggs
1 tsp. cinnamon
1-1¼ cups water
4 Tbsp. oil
1 tsp. salt

Soak chestnuts overnight in 4 cups water. Boil chestnuts until tender, adding ¼ tsp. salt. Cook until 1 cup liquid remains. Half mash chestnuts and cool.

Mix oil, ¾ tsp. salt, and cinnamon into the flour. Add water and knead just enough to form dough. Roll ⅛″ thin and cut into rounds the diameter of a gallon jar. Roll dough so it is out of round, that is, 1″ longer on one side.

Separate eggs, beat whites lightly and mix with chestnuts. Place 1 Tbsp. of chestnuts in center of pastry rounds, fold over and seal. Beat egg yolks and make a couple of brush strokes of yellow on top of turnovers. Bake 350° for 30 minutes.

461. Mincemeat Filling

Raisins or currants
Apples (dried or fresh)
Lemon rind
Moromi or miso
Kuzu
Optional spices

Stew equal amounts of raisins and finely chopped apples with a small amount of water and a little salt. Stew until soft and a very thick sauce consistency.

For 2 quarts of sauce add about 1 tsp. grated lemon rind (or to taste) and ¼ cup moromi (or to taste). Add spices at this time as desired and thicken with diluted kuzu powder.

Use this as a sauce or filling for pie, cookies, in breads, etc.

462. Oatmeal Cookies

3 cups uncooked rolled oats
1 cup whole wheat flour
1 cup corn flour or unbleached flour
1 small egg
1 cup peanut or sesame butter
1 tsp. pure vanilla extract (optional)
⅓ cup yinnie syrup or raisin
  syrup (see #233)
1½ cups soba water
½-1 tsp. salt

This recipe uses water saved from cooking buckwheat noodles.

Mix all ingredients, drop on lightly oiled cookie sheet, and bake 30 minutes at 350°.

463. Cranberry Relish

1 cup cranberries
1 cup currants or raisins
½ tsp. salt
½ cup water

Stew equal parts cranberries and currants with a little salt and water to prevent burning. Stew until soft and boil down to the desired consistency. Nuts can be added and this can be used as a relish or in kanten or other cooking.

464. Soft Gingerbread Cake

3 cups sifted whole wheat flour
2 eggs, well beaten
1 tsp. baking soda
1 tsp. ginger powder or
   ½ tsp. ginger juice
1 cup malt extract, yinnie syrup, or
   other natural sweetener such as
   juice concentrate or amasake
1-1½ tsp. cinnamon
3 Tbsp. oil
½ tsp. salt

Blend together the oil, malt extract, eggs, and baking soda. In a separate mixing bowl, combine the remaining dry ingredients. Pour the liquid mixture from first bowl into the flour mixture and mix together well. If you have an electric beater this can be used to make the batter light and frothy. Warm and oil the cake pans. Cut a liner for the bottom of pan. Pour the cake batter directly onto the paper. Preheat oven to 350° and bake 35-45 minutes until tests dry. Loosen edges of cake with a knife and leave cake in the pan until partially or completely cooled. Turn out onto cake rack and remove the brown paper from bottom. This tastes good plain or with a kanten or apple butter frosting. You can also use this recipe to make gingerbread cookies.

465. Carob Christmas Cake

1⅔ cups whole wheat pastry flour
½ cup carob powder
1 tsp. yeast, dissolved in 1 cup
   warm soba water
½ tsp. salt
⅓ cup oil
1½ tsp. vanilla extract

Dissolve yeast in warm soba water (water leftover from cooking buckwheat noodles), add oil, mix with remaining ingredients and bake in preheated 350° oven for 30 minutes.

466. English Christmas Pudding

1½ cups bulghur wheat
1 cup whole wheat flour
1 cup nuts (almonds, walnuts, or
   filberts)
1 cup raisins
1 cup currants
Apple butter, malt extract, yinnie
   syrup, or carrot concentrate as
   sweetener
3 cups boiling water
¼ cup oil

Roast bulghur in ¼ cup oil until it smells good. Add to 3 cups boiling salted water, cover and keep boiling for 5 minutes, then turn flame very low for another 20 minutes. Roast and chop nuts. Simmer raisins and currants together in salted water (or apple juice) for 15 minutes.

Roast the whole wheat flour until it smells good. Add sweetener to taste. Add all remaining ingredients. It should be mushy. Now add a pinch more of salt and mix until the batter becomes stiff.

Pack into an oiled bowl or basin and tie a piece of cheesecloth around the whole thing. Place in a large pot (with lid) so that it does not touch the bottom. Stand it on chopsticks or a perforated steamer. Put in 2″ water, cover tightly and steam all day. Maintain the water level. It can be pressure-cooked for 3-4 hours instead. In England, it is cooked for at least 12 hours and again for 3-4 hours before serving.

To serve, unmold onto platter and slice like a cake. Traditionally, it is garnished with holly sprigs.

Pronunciation guide
a – ah   i – ee   u – oo   e – eh   o – oh

Glossary

Aemono – Style of vegetable cooking with salt, boiling water, and heat. After vegetables are soft, sesame butter or another condiment is added.

Age – Deep-fried tofu, often made in a bag-shaped pouch.

Albi (also Satoimo or Taro) – Oriental root vegetable or tuber, similar to a small potato, with a sticky interior. *Satoimo* is the Japanese name, *taro* is Tahitian, and *albi* is unknown.

Amasake – Liquid sweetener made from sweet rice fermented with koji enzyme.

Bancha – Japanese roasted green tea.

Barley malt syrup – Natural sweetener, usually made from barley extract and sprouted corn.

Bean threads (also harusame, 'longevity noodles,' or saifun) – Transparent noodles made from bean, potato, or other starch. *Harusame* is the Japanese name, *saifun* is Chinese.

Bechamel – Sauce made by roasting flour in oil and adding liquid. Common in French cooking.

Bonita (hana katsuo) – Japanese fish usually found dried and shaved, used for soup stock or condiment.

Bulghur – Partially cracked wheat, common in Middle Eastern cookery.

Chapati – Flat wheat bread, a staple of India.

Chawan mushi – Japanese custard made with egg and ginkgo nut.

Chirashi sushi – Cold cooked rice with vegetables sprinkled on top.

Chirimen iriko – Small dried fish used for soup stock, tempura, nitsuke, vegetable pancakes.

Chiri nabe – Unseasoned stew with tofu, served with lemon sauce.

Chuba iriko – Small dried fish from Chuba (now Iwate prefecture), Japan. Silver color.

Daifuku – Sweet rice mochi with azuki paste inside.

Daikon – Long white Japanese radish.

Dashi – Soup stock made with kombu seaweed or kombu and dried fish.

Dashi kombu – Thick kombu used for making dashi, or soup stock.

Do – Tao, or way. See Introduction, pg. 10.

Fu – Dried wheat gluten.

Furikake – Condiment made from powdered fish or nori seaweed.

Gefilte fish – Jewish delicacy made from three kinds of cooked fish (white fish, pike, and carp) compressed into cakes or balls, marinated and served cold.

Goma ai – Mixed vegetables cooked and served cold with sesame dressing.

Gomashio – Common Japanese condiment of sesame seeds and a small amount of sea salt, roasted and ground together. *Goma* is sesame and *shio* is salt.

Gyoza – Pan-fried dumplings stuffed with vegetables.

Halvah – Middle Eastern dessert made with ground sesame seeds mixed with nuts and honey or another sweetener.

Hangetsu – Vegetables cut in half-moon shapes.

Hasugiri – Vegetables cut in diagonal rounds.

Hiziki – A dark Japanese seaweed of the brown algae family, rich in calcium and iron.

Ichogiri – Vegetables cut in quarter-moon shapes.

Imoni – Nitsuke of *imo,* or one of the Japanese potatoes.

Jinenjo – Wild mountain potato of Japan.

Kampyo – Edible dried gourd strips, often used for tying foods.

Kanten – Seaweed gelatin, also called agar-agar or Ceylon moss.

Karinto – Deep-fried rolled-out dough shapes.

Kasha – Cooked buckwheat groats, Russian-style.

Kayu – Soft-cooked rice or other grain cooked a long time.

Kenchin – Sauteed vegetable stew with oil.

Ki – Life force or energy.

Kinpira – Burdock and carrot dish – cut *sengiri,* sauteed, and seasoned with soy sauce.

Kirigoma – Roasted and chopped sesame seeds.

Koguchigiri – Vegetables cut in thin rounds.

Koi koku – Traditional Japanese stew made with carp and burdock.

Koji – Enzyme used in fermentation of traditional Japanese foods.

Kokkoh – Grain cereal or 'grain milk' for babies made from rice, sweet rice, oats, and sesame seeds.

Kombu – Japanese seaweed of the brown algae family, often used for soup stock, nitsuke, condiments, etc.

Konnyaku – A translucent gelatinous cake made from yam starch.

Kuzu – High quality starch similar to arrowroot, extracted from the root of a Japanese plant, used medicinally and also in cooking as a thickener.

Mawashigiri – Crescent-shaped wedge cut, used for round vegetables.

Mekabu – Mineral-rich root of wakame seaweed.

Mijingiri – Minced cutting style for vegetables.

Mirin – Sweet rice wine used in Japanese cooking.

Miso – Basic Japanese staple made from fermented soybeans, salt, and barley or another grain. Often used as a soup base concentrate.

Mochi (or Omochi) – Pounded, steamed sweet rice made into glutinous cakes, traditionally served in Japan at New Year's.

Moromi – Whole fermented soybeans, just before squeezing for soy sauce.

Moyashi – Bean sprouts.

Mugi – Barley.

Mushi-mono – Steamed dishes.

Musubi – Seaweed or other food which has been tied in a knot. Rice balls are also called musubi.

Nabe-mono – General name for many kinds of Japanese stew. Nabe means pot.

Nagaimo – Cultivated *jinenjo.*

Nappa cabbage – Chinese cabbage or *hakusai* (Japanese name).

Natto – Fermented soybean dish usually prepared with special enzyme.

Nigari – Bitter liquid (bitters) that drips from damp sea salt, traditionally used to solidify tofu.

Nishime – Style of cooked vegetables cut in fairly large pieces, cooked slowly, and seasoned with soy sauce.

Nitsuke – Style of cooked vegetables cut fairly small and cooked for a short time.

Nori – Versatile seaweed of red algae family, cultivated in Japan and available in thin sheets.

Nuka – Rice bran, roasted and mixed with salt for pickling vegetables.

Oden – Traditional Japanese stew with daikon, carrot, burdock, musubi kombu, etc.

Ohagi – Lightly pounded cakes of cooked sweet rice, similar to mochi.

Ohitashi – Vegetables lightly boiled in salted water.

Ojiya – Rice porridge with vegetables, often made with leftovers.

Okara – Dry soybean leavings from tofu making.

Oroshi – Grated. *Daikon oroshi* means grated radish.

Polenta – Cornmeal.

Puri – Deep-fried puffed dough, often filled with vegetables as a staple sandwich in India.

Rangiri – Large, irregular diagonal wedge cutting style for vegetables.

Renkon – Lotus root.

Saifun (harusame) – Bean thread noodles.

Sainome – Diced vegetables.

Sake – Japanese rice wine.

Sarashinegi – Scallions chopped and passed under water.

Sasagaki – Pencil-shaving style of vegetable cutting.

Seitan – Wheat gluten which has been sauteed with fresh ginger and soy sauce.

Senbei (arare) – Small Japanese snack crackers made from rice flour with seasonings.

Sengiri – Matchstick vegetable cutting – like julienne slicing.

Sesame butter – A paste made by grinding roasted unhulled (whole) sesame seeds. Good for spreads, sauces, and dressings.

Shiitake – Dried Japanese mushroom.

Shingiku – Spring chrysanthemum, an Oriental green vegetable. Watercress can be substituted.

Shio kombu – Condiment made from kombu seaweed that has been cut into small pieces and cooked for a long time in soy sauce.

Shiro ai – Cooked dishes with white sesame seeds or tofu added later. Shiro means white.

Shiso (or chiso) – Leaves of the beefsteak plant.

Shiso condiment – Beefsteak leaves that have been pickled, then dried and powdered.

Shoyu – Soy sauce.

Soba – Traditional Japanese buckwheat noodles.

Somen – Thin, round, white or whole wheat noodles, often served cold in summer.

Sukiyaki – A style of vegetable and noodle dish cooked at the table with very little liquid.

Suribachi – Japanese bowl (ceramic mortar) with grooves on the inside, used for grinding seeds and other foods.

Suricogi – Wooden pestle for use with suribachi.

Sushi – Cooked rice flavored with rice vinegar, often rolled with other ingredients in sheets of nori and served cold.

Sushi mat – bamboo mat for rolling sushi or boiled vegetables.

Tahini – Ground sesame paste made from hulled sesame seeds, less nutritious than sesame butter. Traditional Middle Eastern food.

Takuan – Dried daikon pickles made in winter.

Tamari – Liquid obtained in miso making, used in Japan as a thick sauce. Shoyu, or traditional soy sauce (mistakenly marketed as 'tamari') is made from wheat and soybeans and is not a miso product.

Tanzaku – Flat, rectangular slices in vegetable cutting.

Tawashi – Japanese natural fiber brush used for scrubbing vegetable skins.

Tazukuri – Small dried blue fish.

Tekka – Condiment made by cooking minced burdock, carrot, and lotus root with miso until crumbly and dry.

Tempura – Style of cooking batter-dipped foods in deep hot oil.

Tendon – Large bowl of rice topped with tempura.

Tofu – High protein cheese-like cake made from soybean liquid and nigari.

Udon – Large, flat white or whole wheat noodles, often served in soup.

Umeboshi – Japanese plums pickled with salt and beefsteak leaves (shiso), used for seasoning and also medicinally.

Umeshoban – Umeboshi (salt plum) boiled in bancha tea with a little soy sauce (shoyu) added.

Unagi – Eel.

Wagiri – Thick round vegetable slices.

Wakame – Kelp-type seaweed, native of Japan, often used in miso soup. Very tender.

Wok – Chinese round cooking pan.

Yaki miso – Baked miso.

Yang – Contractive, having a contractive nature or effect. 'Yangize,' 'yangization.' Opposite of and complementary to yin.

Yin – Expansive, having an expansive nature or effect. 'Yinnize,' 'yinnization.' Opposite of and complementary to yang.

Yinnie syrup – Natural sweetener made from milled rice, barley, and koji enzyme.

Yose nabe – A kind of stew with vegetables, fish, chicken, and tofu.

Zoni – Mochi cooked in soup with vegetables.

Cutting Styles

Thin rounds (koguchigiri)

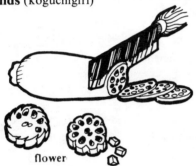

flower

Matchsticks (sengiri)

Thick rounds (wagiri)

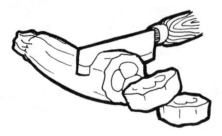

Shaved (sasagaki)

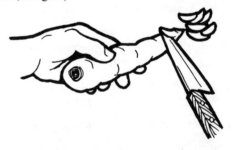

Diagonal rounds (hasugiri)

Crescents (mawashigiri)

Half-moons (hangetsu)

Quarter-moons (ichogiri)

Diced (sainome)

Minced (mijingiri)

Irregular wedges (rangiri)

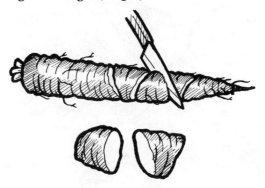

Flat rectangles (tanzaku)

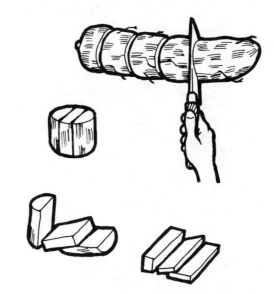

Cabbage strips

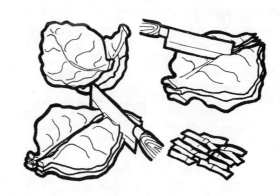

Quartering and slicing

Flower design

Wedges

Pine needle

Chrysanthemum shapes

Fan shape

Topical Index

Grains

Grains with Vegetables

Noodles

Soups and Stews

Beans and Tofu

Fish and Fowl

Breads and Snacks

Desserts

Beverages

Index